THE RECOVERY OF BLACK PRESENCE

Dr. Charles B. Copher

THE RECOVERY OF BLACK PRESENCE

An Interdisciplinary Exploration

Essays in Honor of
Dr. Charles B. Copher

Edited by
Randall C. Bailey
and
Jacquelyn Grant

Abingdon Press
Nashville

THE RECOVERY OF BLACK PRESENCE:
AN INTERDISCIPLINARY EXPLORATION

Copyright © 1995 by Randall C. Bailey and Jacquelyn Grant

All Rights Reserved.

Library of Congress Cataloging-in-Publication Data

The recovery of Black presence: an interdisciplinary exploration: essays in honor of Dr. Charles B. Copher / edited by Randall C. Bailey and Jacquelyn Grant
      p.   cm.
    Includes bibliographic references
    ISBN 0-687-35735-7 (alk. paper)
    1. Black theology. 2. Bible–Black interpretations. I. Copher, Charles B., 1913– . II. Bailey, Randall C., 1947– .
III. Grant, Jacquelyn.
BT82.7.R43   1995
230'.089.'96 – dc20

        94-43238
        CIP

An earlier version of Chapter 9, "Slave Ideology and Biblical Interpretation," was published in *Semeia* 47 (1989), 9-23. Used by permission.

An earlier version of Chapter 12, "Interdependence as a Normative Value in Pastoral Counseling with African Americans," was published in *The Journal of the Interdenominational Theological Center* 18/1 & 2 (Fall 1990 & Spring 1991), 119-47. Used by permission.

The poem "Mother and Son" (p. 207) is from *Selected Poems* by Langston Hughes, copyright © 1926 by Alfred A. Knopf., Inc., and renewed 1954 by Langston Hughes. Reprinted by permission of the publisher.

CONTENTS

Preface 7

PART ONE: BIBLICAL STUDIES

Chapter 1: Copher: What's in a Name?
G. Murray Branch 13

Chapter 2: "Is That Any Name for a Nice Hebrew Boy?"
   Exodus 2:1-10: The De-Africanization of an Israelite Hero
Randall C. Bailey 25

Chapter 3: The Theology of the Book of Daniel and the
   Political Theory of W. E. B. DuBois
Stephen Breck Reid 37

Chapter 4: In Search of a Face for Simon the Cyrene
Boykin Sanders 51

Chapter 5: The Individual and the Group in Luke: A Study
   of Malina's Hypothesis of the Dyadic Personality in
   First-Century Mediterranean Society
H. Wayne Merritt 65

Chapter 6: Oppression and Identity in the Gospel of John
David Rensberger 77

Chapter 7: When the Vultures Are Finished, Can There Be Life?
   The Valley of Dry Bones and the Future of the Black Church
John W Waters 95

Chapter 8: Toni Morrison's Song of Solomon: The Blues
   and the Bible
Abraham Smith 107

PART TWO: THEOLOGICAL STUDIES

Chapter 9: Slave Ideology and Biblical Interpretation
Katie Geneva Cannon 119

Chapter 10: Womanist Jesus and the Mutual Struggle
   for Liberation
Jacquelyn Grant 129

Chapter 11: Symbols of Revelation: The Darkness of
   the Hebrew Yahweh and the Light of the Greek Logos
Octavius A. Gaba 143

Chapter 12: Interdependence as a Normative Value
   in Pastoral Counseling with African Americans
Carolyn L. McCrary 159

Chapter 13: Black Methodist Protestants, 1877–1939: Protest and
   Change Among African Americans Within Predecessor
   Organizations of The United Methodist Church
James M. Shopshire 177

Chapter 14: The Transmission of Faith to Young
   African American Children
Janice E. Hale 193

Charles B. Copher: *Curriculum Vitae* and
   Selected Bibliography 209

Abbreviations 213

Notes 215

Contributors 249

PREFACE

This volume, dedicated to Dr. Charles B. Copher, is long overdue, for Dr. Copher is the biblical scholar on whose shoulders the current generation of Black biblical scholars in the United States now stands. He is the third African American to receive the Ph.D. in Old Testament, which he earned at Boston University in 1947. Since that time he has served on the faculty of Gammon Theological Seminary and then of the Interdenominational Theological Center in Atlanta, where he was later appointed to be the first Dean of the Faculty and then as Vice-President for Academic Affairs. Dr. Copher has a distinguished career as both biblical scholar and church worker. This is evidenced in his many publications and years of service not only as a local pastor but also on the Judicial Council for The United Methodist Church. He has pioneered the investigation of Black presence in the ancient world in general and in the biblical text in particular. We all owe a great debt to him in this regard.

Given the breadth of his career and his multiple contributions to theological education, it was decided early on in this process not to limit this celebratory volume to the field of biblical studies. Similarly, given his contributions to race relations in this country, it was also decided not to limit the contributor list to Black people. Rather all people who have taught biblical courses at the ITC, all alumnae/i who have gone on to receive academic terminal degrees, and alumni/ae pastors of distinction were invited to contribute essays which speak to the importance of Black and Afrocentric studies to the varied disciplines of theological education. This volume is but a sample of the pieces offered for consideration. Given the scope of the work, the decision was made to have it co-edited by the present chairpersons of the biblical and theological areas of the ITC faculty, Randall C. Bailey and Jacquelyn Grant.

As Charles Copher wrestled with what to teach Black seminarians in biblical studies in the 1960s, at the peak of the Black Power and Civil Rights Movements, James Cone was responding to the challenges of those movements in the area of theology. Black religious scholars in other disciplines began the arduous task of recovering the Black Presence in their various disciplines. In so doing, they were in one way or another aiding the paradigm shift from Eurocentrism to Afro-centrism in academic and more popular pursuits. Afrocentrism has its origins in various expressions of Black nationalism. Irrespective of one's ideological perspective on Afrocentrism, the central task of its proponents is the affirmation of the Black Presence and the reversal of the historic devaluation of Africa and the African world, both in academic and in non-academic circles. Out of this Afrocentric ap-proach comes an African American perspective as the basis for under-standing reality. Gayraud Wilmore lists five points or components of this perspective: (1) freedom from White control and domination; (2) positive imagery of Africa as the land of origin; (3) social justice; (4) creative style and artistry; and (5) the unity of the secular and the sacred.[1] No longer is the European experience normative for interpret-ing Black reality, but the African world is elevated to a level of importance heretofore unknown to the western world. The essays in this volume represent various expressions of this Afrocentric thought.

The book is divided into two parts. Part One is devoted to the area of biblical studies. The dedicatory essay is by G. Murray Branch who served, along with Dr. Copher, as Professor of Old Testament on the first faculty of the ITC. In this essay, Dr. Branch examines the Hebrew verb root *kpr*, which phonetically sounds like the last name of our honoree. He uses the nuances and English synonyms of this root as a paradigm for discussing the career of Dr. Copher, and interweaves anecdotes which exhibit the depth of mutual admiration between these two giants of Black biblical studies.

The next two essays, by Randall C. Bailey and Stephen Breck Reid, examine logical extensions of the ground breaking work of Dr. Copher in Hebrew Scripture studies. Bailey examines the birth narrative of Moses in Exodus 2:1-10 and argues that it is a late tradition (Priestly) in the Pentateuchal strands designed to present Moses as an Israelite, in contrast to the earlier Moses traditions (Yahwist and Elohist) which present him as an Egyptian. Reid uses sociological methods to com-pare readings of the book of Daniel to the thought of W. E. B. DuBois, examining the concept of double consciousness of oppressed people in this country and showing how such a hermeneutic helps to offer a fresh reading to the biblical text.

The next three essays in this section of the book, by Boykin Sanders, H. Wayne Merritt, and David Rensberger, speak to New Testament exegetical studies. Sanders reviews the treatments in Euro-centric scholarship of the figure of Simon of Cyrene, especially as presented in the Second Gospel, and then appeals to the studies of Bruce Malina to argue that viewing Simon as other than a Black north

African is contrary to the canons of first-century literary under-standings of character presentations. Merritt, on the other hand, uses Malina's work along with structuralist criticism to argue for an under-standing of characters in the gospels not as rugged individuals, but rather as characteristic or symbolic of the ethnic groups from which they come, and against stressing the racial or ethnic identification of these individuals qua individual. Continuing his previous work on the Fourth Gospel by examining the narrative depiction of marginalized individuals in that work, Rensberger notes the various nuancing in the presentations of what he calls the oppressed and oppressors, which show the complexities of these designations and not monolithic cate-gorizations.

The final pieces in this section of the book are related to contem-porary works and situations. John W Waters presents an exposi-tional/homiletical piece reflecting on the well-known "dry bones" passage in Ezekiel for his understanding of the plight of Black people in the U.S. Abraham Smith presents a literary critical reading of Toni Morrison's *Song of Solomon*, and then examines her use of biblical names for the characters in the novel. In this way he both explores a usage of biblical themes in Afrocentric literary traditions and passes on Morrison's implied caution not to appropriate any tradition uncriti-cally.

Part Two is devoted to various other theological disciplines. Ex-ploring the use of the Bible and biblical interpretation as tools for undergirding slavery, Katie Geneva Cannon demonstrates the connect-edness of ideology and hermeneutics. The primary goal of White interpreters of the Bible, she argues, was the creation and maintenance of slavery by the intentional manipulation of biblical interpretations. Exposing three myths of White Christian apologists, Cannon shows how the oppressive ideology and practices influenced hermeneutical principles and interpretations.

In the area of theology, Jacquelyn Grant presents a womanist interpretation of Christology, analyzing three ways in which Christi-anity in general and Christology in particular have been held captive to the various oppressive structures existing both in the church and in the society. She argues that Christian institutions and doctrines have been imprisoned by sexism, racism, and classism, and that what is needed is an eradication of the various forms of oppression which continue to violate humanity and divinity. Octavius A. Gaba examines the use of the images of "light and darkness" in the Christian under-standing of God. He challenges tendencies of associating God exclu-sively with either one or the other, arguing that God's nature includes both aspects, light and dark, and to rob God of either is to do an injustice to the reality of God.

Using the concept of "interdependence" in the area of psychology and pastoral care, Carolyn L. McCrary explores a model for womanist pastoral care. Drawing from the work of psychological theorist W. R. D. Fairbairn, theologian Howard Thurman, and Bantu philosophy, McCrary challenges the traditional western idealization of independence, and proposes interdependence, consistent with the communal concept of traditional African religion, as a normative construct for understanding reality.

Beginning with the particular story of a Black Church congregation in the Methodist Protestant connection as seen from the perspective of sociology of religion, James M. Shopshire explores the protest tradition of Black Methodism. Through careful examination of the minutes of the Georgia Annual Conference, Shopshire contextualizes the issues for the purpose of interpreting even apparently protest-free situations. He uncovers some of the more subtle survival and protest agenda items in situations of racial hostility.

Finally, in exploring ways in which the faith is transmitted to Black children, Janice Hale investigates both the African and the African American cultural traditions which in fact teach and reinforce faith. From African cosmology to Negro Spirituals to the folkloric traditions of storytelling and proverbs, Hale interprets the subversive transmission of faith during dangerous times of slavery to more recent times of racial oppression.

Several persons were very helpful in completing this book. They include: Michelle Jacques, Constance Pope, Nannett Ephraim, Jacquelyn Hurston, Herbert Marbury, Imani Bailey, Alika Gallaway, Kenneth Jones, Kevin King, and Paul Roberts. For your assistance, we are grateful. We also thank the Status, Tenure, and Welfare Committee, James H. Costen, and Calvin S. Morris, all of the Interdenominational Theological Center, for providing a grant to support this project.

Randall C. Bailey
Jacquelyn Grant
Atlanta, Georgia
June 1994

PART ONE

Biblical Studies

CHAPTER 1

Copher: What's in a Name?

G. Murray Branch

Today, as I begin to write this essay, is Yom Kippur, the most holy day in the Jewish calendar. It falls on the tenth day of the Jewish month Tishri. Yom Kippur began at sundown yesterday evening at 6:37 Eastern Standard Time in the U.S.A. It is a day of prayer for forgiveness of sins against God and humans.

The primary basis in Torah for the day of days is Leviticus 23:27-32. In the key passage the Lord spoke to Moses, saying:

> Mark, the tenth day of this seventh month is the Day of Atonement. It shall be a sacred occasion for you; you shall practice self-denial, and you shall bring an offering by fire to the LORD; you shall do no work throughout that day. For it is a Day of Atonement, on which expiation is made on your behalf before the LORD your God. Indeed, any person who does not practice self-denial throughout that day shall be cut off from his kin; and whoever does any work throughout that day, I will cause that person to perish from among his people. Do no work whatever; it is a law for all time, throughout the ages in all your settlements. It shall be a sabbath of complete rest for you, and you shall practice self-denial; on the ninth day of the month at evening, from evening to evening, you shall observe this your sabbath. (TANAKH)

Yom Kippur is the culmination of the ten days of repentance which begin with Rosh Hashanah or the New Year (cf. Num 29:1 ff). These ten days, from the first to the tenth of Tishri, are often called the High Holy Days in Jewish families and neighborhoods. They provide an opportunity for a turning to God even by persons who at other times seldom attend synagogue services. The Haftorah (prophetic portion) for the Sabbath between Rosh Hashanah and Yom Kippur is Hosea 14:2-3:

> Return, O Israel, to the LORD your God,
> For you have fallen because of your sin.
> Take words with you

and return to the LORD.
Say to Him:
"Forgive the guilt
And accept what is good. . . ." (TANAKH)

Those who do return use these days as an occasion for self-examination of the most rigorous kind since most Jews now acknowledge that it was a recurring pattern of falling away from the Lord by their mothers and fathers in earlier generations that brought upon them national disasters and eventually the loss of independence and destruction of their state. Jewish tradition now teaches that a Jewish person cannot return to God's favor on Yom Kippur unless he or she has made amends for sins against God and against neighbors.

Kpr—A Hebrew Language Root Rich with Meanings

The Hebrew verb root *kpr* (pronounced *kó-fer*) is basic to our understanding of the significance of the Day of Atonement. It also appears in the family name of Charles B. Copher when written using Hebrew characters. Although the writing of this tribute to a long-time friend and faculty colleague was begun on Yom Kippur in 1992, this line of thinking about him started more than forty years ago. It was in 1947 or thereabouts that Dr. Copher returned to Atlanta, Georgia, as a member of the Clark College and Gammon Theological Seminary faculties. In 1947 I moved to Atlanta to join the faculty of Morehouse College and Morehouse School of Religion to teach Bible and World Religions in the College and Old Testament courses in the School of Religion. Lectures by visiting scholars and other activities in the Atlanta University Center schools brought together the two of us around mutual interests. In the winter of the following year, however, we found ourselves together in New York City in a situation which made it convenient, even unavoidable, for us to become much better acquainted.

In the 1940s and 1950s the National Association of Biblical Literature and Exegesis (later known as the Society of Biblical Literature) met regularly during the Christmas-New Year holidays at Union Theological Seminary in New York City. Although Charles Copher and I did not travel together from Atlanta to New York City, nor did we register at the same time for the three days of professional meetings in late December 1948, we found ourselves assigned for housing to adjacent rooms with an intervening bathroom in Hastings Hall—the dormitory part of Union Seminary's quadrangle. This housing arrangement, whether providential, fortuitous, or by design of the Registration Desk, was welcomed by us because this proximity afforded us a convenient opportunity to become much better acquainted after the evening sessions when we were able to relax and carry on leisurely conversations in our rooms, then resume them the following morning at breakfast.

Among the things I learned about Copher was that only recently he had returned to Atlanta after having completed the Ph.D. degree in Old Testament studies at Boston University. He learned that two years earlier I had taken a Master's Degree in Old Testament at Drew University. It was clear at once that the two of us had similar interests in the Old Testament and related studies. Just how the conversation about the name Copher originated I do not now recall. Even then I was curious about how people acquire their names, but I am inclined to believe that it was Charles himself who stressed the name, Copher. In any case, he went to the study desk in the room, took a piece of paper and wrote on it the three Hebrew letters which spell his name— *kpr*— a Hebrew root known to both of us as having great significance in Israel's priestly tradition and to a lesser extent elsewhere in the sacred literature.

Years ago, while working on a Master's thesis dealing with the book called Malachi, I found that the author of Malachi, though unknown to us by name, in all probability carried on his prophetic activity at a time when the great prophetic tradition was giving way to a priestly resurgence. This change is seen in Ezekiel and to some extent in Malachi, who was likely living in the early Post-Exile period and especially in the time of the Priestly Code. The highest tribute to the priest's role and function is found in Mal 2:4-7:

> Know, then, that I have sent this command to you, that my covenant with Levi may hold, says the LORD of hosts. My covenant with him was a covenant of life and well-being, which I gave him; this called for reverence, and he revered me and stood in awe of my name. True instruction was in his mouth, and no wrong was found on his lips. He walked with me in integrity and uprightness, and he turned many from iniquity. For the lips of a priest should guard knowledge, and people should seek instruction from his mouth, for he is the messenger of the LORD of hosts.

Hebrew vocabulary is subject to a wide range of English translations once one becomes familiar with the essential meanings of Hebrew roots. Accordingly when I was invited to contribute to a proposed volume in honor of Dr. Copher's eightieth birthday, I immediately responded in the affirmative and indicated as a subject for my paper: "Copher: What's in a Name?" Memories of our shared experiences—in classrooms and in chapel services; of his lectures at Dexter Avenue Baptist Church in Montgomery, Alabama; of special occasions at the ITC, especially of our ITC retirement dinners in 1978 and 1979 respectively; all the way back to pre-ITC days at Union Theological Seminary's Hastings Hall in 1948—these memories dashed through my mind.

Initially the plan for this essay was to quote and comment on all biblical passages in which the Hebrew word *kpr* appears in the Hebrew Bible. Eventually I realized it would be too ambitious an undertaking, would make the paper too lengthy, and would not be necessary to accomplish the primary purpose of honoring Dr. Copher. So I have selected representative Old Testament passages where *kpr* occurs, quote relevant phrases or clauses in English, and then suggest some possible connections of those English terms with the honoree.

Copher—A Man of Intensity, Diverse Interests, and Abilities

The original meaning of the Hebrew root *kpr* is dubious.[1] Perhaps the original meaning of *kpr* is to cover, or to cover over, specifically with bitumen or pitch, as in Gen 6:14: "Make yourself an ark of cypress wood . . . and cover it (*kaper*) within and without with pitch (*koper*)." It occurs most frequently in Scripture in the *Pi'el* form, appearing as such in at least 15 books of TANAKH, in all three divisions, but most often in Leviticus.

Students of biblical Hebrew learn that the distinguishing significance of the *Pi'el* form of the verb is that it indicates intensive, sustained, or repeated action. For example, the Hebrew verb *dbr*, meaning "to speak," is used characteristically in the *Pi'el* because speaking is a sustained activity. Another example is the verb *šbr*. In the *Qal*, *šbr* means "to break," but in the *Pi'el*, *šbr* would be rendered "to shatter." In as much as the preponderance of the root *kpr* is in the *Pi'el*, we must understand that the actions of making atonement (Exod 29:37; Lev 9:7), covering sin (Gen 6:14), purging or making expiation (1 Sam 3:14), forgiving and being forgiven (Ezek 16:63), or reconciling and being reconciled (Ezek 45:15) to God and neighbor (the purpose of Yom Kippur), are intensive or repeated actions divinely ordained so as to become a fixed part of our human nature as sons and daughters of the gracious and ever-living God who created and sustains us.

It is indeed appropriate that the three letters of the Hebrew root *kpr* also spell the name Copher. It is also pertinent to our honoree's person and character that the form of this root appearing in the biblical text with overwhelming frequency is the *Pi'el*, since Charles B. Copher is a very talented man of marked intensity with interests that are wide-ranging. He is a gifted scholar and skilled teacher, a convincing preacher and a helpful pastor, a stimulating lecturer and a fascinating conversationalist. Whenever he talks, he speaks with intense fervor and at a volume such that even those members of the congregation who "have ears but hear not" can hardly miss getting the message.

In the second half of my teaching at the Interdenominational Theological Center, when Dr. Copher's main duties were moved from the classroom to the office of the Vice President of Academic Affairs and Dean of the Faculty, early in each semester I invited him to give two lectures on his area of special research—The Black Presence in the Bible and in the Biblical World—to students enrolled in my Old Testament History and Old Testament Literature courses. Whenever I heard him lecture there or elsewhere, my thoughts invariably went back to the days of the early 1940s when I was a graduate student at Drew University and entered a course taught by Dr. Edwin Lewis, Professor of Systematic Theology and one of the editors of the *Abingdon Bible Commentary*. Professor Lewis was not only a stimulating teacher of theology, but he was also fascinating to listen to because he had a unique quality of voice and an odd style of phrasing for emphasis. Moreover, he could be heard all over the first floor of the Seminary Building. Mrs. Lewis, his wife, visited his classes from time to time, just to listen to his lectures. Although Dr. Copher does not have such an odd style of delivery, he too could be heard easily on the second floor of the ITC classroom building. Students who listened to his lectures were helped greatly in their understanding of the importance of Old Testament studies to their ministries and came to a new or deeper appreciation of the presence and participation of peoples of African and also of Negroid derivation in the formation of biblical religion and culture in the ancient world.

It must be said not only that Dr. Copher was outstanding as a biblical scholar, professor, and churchman, but also that he was a person skilled in horticulture, land terracing, and the building of stone walls. When the recently organized and chartered Interdenominational Theological Center began holding classes in September 1959, Charles and his wife, Marie, were having a new house built in northwest Atlanta. They themselves did much of the landscaping and beautifying outside the house. The grounds were so well laid out and attractive, because of the abundance and variety of flowers and plants, that a visitor easily could have taken the householder to be a nursery owner rather than an academician. When I looked at and felt his hands, which were rough and calloused as though he had been farming for years or working as a stone mason, I gained a new level of respect for him as a man of many and contrasting gifts.

Dr. Copher's diversity of talents was matched by an unusual mix of personality traits. He took his calling as a Christian minister seriously, yet he used humor often and engaged in boisterous laughter as much as anyone in the ITC family. Hardly a semester passed in which a student or two would not come into my office and say to me, "Professor Branch, how can I tell when Dr. Copher is serious?" His habit of kidding, joking, and "pulling the legs" of others sometimes has been baffling to some of his ITC faculty, staff, and other friends, especially to those who have not been in close association with him in several kinds of circumstances.

Years ago, when Urban Ministry programs had been established and operating in a few places (such as Chicago) for the purpose of providing clergy persons with real life experiences of trying to make it for a week in a large inner city as unemployed, unknown, near paupers without family or friends, Copher, without telling his ITC friends, accepted the opportunity for that kind of exposure. After he had gone through that sobering experience, someone mentioned it after the close of an ITC faculty meeting. Many of the people still in the room, including me, took the report to be a joke. Later we learned that it was true. Charles Copher actually had taken upon himself the role of an unknown, shabbily dressed, nearly destitute man, living for several days in the inhospitable environment of an inner city, being helped now and then by a person who still knew the meaning of "the milk of human kindness."

Let me say again that the three letters of the Hebrew verb *kpr*, which have been translated by a dozen or more English terms and which also spell the family name of Charles B. Copher, are significant in that they convey important features about the man whom this volume honors. He was, among other things, a professor, a priest, a pastor, and a preacher.

Professor

Dr. Copher spent more than half of his four score years of very active life in institutions of higher learning as a professor, the dean of a theological faculty, and a lecturer. After his retirement from the Interdenominational Theological Center, the Charles B. Copher Annual Faculty Lecture Series was established in 1979, with Dr. John W Waters, Professor of Old Testament, as the initiating lecturer. Inasmuch as the basic meaning of the Hebrew root *kpr* appears to be "to cover, to cover over, or to purge away," perhaps we should think of Dr. Copher's long years of service in academia as having been dedicated to covering ignorance and purging errors, "old wives' tales," and nonsensical notions, which so readily become attached to folk religion.[2]

Priest

As a priest and minister in The United Methodist Church, Dr. Copher surely was called upon to be solicitous of the well-being of the congregation and those to whom he ministered. Perhaps God said to him, even as Moses said to Aaron, "Draw near to the altar and sacrifice your sin offering and your burnt offering, and make atonement for yourself and for the people; and sacrifice the offering of the people, and make atonement for them; as the LORD has commanded" (Lev 9:7, NRSV; the KJV reads "make an atonement").

Pastor

As a pastor and counselor to congregations or students in Ohio, Massachusetts, Georgia, or wherever, Dr. Copher surely spoke words of comfort or encouragement, offered prayers, and read portions of Holy Writ such as Psalm 65:1-3:

> Praise is due to you,
>   O God, in Zion;
> and to you shall vows be performed,
>   O you who answer prayer!
> To you all flesh shall come.
> When deeds of iniquity overwhelm us,
>   you forgive our transgressions.[3]

Preacher

As a Christian preacher, Dr. Copher could not have avoided being influenced to some extent by the Apostle Paul. Prior to his mystical religious experience on his way to Damascus, Saul of Tarsus was an acknowledged Pharisee, who had been "brought up at the feet of Gamaliel" (Acts 22:3). His personal experience with the risen Christ transformed him from an ardent persecutor of men and women who were followers of The Way, to an indomitable champion of Christ the risen Lord, and a most persistent Apostle to the Nations. Out of his own unforgettable experiences of radical transformation, he wrote to the Church at Corinth:

> So if anyone is in Christ, there is a new creation: everything old has passed away; see, everything has become new! All this is from God, who reconciled us to himself through Christ, and has given us the ministry of reconciliation; that is, in Christ God was reconciling the world to himself, not counting their trespasses against them, and entrusting the message of reconciliation to us. So we are ambassadors for Christ, since God is making his appeal through us; we entreat you on behalf of Christ, be reconciled to God. (2 Cor 5:17-20)

Paul's doctrine of reconciliation is repeated in Rom 5:10:

> For if while we were enemies, we were reconciled to God through the death of his Son, much more surely, having been reconciled, will we be saved by his life.

Given Paul's solid grounding in Pharisaic theology with its belief in resurrection, and given Paul's conviction that he had been fully reconciled to God, he may have derived his reconciliation doctrine from his knowledge of the many-faceted senses in which the Hebrew root *kpr* has been understood. In the Hebrew text of Lev 7:7*b*, *kpr* is found, and is rendered in TANAKH as "it shall belong to the priest who makes expiation thereby." In the KJV, the NRSV, and several other English translations, Lev 7:7 is placed at the end of chapter 6 as verse 30. The King James translators rendered Lev 6:30 "And no sin offering, whereof any of the blood is brought into the tabernacle of the congregation to reconcile (*ykpr bw*) withal in the holy place, shall be eaten: it shall be burnt in the fire." The NRSV says "for atonement in the holy place."

In my view, Charles B. Copher was the most effective minister of reconciliation in the Interdenominational Theological Center family, especially after he assumed the duties of Dean of the Faculty—a title which he was given the first year we occupied the newly constructed campus of the ITC at 671 Beckwith Street in Atlanta. The fledgling Theological Center had spent its first year of operation in South Atlanta on the campus of Gammon Theological Seminary. In the early years there were some "growing pains," some problems of inter-relations among newly combined faculty and staff persons, and among the four denominations and seminaries, which were first constituents of the new venture in ecumenical, cooperative theological education.

Because Gammon was the largest of the original four seminaries and provided a majority of the faculty and staff persons for the ITC, and because The United Methodist Church contributed through Gammon the most funds and other benefits for the Center's operation, Gammon exerted more influence than the other three combined upon the curriculum, policies of management, and decision-making. Thus, on occasion, friction arose, which for the most part was readily smoothed over. Dr. Copher had been for some time a respected person on the Gammon faculty, was a member in good standing of a United Methodist Conference, and is by nature an accomplished conciliator. Accordingly, he was in an especially favored position to exercise the ministry of reconciliation.

His paramount opportunity to pour oil on troubled waters came, however, after he assumed the office and full responsibilities of Vice President for Academic Affairs and Dean of the Faculty. In the wake of the Montgomery Bus Protest and student sit-ins in Greensboro, North Carolina, and elsewhere, freedom fever spread to all sectors of the country and overseas to colonized peoples on the African continent and elsewhere. Ferment among seminarians surfaced first among Black students enrolled at Colgate Rochester Divinity School, which claimed the largest number of Blacks in the student body of any predominantly White seminary. Those students at Colgate Rochester charged that their seminary was not adequately preparing them for ministering to Black churches and to the needs of the communities in which they expected to be called to serve. Administrators and faculty persons at Colgate Rochester became so concerned about what their students were saying that they invited a team from ITC—consisting of President Harry V. Richardson, Dr. Copher, myself, and Rudolph Smith, a well-respected student—to participate at their expense in two back-to-back, two-day weekend consultations on the Colgate Rochester campus, along with a similar team from the School of Theology of Howard University.

The ITC team returned to Atlanta from Rochester thoroughly sobered. We were conscious of the problems faced by seminarians and by the ITC in particular. We talked among ourselves. Yet we were not fully prepared for the demonstration not long thereafter by the ITC students. One Tuesday morning in the spring of 1968, ITC students and a goodly number of faculty persons assembled for what was expected to be a regular, twice a week chapel service. The scheduled speaker was a Professor of Psychology and Clinical Counseling from the Candler School of Theology, if I recall correctly; as Chair of the ITC Chapel and Assemblies Committee, I presided. The house was full. We sang the first stanza of an opening hymn. Suddenly the organ and singing stopped. The congregation sat down as two students arose at the back of the room, one on either side. They walked briskly down the sloping aisles of the large lecture hall in the classroom building then used as a chapel. They stopped at the front, still one on each side, and turned to face the assembly. In alternating fashion they began reading an extended list of complaints and charges against selected persons in authority at the ITC. The thrust of the charges was that certain persons in positions of authority at the ITC treated seminary students as though they were children and that they, the students, received too little a part in making decisions that affected their lives and ministry. The reader will not be surprised that the chapel ended with the reading of that bill of particulars. A special faculty meeting was called immediately, and students gathered in the Student Lounge on the ground floor of the classroom building. Later, perhaps that afternoon, several faculty members gathered with students in their lounge for a further airing and clarification of grievances.

Against that broad and varied background, Dr. Copher's skills at peacemaking became critical because, while he himself was not a direct target of criticism, the Secretary in the Dean's office was one of those singled out by students to receive the brunt of complaint. I do not know what Dean Copher did or said to his Secretary, but his reconciling capabilities must have been at their highest level of graceful precision inasmuch as the lady had no stroke, heart attack, or other recognizable disabling experience, and continued to work as Secretary in the Dean's office thereafter for a considerable span of time. It is my impression also that she promptly became less officious in her manner of dealing with other people, especially with ITC students.

Among the consequences of that student action was an agreement, arrived at through faculty discussion and soul-searching, that each of us would consciously endeavor to "blackenize," as far as possible, the courses for which each had teaching responsibility. To that end many of us wrote a preliminary paper on how that would be done. A series of faculty sessions was held, one each month in addition to the regular faculty business meeting. One teacher after another shared with the group how he or she would go about lifting up the participation of Black persons in and their contributions to his or her discipline and field of study. Those discussions led Copher on a line of research, investigation, and study of the Black presence in the Bible and in the biblical world, which has brought much benefit to many hundreds and thousands of persons who have read his articles or heard his lectures over the last quarter century. His expectation at the outset was to have produced a book on the subject long before now, but fresh leads continue to appear such that he has been unable to terminate the investigation.

One of the effects of Copher's work has been to irritate and trouble those who hold on to unexamined and false stereotypes about Negro inferiority and the non-contributions of Black Africans to human history and culture. Still others, taking a cue from him and his work, have produced numerous books and articles of their own on the same general theme. If the truths and information about the history and culture of Black Africans, including Negroid peoples throughout the world, continue greatly to expand and to be stimulated by Copher's work, perhaps it will help to cover ignorance, purge prejudice, expiate the sin of racism, and bring nearer the day of reconciliation among all the peoples of earth, thus fulfilling the promise of his name.

Chapter 2

"Is That Any Name
for a Nice Hebrew Boy?"
Exodus 2:1-10: The De-Africanization
of an Israelite Hero

Randall C. Bailey

Scholars in other disciplines have long argued that Moses was an Egyptian.[1] In the previous century Count Volney, quoting Strabo, made such claims on the basis of historical reconstruction of events during the suppression of the monotheistic Aton cult.[2] Similarly, early in this century Freud, in *Moses and Monotheism*, made such a claim on the basis of the lack of conformity on a mythic level of the Moses birth narrative, found in Exod 2:1-10, with the elements and structure of the classic "exposed child" myth.[3] Later in this century John G. Jackson revived these claims.[4]

It is safe to say that none of these arguments has been taken seriously by the guild of biblical scholars. The closest we have come is in acknowledging that the name Moses is Egyptian. We have not, however, extended this acknowledgment to the possibility that the bearer of the name was Egyptian.[5] Instead we have argued about the inconsistencies between the genealogy of Exod 6:20 and its parallel in 1 Chr 6:3*b*, in which Moses' name appears before Miriam's; about the narrative of Exod 2:4, where she is older than he; and about the grammatical irregularities of the etiology found in Exod 2:10. The one exception to this arguing against the possibility of Egyptian origins for Moses among contemporary biblical scholars is George V. Pixley, who concludes that "The liberator's name then would seem to confirm the tradition that he was sprung from the dominant Egyptian class itself."[6]

This lack of acceptance, in fact this lack of serious entertainment of the thesis, is based in the claims found in Exod 2:1-10 that Moses was an Israelite of Levitical stock who got his name from an Egyptian princess. This makes sense, for what would an Egyptian be doing leading the Israelite people from slavery to freedom and being called the "servant of YHWH"? They argued that Deutero-Isaiah's use of the designations "the shepherd of YHWH" (Isa 44:28) and "the anointed of YHWH" (Isa 45:1) for Cyrus, the king of Persia, should not cause us to rethink these possibilities with Moses. Are these scholars outside the biblical field trying to make a John Brown out of Moses?

As I examine the materials in Exod 1–3, I shall demonstrate (1) that there is evidence to be found in Exod 2:14b–4:23 which would point the reader in the direction of seeing Moses as an African; (2) that the narrative found in Exod 2:1-10 is a very late addition to the final form of the text; and (3) that the intention of the writer of this birth/adoption narrative, who added this tradition to the text, is to systematically plant the seeds which will counter the evidence to come later in chapters 2 and 3 that Moses was an African. In other words, as one looks at the materials in the latter units, the clear message is that Moses is Egyptian. I shall then show that many aspects of the narrative in Exod 2:1-10 are intentionally geared to counteract these impressions. In fact the writing of this unit is so skillful that logical questions of discontinuity, which ought to arise from reading the succeeding narratives, have either been ignored in the scholarship or have been resolved in line with the claims of the birth/adoption narrative. Thus, my investigation should lead to a better appreciation for the narrative skills of the writer of the unit in 2:1-10.

The Introduction of the Reader to the Character Moses

I begin the investigation by noting that there has been much discussion on the relationship of the units in Exodus 1–2 to each other. On the one hand, Exod 1:11-14 bespeaks the oppression of the Israelites in the form of economic exploitation by the Egyptians. The subject of such economic oppression is then dropped and not picked up again until 2:23, a summary which states, "And after many days the Egyptian king died and the children of Israel suffered under the economic exploitation and cried out. . . ." Interpolated into this subject of economic exploitation is a series of narratives, in Exod 1:8-10 and 15-22, which bespeak Pharaonic genocidal attempts upon the people by a king "who knew not Joseph." It is interesting that neither the economic oppression nor the genocidal plan tradition acknowledges the other, thereby suggesting that they are independent of each other. Even the summary statement of Egyptian exploitation in 2:23*f* does not conflate these two traditions of economic exploitation and geno- cide.[7] Similarly, in 2:23 the significance of the death of the king of Egypt is that the oppression did not cease. There is no indication that Moses, a fugitive murderer, was now safe to return to Egypt. Thus, this summary does not presuppose these other narratives found in Exod 1 or 2.

Exodus 3:1 begins the call narratives of the deliverer/liberator, Moses. The subject of economic exploitation and oppression is the main problem, as vv. 7 and 9 claim. There is no mention in these units of the subject of genocide. Again there appears to be no knowledge in these units of the genocidal policies of 1:8-10 and 15-22. Thus, one sees that Exod 1:11-14; 2:23-25; and 3:1*f* all deal with the subject of economic oppression to the exclusion of the genocidal policies.

There are two other indications that the materials in Exod 3:1–4:10 predate and do not presuppose the materials in 2:1-22. The first is the way in which the main character, Moses, is identified. Exodus 3:1 gives us his name and occupation (a shepherd), and his employer's name and their relationship (Jethro, his father-in law).[8] It appears this writer is introducing the characters to us for the first time. Otherwise there would be no need to tell the reader of his occupation and his relationship to his employer, since these data are found in 2:11*f*.

The second indication that the narratives of 3:1–4:10 do not presuppose the narratives of ch. 2 is that in 3:11 the main character asks a question about being commissioned to go to say to Pharaoh, "Let the people go." His objection is not that he will face murder charges upon his return, as 2:11-15 would indicate. Rather his objection, "Who am I that I should go to Pharaoh and bring the Israelites out of Egypt?", seems to be one of his suitability in regard to his personal qualifica- tions for the task.

Thus far, I have noted that the subject of economic exploitation is begun in ch. 1, picked up at the end of ch. 2, and continued into ch. 3. Similarly, I have argued that 3:1 functions to introduce the main character, Moses, and his father-in-law, Jethro, as though the reader does not know him or their relationship. Finally, I have argued that none of these narratives demonstrates awareness of the intervening narratives of Exod 1:8-10 or 1:15–2:22, the genocide plans, the birth of Moses, or the flight of Moses to Midian and/or of his marriage. Scholars have long agreed on the composite character of the narratives found in Exodus 3.[9] They have done so, however, from the perspective of the Exod 2:1-10 introduction to Moses. If my contention is correct, namely that in the first development of the tradition, Moses, the main character of the Exodus narrative, is first introduced to the reader in Exod 3:1, then what is the implication of this for interpretation?

In the earliest narrative, which is part of the J tradition, Moses, an Egyptian, notes the burning bush (v. 2), and the deity notes that he has turned to observe this (v. 4a). The deity then describes the economic oppression (v. 7) and the deity's intention to liberate the people (v. 8). The first thing to note is that the main character is Egyptian. This is clear from his name, which is of the order of Ramses, etc. While Noth and others have argued that this was not a fact known to the ancient writers, it appears that this line of argument is an attempt to buttress their contention that the modern reader should not put much emphasis on this connection.

Second, in this J narrative, the statement of the deity in 3:7a is, "I have surely seen the oppression of *my* people" (*'mî*), not "*your* people" (*'mk*). Thus, as far as J is concerned, the deity is talking to an Egyptian about the liberation of a foreign people. In addition the means of this liberation is through divine descent, "I have come down" (3:8a). In the E narrative, interestingly, there are several aspects of the J narrative which are not changed. The first is the name of the main character, Moses. The second is the designation of the people as "my people." This identification of Moses as a non-Israelite is furthered by the instructions to tell the people that he was sent to them by *'elohê 'abotekem*, "the God of *your* ancestors," not "*our* ancestors."[10]

As scholars have long noted, much of the theology of this J passage, however, caused trouble for E, who later redacted the material. The major problems for E in this narrative were the divine descent, implication of liberation completely through non-human auspices, and direct address to a human. Thus, the narrative is augmented by the deity speaking through the fire and a commissioning of the liberator within the genre of prophetic call. Thus, we have the previously noted questioning of the individual of their personal qualifications, "who am I," followed by the words of assurance, "I shall be with you" (v. 11), and the commissioning (vv. 15-16).

E also recognized the problem of such a commissioning of an Egyptian. This problem is solved, however, not in terms of altering the ethnic identity of the character. Rather, the problem is solved by educating the character. This is done by the question, "If I come to the Israelites and say to them, 'the God of your ancestors has sent me to you,' and they ask me, 'What is his name?', what shall I say to them?" (3:13). As can be seen from my form critical remarks above, this is an extraneous element to the call narrative structure. In fact it comes between the deity's response to Moses' questioning of his suitability and the deity's charge to Moses. In the call narrative genre the response and charge usually follow each other. The question, therefore, arises as to the function of this additional element.

Many scholars have argued that this additional element should be understood as E's attempt to equate Yahweh and Elohim, and thus should not be taken as a serious effort at data collection on Moses' part. It appears, however, that from the narrative level the question is one which is seeking information which is not known. The question is, who possesses the knowledge or the answer to the question posed in the narrative, "What's your name?" Moses or the people? The suggestion of the narrative is that Moses is saying, "When I, as an Egyptian, go to your people, Elohim, they might not believe me and try to test my authenticity. If this is the case, how do I pass their test?" In other words, they know the answer (i.e., the name of the deity), but he does not. This appears to be a logical question for an Egyptian to ask an Israelite deity. Thus, the answer to the question is for Moses' benefit.[11] This could also explain why the answer to the question begins, not with the requested name, but rather with a description of the nature and function of the deity.[12]

A third problem for E is how to explain the location of this Egyptian character in Midianite territory married into this priestly family. The solution, nuancing Coats, is the creation of the Midianite marriage narrative utilizing the established literary motif of the stranger/foreigner at the well defending the women leading to betrothal and marriage, as happens in Genesis 24.[13]

If my reconstruction of the tradition is correct, then the identification of this foreign man by the Midianite women as Egyptian in 2:19 seems quite clear and understandable. Interestingly, most of the scholarly speculation on this verse has been on his apparel, not on his physical appearance, language, etc., which is understandable, since the unit is usually read through the eyes of 2:1-10 and not through 3:1-15.[14]

Further, while J is not definite as to the location of this action, only in the *midbar*, the wilderness, E adds the details that this event took place on the mysterious "Mountain of God" (3:1) in the desert outside Egypt. Thus, the Egyptian is commissioned by the deity outside of Egypt. It should also be noted that having an Egyptian function in such a role was most plausible to the J and E readers of the tenth and eighth centuries respectively, who held the Egyptians in such high esteem.[15]

Such was not the case for the writers and readers of the post-exilic period, however. One could not maintain the theocracy's claims of Israelite national separation and purity as exemplified in the Priestly materials[16] and the Holiness Codes[17] with the prime mediator of the law being an Egyptian. Such could not be tolerated. Such must be reshaped and refocused. One can almost hear the P writers saying, "He must be de-Africanized. We must refocus this tradition as we did with the Table of Nations, where we manufactured three sons of Noah to separate Israel (Shem) from those to the south (Ham). Thus, before we can recast the call traditions in Exod 6:2-9, groundwork must be laid."

In hypothesizing the development of this reconstruction it appears that, first, Exod 3:6, where the deity is identified as *'elohê 'abika*, "the God of your [ms, referring to Moses] ancestor," was added to the J and E materials; this would counteract the "my people/your [mp] ancestors" of 3:7, 10, and 16. Next, the vehicle of birth-adoption narrative of 2:1-10 was selected to resolve most of the above-mentioned problems. Finally, the genocide narratives of 1:15-22 were added to give a context for the birth-adoption narrative. It is thus to the unit of the birth-adoption narrative that I now direct my attention.

The Birth of the Liberator and the Aggrandizement of the Mother in Exod 2:1-10

As the opening lines of this narrative say,[18] a son of a Levite married a daughter of a Levite. While most attention in commentaries has been given to the anonymous nature of the introduction of these characters, through the omission of the names, this line of argument has bypassed the function served by such identifying information. It appears the narrator feels the names can be taken care of in the genealogy of Exod 6:17-23. At this point in the story the narrator has to stress/highlight the national and tribal identities of these characters. Names alone will not do that unabashedly. Clearly tribal identification fills the bill. Thus the text suggests "a good Levite male married a good Levite female." What better stock for the lawgiver, especially if he is to be augmented by Aaron? "No, he can't be Egyptian," thinks the reader, "since both his parents are Levites."[19] That settles the nationality question. He's a Levite!

Having resolved the nationality question, the narrator still has to deal with the name. As the broad structure of the narrative shows, the unit is formed on the birth formula, *watahar . . . wateled . . . watiqrah*, she conceived, she gave birth, she named. As one readily notes, the first two elements of the formula, she conceived and gave birth, are found in v. 2. The third element, she named, however, is reserved until v. 10. As has been argued in other contexts, when any element of the birth formula is problematic for the narrator, an intervening narrative is interpolated into the formula in order to resolve the problem prior to the appearance of that element in the text.[20] Thus, once the child is born, the name is not given until there is an explanation of how it is understandable that this Levite child has an Egyptian name. The solution is easy: he is special, because an Egyptian princess adopted him and gave the name to him.[21]

Now, how do we get an Egyptian princess to adopt and name him? Simple: use a variation on the "exposed child" myth, known in the ancient world as a means of introducing leaders, as exemplified in the legend of Sargon's birth[22] and the like. Thus I assume that the writer of this narrative was consciously using this "typical motif," as Gressmann termed it.[23] In other words, just as in post-exilic times the P school turned to Mesopotamian mythology for a nuancing of the creation and flood narratives, so also did they turn to these materials for this birth/adoption narrative of the arch law-mediator. The birth-adoption motif provides for the hero introduction, while giving a context for the etiology and a way to acquire for him access to the royal court. Freud and others point out that this narrative differs from the usual "exposed child myth" which is schematized as "from riches to rags to riches," while here we have "from Levite serf to palace to Israelite slave leader." In the eyes of the narrator, however, this schema fits the riches, rags, riches, model. This is not the proof that he was Egyptian, given the basic structure of the myth, as Freud argues. Rather, it is the way in which the myth has to be nuanced in order for the problems to be solved.[24] Similarly, as opposed to having a prophecy about a potential ruler threatening the throne, as is often the case in such narratives, the genocidal stories provide a reversal on the motif in setting the context for the birth/adoption.

The extensive attempt by the rabbinic writings to ground this birth within the "threat to the ruler" motif [25] demonstrates that such an omission within the text itself is readily apparent. The omission could also signal to the reader that the writer had a different purpose in mind in using the "exposed child" motif. In other words, while the motif was helpful in some aspects, it had to be modified, since the writer did not want to portray the child as a threat to Pharaoh; rather, as I am arguing, the writer wants to explain away the name. If this were not the case, one would expect the writer to have added the "threat" element of a usurper to the throne into chapter 1.

In looking more closely at this narrative in Exod 2:1-10, another problem posed by the narrative in Exod 2:19 is solved, namely the statement that Moses was recognizable as an Egyptian. As the birth-adoption narrative says, as soon as the Egyptian princess sees the child, she recognizes that he is a Hebrew. What better confirmation for his identity through outward appearance than for Egyptian royalty, who ought to be able to recognize one of their own, to proclaim that just by looking at him one can recognize him as a Hebrew. The creativity here is ingenious, for once the reader gets through vv. 1 and 6—Levite, Hebrew child[26]—the Egyptian designation in v. 19 is reduced to "maybe it was how he was dressed," as the commentators argue. In fact, it gives the reader the sense that Hebrews were outwardly different from Egyptians, who could be recognized by sight.[27]

Is it enough, however, to just explain away his nationality, to just de-Africanize him? The reader is still left with one who is an Israelite, but who was raised at the Egyptian court. This, therefore, raises two other questions. Can we really trust him to act right? Did he forget where he came from (which is a suspicion raised of all oppressed people who are allowed to go to/are trained at/allowed to sit at Pharaoh's table)?

The way in which this writer chooses to answer these questions is both ingenious and fascinating. The method utilized by the narrator to "show this one approved" is to build up the mother of this child. While some scholars have recently begun to concentrate on the role of the women within this narrative complex, most of the attention has gone to the midwives and the two daughters.[28] It is my contention, however, that it is the mother who is the star of the show, the prime mover, the guarantor of the son! While some birth narratives of important biblical characters do begin with the barren woman motif, such as Sarai/Isaac (Gen 16:1-2), the unnamed woman/Samson (Judg 13:2), and Hannah/Samuel (1 Sam 1:2), others begin with narratives which through their syntax demonstrate the craftiness and guile of the mothers, such as Rebecca/Jacob-Esau (Gen 25:22-24), and Bathsheba/Solomon (2 Sam 11:2-5). The narrative in Exod 2:1-10 is of the second type.

The writer begins the legitimation of the mother at the very outset. Not only is she a Levite woman, she performs in the best tradition of an Israelite woman (in the view of the narrator): she gets pregnant. Immediately upon this announcement of conformity to role expectations, the writer tells us that this woman is of the caliber of Elohim in the Priestly creation narrative of Genesis 1, for she also can look at her creation and pronounce him *kî tôb*, good.[29] In other words the verbal phrase "she saw that he was good" reminds the reader of the response of Elohim to the phases of creation.[30] Thus, the phrase should not be rendered "she saw he was a fine baby," as the NRSV now translates it.

By the same token, while much has been made of the presence of the deity in this narrative in terms of the mother "carrying out the divine plan for the child,"[31] the deity is conspicuously absent from this unit. There is mention of the deity and the rewards of the deity for the midwives in chapter 1, but there is no such reference in chapter 2. Instead, the narrative says, "and she saw." The mother made the evaluation. This mother acts just like the deity acted before. Hers is the evaluation to be watched.

Immediately on the heels of this evaluation the writer tells us about Plan A—to hide the child. In the tradition of Rahab with the spies of Jericho (Joshua 2) and of the Israelite deity with those in trouble, as attested throughout the Psalms, she hid him for three months. This is intriguing, for these are the months when he would most bond with her, on the one hand, and the ones when the baby would cry the most often. In other words, during the months in which it would be most difficult to hide a baby, who does not sleep through the night but awakens the parents by crying in the middle of the night and would thus be easily detected by others, she was able to hide him. Surely she is "able"![32] End of Plan A.

When she wasn't able to hide him anymore, she began Plan B by building a *tebah*, an ark. First Noah, now the *bat levi*, the Levite woman, and then there were no more: these are the only two passages in the Hebrew Bible which use this term for ark. This ark was built by her with pitch and bitumen and all the other stuff necessary to ensure that it would float and protect the child. In other words, she duplicated Noah's act. Just as Noah saved humanity for the world by building an ark and surviving the flood, so also this woman is going to save the nation from drowning in the Nile. The point here is that while most commentators compare Noah and Moses, the narrator has compared Noah and the mother. As with the *'ešet ḥayil*, the capable woman of Proverbs 31, the way to prove a woman worthy is in the view of the biblical writer to show her to be a better man—used non-generically—than her main prototype.

The mother then places her son in the ark and puts it in the reeds along the bank of the Nile while his sister positions herself at a distance in order to see what will be done to the baby boy. The end of Plan B—or is it? On the one hand, in the use of the word *wattetaṣṣab*, "and she positioned herself," with the switch of subject from the mother to the sister, one has to wonder if the mother has dropped out of the action completely. On the other hand, the use of this verb has a foreshadowing of the instructions that will be given to Moses to position himself before Pharaoh, as happens in Exod 8:16 and 9:13. It also foreshadows Moses' response to the people after the exodus when they feel trapped between Pharaoh's army and the sea. As he tells them in 14:13, "Fear not! Stand fast and see the salvation of Yahweh. . . ." Here in our narrative, the sister is told to stand fast and watch the ambiguous "what will be done to him." Will it be salvation or destruction? Is the mother still in control?[33] The reader has to follow the action to see if this is the case.

As the narrative continues, the daughter of Pharaoh and her entourage appear on the scene. Once the ark is discovered and the child identified, the narrator tells us the princess took pity, *watahmol*, (v. 6b) upon him. Thus, one of the major motifs for subverting the will of monarchs is utilized. Someone from the house of the monarch— usually a woman, but in the case of Jonathan, a male—switches allegiance from the monarch to the Israelite potential savior. Such is the case with Rahab (Josh 2:1-22), Michal (1 Sam 19:11-17), and Abigail (1 Sam 25:1-42).[34]

Now the sister pops up with the speech which will save the day: "Shall I go and get you a Hebrew nurse from the women to nurse the child for you?" Noth and others point to the conflict between the order of the names in the genealogy of Moses and Miriam in 1 Chr 6:3, where the order implies that she is younger than he, and in this narrative, in which she is depicted as older.[35] Childs and others marvel at the ingenuity of this young girl to say just the right thing at the right time. The reader, however, recalls the comparison of the mother to Elohim and Noah, the foreshadowing of positioning and having pity, and then realizes that this must be part of Plan B. The mother knew what would happen. She knew Pharaoh's daughter would show up and switch loyalty. She told the daughter what to say, just as the deity will tell Moses what to say. It worked. This woman is ingenious!

To cap off the narrative, Pharaoh's daughter offers to pay the mother for raising her own child. She is offered *śekarek*, which is generally used to denote one's just wage, that payment which one deserves and for which one has worked. In fact the flawlessness of this plan shows that she has earned this payment. Imagine being paid to raise your own child! This woman is as good as Abram, who convinced his wife to lie only to be rewarded by Pharaoh to take her back (see Gen 12:10-20).

Through such a portrayal of the mother, the narrator asks, "Can we trust such a woman to rear the child in the way he should go? Is she not crafty enough to make sure he is able to withstand the seduction of being in Pharaoh's court? Can we rely on a child reared in such an environment to act right and withstand the onslaught of that revered Egyptian wisdom?"[36]

The answer is yes for three reasons. First, the narrator says *wayig-dal*—"when the child grew up" (v. 10). This is only the third time a third person masculine singular verb has appeared in the unit. The first two were in the very beginning with the father going and taking a wife. Now the child grows up. Both of these are natural phenomena. What is unusual here is that unlike Gen 21:8, when the *wayigdal* is accompanied with *wayiggamel*, "and he was weaned," implying a short time, here there is no such qualification. The time is unspecified. Therefore, in the omission of the qualifying "weaned," the implication is "when he got older." Thus she had a longer time to shape him.[37]

Second, we can trust the mother's training to last, since the actions and speeches of the Egyptian princess—pity on a Hebrew, tricked into paying the mother to raise him, and bad grammar on the etiology—show that he will be able to withstand Egyptian wisdom like this. Clearly, she is no queen of Sheba![38]

Finally, we can trust this woman to train her son to identify with his people, for as the following narrative (2:11-14) will show, he defends them against the Egyptian taskmasters. Is there any more proof needed that this nameless woman, this *bat levi* can train up the law-giver in the way he should go? It appears not.

Conclusion

Both Exum and Weems raise the ideological question regarding the use of women in the beginning frame of the book of Exodus. It appears that my reading would suggest that women are used literarily in the frame as foils for the so-called "wise/shrewd Pharaoh." This happens in the case of Hebrew as well as Egyptian women. Thus, their primacy in the narrative appears not to be for the highlighting of women's accomplishments. Rather they are used as debunkers of a venerated male who can be tricked by women of low and high status, by named and unnamed women. At the same time the reader must keep in mind that this "venerated male" is symbolic of a "venerated nation." Thus, there is a backhanded nature to the use of these women, similar to the Deuteronomic use of woman, such as Michal, who foils her father at his own job in 1 Sam 19:11-17.

By the same token, the literary artistry of the narrator is to be admired, for the use of the established literary motifs sets the stage to enable the reader to read the remainder of the Moses tradition through the eyes of this narrative. Similar to the way the Priestly writer presents Genesis 1, through which all other creation traditions are usually read, and Genesis 17 with the "covenant of circumcision," through which all other circumcision passages tend to be read, so also with this passage through which the Moses tradition is read. The artistry of structure, vocabulary, imagery, and the like, dismantle later narrative clues to alternative renderings and development of the Moses tradition. Such a reworking of the tradition for ancient readers would not only have a comical flair but it would push all the right buttons for the reorientation of the tradition.

This reworking of the Moses tradition by the writer may be equally effective with the modern reader, especially the one grounded in Eurocentric Jewish and Christian traditions, since it so thoroughly debunks the Egyptian traditions. In other words, the presentation of the birth of Moses fits well our expectation of "deliverer against the odds." Similarly, since those in these religious traditions do not venerate Egyptian wisdom or culture, the ideological thrust of the Hebrew, anti-Egyptian narrator is taken for granted. Thus, it is quite conceivable that a leader like the Pharaoh so farcically portrayed here could exist and could be so skillfully derailed. By the same token, the notion of Moses being an Egyptian is so far removed from the realm of cognitive possibility for most modern readers that the reassurance of the nice Levite boy marrying the nice Levite girl is welcomed.

Finally, my reconstruction suggests that the liberation narratives of Exodus originally spoke to class struggle along with national struggles. It also suggests that coalitions among people across class and national lines within such struggles are a model for consideration for our current liberation efforts. As the tradition now stands, however, debunking it could be dangerous if used to suggest to other oppressed people that oppressive forces are easily undermined and overcome.

CHAPTER 3

The Theology of the Book of Daniel and the Political Theory of W. E. B. DuBois

Stephen Breck Reid

The call of the Gospel requires that we implement the reign of God. Both Scripture and modern social theory provide resources in this task. Social theory, exemplified by William Julius Wilson's description of the declining significance of race,[1] presents a troubling vision. Race and class have produced a combination adroitly used by forces of political domination through three historical periods—from the racial caste system of the antebellum period, through the combination of class struggle and racial oppression characteristic of the "Jim Crow" era in both North and South, to the "transition from racial inequalities to class inequalities" in more recent history.[2] This third period has witnessed the bifurcation of the African American community; in many instances the Black middle class no longer lives in the same neighborhoods as the Black underclass.[3]

The strategy of implementation of the Gospel's vision of the reign of God necessarily changes as the social structures change. The changes outlined by Wilson provide an occasion for a change in strategy. The Black middle class and the Black underclass no longer share the same neighborhood. Therefore new strategies of cooperation must come to the fore.[4] We who are concerned with the life of the church in America find the circumstance of the Black underclass a matter of theological concern.[5] In order to address this we should begin with an examination of sources and norms from a previous era. The politics of the book of Daniel and of W. E. B. DuBois share several elements in content and context, and provide the starting point for this essay.

Before either DuBois or the book of Daniel can appropriately be incorporated into a contemporary Black political theology, I would note their similarities and differences. Further, I will observe the significant ways in which both Daniel and DuBois stand in different contexts than ours and therefore I shall be cautious in my appropriation of them as sources and norms of political theology. Recent treatments of W. E. B. DuBois as a source of theological reflection make this task easier.[6] The Black community has debated Black political theory and strategy from the nineteenth century to the present. The differences between Booker T. Washington and W. E. B. DuBois in the nineteenth and early twentieth centuries, and between Martin Luther King, Jr. and Malcolm X in the mid-twentieth century, immediately come to mind. Often that debate in churches has been forced to come to terms with Scripture. In conversation with the book of Daniel and the writings of W. E. B. DuBois, I want to explore the possibilities and the limits of their perspectives as a basis for Black political theology today.

Traditionally, Black church interpretation represents intratextual theology: it builds from a scriptural foundation as opposed to a philosophical position.[7] Therefore this essay will outline first the position of the book of Daniel, then describe the position of W. E. B. DuBois. These will be seen to exhibit certain core values which may serve as the beginning of an intratextual Black political theology.

Reading the Daniel Legends

Before I proceed I must establish a proper reading strategy in order to make the best use of the Daniel legends as a resource. The constant evolution of art and literature in African-American culture requires concomitant reappropriation of the biblical text as ours.[8] A proper reading strategy presents a problem because almost all of the exegetical work on the book of Daniel misses what I feel is a key dimension of the text. A work such as Daniel has several different kinds of meaning: among others, sense, feeling, tone, and intention.[9] Contemporary readers in the U.S. often miss a proper understanding of the tone of the work because of a lack of comprehension of the world of colonial Palestine in the Second Temple period—colonial in the sense that it was part of the political world of the Ptolemies, the Seleucids, and eventually the Romans. A basic problem is the inability of those readers to grasp the perspective of the writer, namely, the perspective as a colonized person. Without this colonial perspective, a reader reconstructs the intention of a given passage but never enters into the logic of the piece. Often such interpretations give witness not to the world of the writer, the colonized, but rather the world of the dominant society of the modern reader, the colonizer.

Despite an ability to move toward the types of reading strategies, readers often fumble with errors in reading.[10] The specific error in reading here involves what I. A. Richards has called "a lack of reading."[11] A competent reader must understand Daniel in the broad context of other colonial literature. Just as one who has never read any poetry has difficulty reading the poetry of Countee Cullen or Shakespeare's sonnets, those of us who have never traveled self-consciously into the colonial world will struggle to grasp the book of Daniel. Scholars socialized to deny their condition of colonizing and/or colonization as not relevant data will also produce the same error of reading. Studies of Daniel and of apocalyptic literature in general lift up two unresolved topics: the blind alley of the search for the Hasidim (referred to in the book of Daniel), and the contours of manticism (the use of mania—that is, ecstatic/religious experience) to interpret appropriate action in the present.[12] Today the competent reader should add to this mix "colonialism."

Overlooking the issue of colonialism or approaching it only obliquely happens to scholars outside of biblical studies. Macro-sociologists as well as micro-sociologists have tended away from using the nomenclature of colonialism. Macro-sociologist Gerhard Lenski reserves the term "colonialism" for industrial societies.[13] Rather he describes agrarian society types which have colonial tendencies as "conquest states."[14] The agrarian society types which dominated Africa and Europe and Asia during the Second Temple period forged together warfare and agriculture to form the tandem enterprises that drove society. Beneath the cultural hegemony of the Hellenistic Age the threat of deadly force remained close to the surface (Dan 2:18; 3:22).

Attempts among micro-sociologists and anthropologists to explain the power elements in prophetic, millennarian-visionary, or ecstatic experience has for some time tried to deal with the role of social location.[15] Thomas Overholt brought together the work of anthropologist and micro-sociologist on manic activity in an examination of biblical prophecy. He uses the categories of I. M. Lewis: central and peripheral prophecy, and ecstasy. Thus he gives attention to the social location and stratification question.[16] Overholt avoids the inflammatory language of colonization and cultural hegemony; nonetheless, most of the sources he cites come from colonized peoples, such as Native Americans.[17]

A competent reader attempts to reconstruct the social world of the Second Temple period (especially the Hellenistic part). In order to successfully complete this task, a reader draws as clearly as possible a picture of the colonizer and the colonized.[18] However, experienced and competent readers know all too well that the colonizers left indistinct footprints in the soil of ancient Judea. A new perception of Antiochus IV Epiphanes (and by extension to the colonizers he led) provides a new understanding of the events of the era.[19]

A competent reader remains cautious. The writings of the colonized probably will not provide an altogether accurate rendering of the colonizers' world. The converse probably also holds true. The Bible in general, and post-exilic biblical texts in particular, come from the crucible of colonial life in faith. As such, one might well hypothesize that post-biblical texts give the modern reader predominantly the perspective of those who have been colonized.

A Reasonable Strategy for Reading the Book of Daniel

First, a reader notices that the colonized world is binary. Hence, "oppositional literature" provides an apt description of material such as Daniel. Further, the reader recognizes the role of dualism in apocalyptic literature.[20] The binary world of the colonizer and the colonized fits well within these proposals about apocalyptic literature.

The ideological battle for the community that heard and read the book of Daniel is not Hellenism or cultural monism. The option of cultural monism is seldom there for the colonized; it requires isolation from the dominant culture. During the Second Temple period, only the Qumran community comes close to this proposal. On the contrary, the battle in the rhetoric of Daniel concerns how the community of faith can remain appropriately bicultural.[21] We find parallels to the debate on the appropriate response to cultural hegemony in other places today, such as North America and South Africa.

Designations of the genre of Daniel 1–6 should take into account the context of responses to colonialism. For instance, Humphreys calls it a tale of the wise courtier[22] and Müller calls it *Märchen*.[23] The tales of the wise courtier depict a Jewish/Hebrew colonial subject who demonstrates superior or exceptional wisdom in a foreign court. *Märchen* are mysterious tales meant to provoke the reader's sympathy for the principal figure, in this instance a colonized subject. Lacocque argues that this is haggadic midrash, which we might understand as narrative ethics in a colonized situation.[24] The genre of Daniel 7, 8 and 10–12 likewise reflects a tone that obliquely censures the colonial situation of second century BCE rulers and their Jewish collaborators.

The genre of theriomorphic (animal form) historical allegory depicts the colonizer in theriomorphic form.

Images and Power

The issue of image and reality continues through the narratives. The king is preoccupied with public perception. "All the people involved are described by political status."[25] Perception blends with the issue of difference. "Religious affinity is political affinity and conversely, religious difference is political difference. The Chaldeans' tacit equation is: Difference is suspect."[26] Whether it be the depiction of the empire as animals in the theriomorphic historical allegories (Dan 7–8, 10–12) or the depiction of Nebuchadnezzar behaving like an animal, namely eating grass (Dan 4:28-33), the reader continually notes the ironic tone of this piece of colonial/oppositional literature.

Biculturalism can never go so far as to view the colonizing monarch as comparable to the Jewish deity. On the contrary, what made a *good* colonizer, as drawn by the writers of the book of Daniel, was the awareness that the God of the Jews was superior to the king. Only King Belshazzar, who quickly dies, fails to pledge allegiance to the God of the Jews (Dan 2:27; 3:28-29; 4:34-35; 6:26-28). The *hubris* of the empire and the king gives rise to the loss of humanity according to the theology of the book of Daniel. The story of Nebuchadnezzar makes this point eloquently. "A man [*sic*] who thinks he is like god must become a beast to learn that he is only human."[27]

The Jews exhibit exceptional knowledge rooted in religious experience and piety in both the narrative and visionary elements of the book of Daniel. The location of the Jewish epistemological advantage is in a combination of faith and ethnic background. For instance, in chapter 2, the Chaldeans, a designation that is both professional and ethnic, cannot tell Nebuchadnezzar the content and meaning of the dream. But Daniel can.

At this point my exposition of the book of Daniel maintains that the narrative depicts an epistemological advantage for the faithful Jewish community. The source of the epistemological advantage derives from a life of piety; that is to say, God's self-revelation comes to the pious. Daniel's refusal to defile himself (Dan 1:8) lays an important foundation for this exceptional character. The piety has to do with diet but also with the spiritual discipline of prayer (Dan 9).

Exceptional character imbues Daniel with not only the colonizers' consciousness but also with God's. One might call this a "double consciousness." The historiography of the narratives, such as the four

41

world kingdoms (Dan 7), occurs also in the vision reports. The book of Daniel unifies an ethic of exceptional people drawn together in faith that gives them salvation and vision. The exceptional ethics connect with a salvation eschatology where God breaks the progress of Gentile rule.

Materialist Issues

"Materialist" refers to the socio-political context of a piece of literature. The depiction of the socio-political context emerges from the sociological/anthropological reading of the material culture. Two materialist issues push the rhetoric of the book of Daniel. First, we have professional conflict. The office and profession of scribe existed long before the Second Temple period. Scribes are a part of agrarian societies.[28] By the sixth century, the biblical text describes scribes as an institution on the scene in Judah. The emphasis on writing and scribal activity in the prophetic books of Ezekiel and Jeremiah give witness to this. The Ezra corpus develops the scribe as hero.

The rise of the scribes as a profession or institution effects other institutions such as the priesthood. The writer of Daniel does not sketch a conflict of priest and scribes but approaches this obliquely through the narratives of a scribal hero priest, such as Daniel. In the vision reports, Daniel blends the scribe and the visionary prophet; in other words, the mantic function of the prophet now has a scribal dimension.

This rhetorical strategy is not as disinterested as it may at first seem. Conquest states in the agrarian society type require bureaucrats, or a governing class. A potential conflict arises between the priestly class on the one hand and the governing class on the other.[29] When the occupying or colonial forces replace thoroughly the previous government, the lines between governing class and priestly class are more sharply drawn. However, generally in the occupied nations, the lines between governing class and priestly class become more blurred.

After the demise of Zerubbabel and the Davidic house, the lines between the governing class and the priest and retainers become even more blurred for the Jews. Part of the rhetorical strategy of the editor of the book of Daniel involves further blurring of the lines. Daniel as an ideal figure is both colonial bureaucrat and "holy man" at the same time. He is part of the governing class and a priest as well. Through the hero, Daniel, the writer gives instruction to the colonial community—instruction that addresses the blurring of governing class and priestly class. Daniel could work in the court of the king but Daniel could not eat the food (Dan 1:8). We should note the distinction between economic intercourse and other types of cultural exchange.

The second materialist issue is geopolitics. Colonized persons have political power based on alliances. Colonizing persons have *sui generis* political power. The rule of thumb for the competent reader, then, should be to follow the alliances. The book of Daniel contains one of the few pro-African,[30] in this case pro-Ptolemaic, documents in Scripture.

Geographers describe Syria-Palestine as a land bridge. During every historical period, groups have looked to one end or the other of the bridge. The Syrian Wars, beginning in 274 BCE and culminating in the Battle of Panias in 198 BCE, grew from the desire to control the region of Syria-Palestine. Colonized groups (with the possible exception of sectarians) aligned themselves with one or another of the principals, the Ptolemies (Egypt) or the Seleucids (Syria). The institution of the high priest reflects the way the colonizers controlled the community by designating the high priests.[31] Often the conflicts spilled over into the lives of the people of Judea.

Each power—Egypt and Syria—had a history as both allies and enemies. During the Syrian Wars Palestine was largely under Ptolemaic control and developed a coterie of Ptolemaic supporters. Also during that period the literature reports no crisis comparable to that of the Seleucid reign. The theological rendering of the Syrian Wars (Dan 10–12) as *vaticinia ex eventu* indicates a bias against the Seleucids. Through literary artistry, the writer/editor of the book of Daniel transfers the loyalty of the Jewish community from Persia (Haggai-Zechariah) to the Ptolemaic Egyptians. The contrasts of the monarchs in Daniel 2–6 on the one hand, and on the other the Seleucids in Daniel 10–12, make clear the superiority of the Egyptians, and at the same time accent the exceptional character of the Jewish community.

John Collins has proposed that the material now comprising the book of Daniel originated in a community of Jews who moved into Palestine early in the second century BCE.[32] Through the depiction of the characters in Daniel 2–6 we find a colonial but malleable ruler. We have oppositional literature with incisive critique of dominant culture of the period, but the dominant culture is more silly than malevolent. They also happen to be Mesopotamian. The Seleucids win the prize as the draconian malevolent force. Hence, the editor has transferred the loyalty to the Mesopotamian rulers by reading community into a distrust or hate of the Seleucid regime. All this is done through the characterization of the barbarians, the Gentiles.

DuBois's Agenda for a Black Political Theology

W. E. B. DuBois introduces three themes into the consideration of life under the shadow of racism: the descriptive category "double consciousness"; a remedial strategy of cultural criticism; and the body for the implementation of cultural criticism, which he calls the "talented tenth."

Double Consciousness

DuBois's idea of double consciousness resonates with Black experience, whether conscious or unconscious. "It is a peculiar situation, this double-consciousness, this sense of always looking at one's self through the eyes of others, of measuring one's soul by the tape of a world that looks on in amused contempt and pity."[33] The presence of double consciousness represents an element of perspective that continually informs the structure of social knowledge. Assimilation of a colonized people forestalls the epistemological advantage of double consciousness. The dominant (colonizer) consciousness becomes the consciousness of the colonized.

Cultural Criticism and Education

DuBois himself draws a type of cultural criticism that could aid in building a political theology. DuBois's understanding of education and criticism expresses the same holistic approach that his sociological research embodies. As he states, "But I have already said that human education is not simply a matter of schools; it is much more a matter of family and group life—the training of one's home, of one's daily companions, of one's social class."[34] The term culture criticism seems to capture DuBois's goal. "Education must not simply teach work—it [education] must teach Life. The "talented tenth" of the Negro race must be leaders of thought and missionaries of culture among their people."[35] Cultural criticism shapes a strategy of social change. "They call for freedom on the one hand and power on the other."[36] This strategy has a type of pragmatism and holistic quality typical of Black political theology. DuBois outlines five elements: (1) economic cooperation; (2) a revival of art and literature; (3) political action; (4) education; and (5) organization.[37]

The "Talented Tenth"

The persons regarded as the "talented tenth" function as the agents of cultural criticism. The awareness of double-consciousness and skills in cultural criticism require education. "The problem of education, then, among Negroes must first of all deal with the "talented tenth"; it is the problem of developing the Best of this race that they may guide the Mass away from the contamination and death of the Worst, in their own and other races."[38] DuBois clearly understood the task before these persons. "Three tasks lay before me [and the "talented tenth"]; first to show that the Talented Tenth as they have arisen among American Negroes have been worthy of leadership; secondly, to show how these men [sic] may be educated and developed; and thirdly, to show their relation to the Negro problem."[39]

Some of this comes from more than a type of elitism. Some of the impetus of the idea of the "talented tenth" stemmed from the awareness of limited financial resources. "All men [sic] cannot go to college but some men must; every isolated group or nation must have its yeast, must have for the talented few centers of training. . . ."[40] DuBois included the clergy in the "talented tenth." The clergy provided leadership. The exercise of this leadership involved cultural decisions. "The Talented Tenth rises and pulls all that are worth the saving up to their vantage ground."[41]

The combination of "double consciousness" and cultural criticism required a strenuous person. The notion of the "talented tenth" embodied the strenuous person much as DuBois himself. The watchword for the "talented tenth" was "striving" though one might equate that with "struggle."[42] The task of the "talented tenth" was educational but on two fronts from related and sometimes competing ways or view. The "talented tenth" represent a civic virtue and economic self-determination. Yet they protest for a "welfare state" to protect the Black underclass.[43]

The Book of Daniel and the Agenda of DuBois

DuBois and the book of Daniel exhibit similar accents on three issues. First, the book of Daniel depicts the rulers as unwise at best. The Gentile leaders need instruction for success of the community. At the same time, the hero stories describe a certain level of success for those exiled (colonized persons) who apply themselves through education. Daniel and the Jewish elite educate also the Gentile community and find some success in the colonial world. Likewise the "talented

45

tenth" educates the Black community but also obliquely educates the white community.[44] The "talented tenth" also enjoys some economic wealth.

Second, the book of Daniel describes a model of the "talented tenth." The book of Daniel accents how special these young men were (Dan 1:4). Further these men find success and piety together: "The person 'marked' by wisdom will receive a just end."[45] DuBois seems to understand that the "talented tenth" will come from and remain in the upper classes of the Black community. Daniel is characteristic of the civic virtue of DuBois' "talented tenth." However, Daniel's advocacy for his people does not come through as clearly as that in other court legends such as Esther and Akikar.

Third, the parameters of social intercourse in the Daniel legends indicate a "double consciousness." Also, the faith in God as the source of knowledge meant that the Jews described in the book of Daniel have a double consciousness as a twofold knowledge base. They have conventional wisdom available to all and they have religious information available only to the pious. Likewise DuBois's "double-consciousness" is a double epistemological knowledge. One has "white knowledge" or conventional wisdom on the one hand and "Black or faith knowledge" on the other hand. These three elements—unwise colonizers, the "talented tenth," and "double consciousness"—form the basis of a communitarian solidarity between the Black middle class and the Black underclass.

Epistemological Models of Colonial Responses

Evaluation of the communitarian proposals of Daniel and DuBois requires epistemological or analytic models, such as those proposed by Cornel West. These do not appear to be theories of knowledge per se, but ethical-social responses/reactions to racism or colonial existence. Nonetheless, the reactions form the matrix of perception for the interpretation of data—knowledge. In fact, the basis and orientation of West's models is that the response to racism (colonization) generates knowledge. With this in mind, West proposes four epistemological models: assimilationist, exceptionalist, marginalist, and humanist to describe African American response to cultural hegemony.[46]

The assimilationist and the marginalist models maintain that the indigenous culture should by and large accommodate the new culture. Assimilationists maintain that the colonized community should change, wherever the colonized community does not adhere to the dominant culture. A colonized community would fall into a cultural melting pot never to be seen again. Further, the Hebrew Bible does not advocate an assimilationist position as one can discern through the ethics and doctrines.[47]

The marginalist model represents a similar position. Here the base culture is seen as restrictive when compared to the broader dominant culture.[48] During the Second Temple period, or could we call it the colonial period, the marginalist view represents a persistent but always subtle voice. To call this the colonial period seems appropriate to the degree that Judea was part of a larger empire: either Persian, Greek, Seleucid or Ptolemaic for most of the age, though there was a short respite of independence.

The exceptionalist and the humanist models contend that the residue of indigenous culture contains the roots of hope in the face of the new cultural hegemony. In that regard, the exceptionalist and humanist models represent a nativistic religious type.

The anthropologist Anthony Wallace in 1938 defined nativistic cults. The prophetic rhetoric largely assumes a nativistic religion in the face of cultural change. Though one should not oversimplify, the prophets' nativistic bent did not forestall the anti-Baalism of Elijah, Hosea, and Jeremiah. Amos and other eighth-century prophets critique the unbridled latifundization of the land under the emerging royal institutions. At the same time the prophets presuppose royal institutions. Hence they present a nativistic bent, while at the same time viewing religion and culture in a paradoxical relationship.[49] The book of Daniel confirms this nativistic bent.

The exceptionalist and the humanist models represent a spectrum of positive valuation of indigenous culture. The exceptionalist claims the *sui generis* nature of the indigenous culture. Further, the exceptionalist, as the name suggests, is somehow better than the cultural alternative of the dominant or colonizing culture. On the other hand, the humanist does not posit any superiority. Rather, the sense is that in the experience of the indigenous culture something of "human" experience can be discerned.[50] W. E. B. DuBois forged the intellectual framework of the exceptionalist stance. Exceptional describes the man as well as his theoretical position.

There are numerous biblical examples of exceptionalist thought. The post-exilic political theology of Esther and Daniel comes out of an exceptionalist position. Here DuBois can become a conversation partner, for he developed the germ theory in order to argue the superiority of African American culture, connecting this with the political idea of the "talented tenth."[51] The Br'er Rabbit stories give us our best analogy.

Like the legends of Daniel, these stories lack sparkle without the contrast between the ordinary people and the exceptional hero—Br'er Rabbit, Daniel and his friends. We see in the book of Daniel opposition literature. The Hebrew Daniel succeeds while other ethnic groups fail to solve the problems. Fewell correctly asserts that a deconstructionist reading with the emphasis on power positions renders an interesting reading of the text.

West proposes a humanist response to colonization. He derives this category from Enlightenment taxonomy. Here the particularity of the colonized group serves the broader community in developing an anthropology. If we seek a reading from the humanist perspective, then the other works we should consider would be by authors such as Jean Toomer, Zora Neale Hurston, Alice Walker, and Toni Morrison. Such an examination will indicate that in these writings the dominant culture does not dominate the story directly. The "white" characters in no way capture our attention in these works. They are oppositional but not in the same way as Daniel 2–6.

The book of Daniel is an exceptionalist document. However, when the reader does not share the epistemological model of the text, the reader inevitably reads the text differently than earlier readers. Without existential and colonizing hermeneutics, a modern western reader transforms the material into a humanist text. The legends of Daniel provide an exceptionalist political theology, if we dare to see it. After such an epiphany we must choose whether to embrace or rework the exceptionalist position in our own church theology.

Conclusion

The book of Daniel lives not because it becomes an often quoted text in the rest of the Hebrew Bible, nor because it ensconces itself in the Mishnah. Rather it works as a subtext, a filtering text that changes the way other texts are read. The exceptionalist position adapts to the materialist issues of the Roman Empire. It becomes a building block in the political foundation of the Pharisaic movement.

I see in DuBois a similar position. I cannot tell to what degree his position is somehow indirectly derived from the book of Daniel, though I have noted the similarities and differences. Nonetheless, the "talented tenth" assumes a level of mutual care and proximity that "open housing" has eroded, as many Black middle-class persons no longer have to reside in a poor Black community. I suggest beginning our political theology with DuBois and the book of Daniel only to look forward to where we need to go next.

The sociological correlation between DuBois and the audience that resonated with the book of Daniel in Black communities has changed. Now middle-class and upper-middle-class Blacks experience an estrangement from the Black underclass. The book of Daniel and DuBois expected living patterns that do not necessarily exist in as wide ranging patterns as they once did. The question is then, what does Daniel say in the face of the declining significance of race?[52]

The study of Daniel and DuBois reminds me of the core values of Scripture and of African American political thought. Those values assume that the theological intelligentsia identifies with the disenfranchised community. That call to identify with the African American underclass falls afresh on the ears of middle-class African American biblical theologians. The times may have changed with different living patterns but the core values have not. The task for biblical theology requires the move from a necessary descriptive analysis such as presented in this essay to a programmatic piece outlining strategies for racial solidarity.

CHAPTER 4

In Search of a Face for Simon the Cyrene

Boykin Sanders

In recent years there has been a renewal of interest in the subject of Blacks in the biblical world.[1] Dr. Charles B. Copher has contributed much to the subject, focusing especially on contributions made by Blacks to Old Testament history and literature. In his seminal article "Three Thousand Years of Biblical Interpretation with Reference to Black Peoples," Copher makes note of Black persons in the New Testament as well: "Of the twenty-seven books that constitute the canon (NT), only one, the book of Acts, chapters 8:26-39 and 13:1, contains references to Black persons and peoples."[2]

This essay attempts to add to Copher's observation by focusing on the much debated reference to a Simon of Cyrene in Mark 15:21 (cf., Matt 27:32 and Luke 23:26). It seeks to construct a reasonable face for Simon, (1) by taking issue with scholarly attitudes and opinions regarding the intent of the NT Gospels in general and the Simon episode in particular; (2) by calling attention to what "facts" there are for Simon in canonical and non-canonical sources; and (3) by gathering those "scraps" along with further observations regarding styles of the synoptic writers and offering what I consider to be the most reasonable face for Simon of Cyrene: a native North African Black person who was commandeered by Roman authorities to carry the cross to the execution site.

Current Views Regarding History, Ethnography, and the Simon Episode in NT Interpretation

Contemporary NT scholarship is unusually influenced by the assumption that little if any reliable information can be gathered about the history of individuals and groups that appear in the NT Gospels. There are two general reasons for this view.

First, NT scholars are generally of the view that earliest Christians focused on current and future concerns of faith rather than on present, non-faith issues or particulars of the past, an assessment that is not without merit. For example, in the letter to the Philippians, Paul advises that he is "straining forward to what lies ahead," having renounced both his ethnic and religious connections of the past (Phil 3:13). In the letter to the Galatians, Paul instructs that the past is of no use for the new Christian life, for in Christ "there is no longer Jew or Greek, there is no longer slave or free, there is no longer male or female; for all of you are one in Christ Jesus" (Gal 3:28). The writer to the Colossians speaks of a newly created humanity wherein past ethnic identity and social status (e.g., Jews, Greeks, barbarians, Scythians, slaves and free persons) become inconsequential (Col 3:10-11). Ephesians declares that two previously distinct ethnic groups (Jews and Gentiles) have now merged into a new creation through the cross (Eph 2:15-16). And John manipulates the language "the Jews" in such a way that it no longer has an ethnic designation but now refers to any who stand in opposition to the Johannine Christian community.[3] Thus, Nils A. Dahl resonates with this style when he claims that the Greek term *éthnē*, "nations," in NT times "had become a designation of the big collective of non-Israelites, the Gentiles, with little or no attention paid to the ethnic components of this mass."[4]

Second, scholars operate with the thesis that the Gospels do not contain the true words and deeds of the historical Jesus. Rather, they are kerygmatic in nature and focus on the needs of Christians whose worlds and issues were different from those of Jesus, their founder. In particular the Gospels target the needs of readers who struggled with apocalyptic issues and the writers of the Gospels have sought to address them by use of material that is said to go back to the historical Jesus. Martin Dibelius, a early form critic, puts the matter as follows:

> For the creators of the tradition, Messiah implied fulfillment already: As Messiah Jesus went to his death, his messiahship was confirmed by the fact that God did not forsake him in his death, and will come again to inaugurate his reign. What we must realize is this: The life of Jesus runs its course before Easter, whereas the tradition about his life was formed after Easter and conditioned by events of Easter.[5]

Thus, with the view that the writers of the Gospels and their readers were highly affected and motivated by ideas of an imminent end and/or the second appearance of Jesus the Lord, scholars generally view the Gospels as repositories of early Christian issues, not biographies of the historical Jesus.[6]

In more recent scholarship this perspective has been challenged.

Some scholars find problematic the notion that all components of Gospel materials were subsumed under a cross-resurrection and Jewish apocalyptic theology.[7] Others call for control of the tendency by some to make the canonical Gospels the standard by which non-canonical Gospel materials are judged vis-à-vis the Jesus legacy. Here the aim is to recognize traditions about Jesus that were not transmitted in the orthodox key.[8] Still others believe there is reasonable cause to turn again to the historical Jesus issue in view of what is now known about biographies of famous others in the time of Jesus.[9] Yet, despite these innovations in the study of the Gospels, what Dibelius noted about their nature remains essentially unaltered today. In a word, the materials of the canonical Gospels have as their focus the cultic needs of first century Christian communities, not the historical Jesus.[10]

This thesis regarding the intent of the Gospels is not without consequences for assessing and interpreting the Simon of Cyrene episode of Mark 15:21 and parallels. In general, scholarly opinion is that the episode is historically unreliable, especially since it conflicts with well-known customs and traditions in Roman and Jewish history. For instance, some point out that the Simon episode is incongruent with what is well-known about Roman practices regarding condemned prisoners. In brief, a condemned prisoner was expected to carry his own cross.[11] Others find episodes and/or events within its contexts especially troubling (e.g., Mark's date for the crucifixion, Mark's seeming confusion regarding the Passover and the Lord's Supper, and Mark's report of two trials for Jesus—one before the Sanhedrin in Mark 14:53-65; the other before Pilate in Mark 15:2-5), and wonder about their intent.[12] Others point to what amounts to an extraneous theme in relation to the death of Jesus, e.g., the tendency of Luke in particular to blame Jews for Jesus' death when historical facts do not support such a view.[13] Furthermore, there are historical problems with the position that the death of Jesus in Jerusalem followed the predictions of scripture.[14]

As the Simon episode appears in documents with a cultic focus and within a setting where there are historical contradictions and extra-historical themes, the scholarly tendency has been to focus on its theological function. For example, several believe that the Simon tradition of Mark 15:21 is employed by Mark to illustrate for Peter (and so the church) that the requirements of discipleship are according to Mark 8:34: "If any want to become my followers, let them deny themselves and take up their cross and follow me."[15] Brian K. Blount, recognizing the similarities between the "take-up-the-cross" language of Mark 8:34 and that used for Simon's cross carrying in Mark 15:21, believes that Simon functions as a model disciple for Mark. Thus, although the Simon episode conflicts with Roman customs regarding condemned prisoners, Simon's bearing of the cross on behalf of Jesus is justifiable under the rules of Greco-Roman rhetoric. As he states, "Mark maintains the plausibility of Simon carrying the cross by placing the scene (the Simon scene) after the scourging. So weakened, Jesus predictably needs help bearing the cross."[16] Frans Ventur makes the case for Simon the crossbearer even more graphic:

> The centurion jerked his head in the direction of Jesus. "Come carry the cross," he ordered Simon. He (Simon) looked at Jesus lying in the dust, utterly exhausted. He looked defenseless, his hand limp and motionless, his narrow face reddened with blood. Simon saw how his wounds had bled into his sandals. . . . "Where are your disciples? Why don't they carry the cross?," shouted Simon to the prisoner. Jesus looked at him, his eyes gentle but filled with pain. He looked pleadingly, as if he thirst and was begging for water, at the big man who stood menacingly over him. . . . "Pick up the cross," the centurion said again. . . . Simon shuffled forward. . . . He closed his eyes and seized it. . . . As he stood upright, he heard the mob's derision. "There goes a new disciple!" they shouted."[17]

Thus, when one brings together scholarly perspectives regarding the reader-response nature of the Gospels,[18] stress on the theological character of the section in which the Simon episode appears and the view that Mark in particular focuses on the nature of true discipleship, it is not hard to see why it is more typical to raise functional rather than historio-ethnographic questions of the Simon episode. For instance, Frank J. Matera not only does not believe that there was ever such a thing as a pre-Markan Passion narrative, i.e., an older or more historic account regarding Jesus' sufferings and death in Mark 14 and 15, but finds the material of Mark 15:20b-24 (the section containing the Simon episode) to be related to an idea outside of its own section:

> We suggest that instead of a pre-Markan narrative or a present historic tradition, we have a series of loosely connected phrases which Mark assembled (Simon, the place of the crucifixion, the wine, the garment, the inscription) by use of kai and relates in the historic present for the sake of vividness. In this fashion the entire section serves as a preface for the second mocking.[19]

In addition, information regarding Simon's sons (Rufus and Alexander) in Mark 15:21 was discarded by Luke "because they (Simon's sons) were no longer known by his (Luke's) community."[20] Simon's sons were Christians and were well-known by Mark's community, and Rufus's activities in particular are referred to by Paul (cf. Rom 16:13).[21]

Furthermore, geographical and/or ethnographical information given regarding Simon, (e.g., Simon is Cyrenian and thus North African), should not be taken seriously. What Luke intends by use of that information, given what is known about his tendencies, is to illustrate the universal nature of the Christian movement. Cyrene in his mind "marks the outer western boundary" and is thus "a distant and foreign signification": "Simon . . . from Cyrene . . . fits neatly within the pattern of inclusion which Luke-Acts has demonstrated towards its farthest western region."[22]

The above commentary, provided by scholars who work within the parameters of current emphases in the study of the Gospels, offers a plethora of insights about factors or issues for the Jesus movement beyond the time of Jesus' own personal history. It is motivated by the thesis that the historical Jesus issue was a focus of neither the writers nor of the first readers of the Gospels. In fact, the tendency is to think that it was not long before the Jesus movement forgot its roots. Recently, this has caused a number of scholars to postulate that in a Gospel such as Mark's (written approximately 40 years after Jesus' death) there are only two sayings that undisputedly go back to the historical Jesus.[23] Yet there is the lurking issue of whether the writers of the Gospels intend to address only the pastoral and/or cultic needs of readers in the materials they chose to present. In other words, when Mark's first readers came to the place in the Marcan manuscript where it was stated that a certain Simon of Cyrene was compelled to carry the cross, were they reminded of an event and person related to the actual circumstance of Jesus' death, or did they think only about what the episode meant for their own lives?

The Face of Simon in Mark 15:21 and Parallels, and in Non-Canonical Sources

While historical-critical scholars generally hold to the view that the Gospels are evangelical or fictive in nature, there is also the belief that the Passion Narratives contain some of their oldest traditions.[24] In short, the Simon episode is thought to be one such tradition due to its brevity and lack of connection to its setting.[25] Because of this, Vincent Taylor took it to be a case of local knowledge on the part of Mark and his readers regarding events surrounding Jesus' death.[26] Similarly, Martin Dibelius viewed it, along with the story of the young man who fled naked in Mark 14:51, as eyewitness accounts.[27] Furthermore, the episode stands out in two other ways when compared to materials of its context.

First, the reader would not have expected a Simon story in view of what Mark had promised in Mark 10:33-34 regarding things or events that would take place in Jerusalem in connection with the suffering and death of Jesus. In that text (commonly referred to as Mark's third Passion prediction) the reader is told about several things that would take place in Jerusalem, but the Simon episode is not one of them. For example, the notation of 10:33a "we are going up to Jerusalem" is provided for in the material of Mark 11:1-10. The subsequent events of Mark 11:15–13:37 make reasonable the next prediction of 10:33b, "And the Son of Man will be handed over to the chief priests and the scribes." The notation of 10:33c, "and they will condemn him to death" is fulfilled in the trial before the Sanhedrin and the condemnation to death (Mark 14:64). The notation of 10:33d, "and they will hand him to the Gentiles" is related to Mark 15:1, where the Jews deliver Jesus to Pilate. "They will mock him" of 10:34a (cf. Mark 14:65e) is covered by the mocking of the Roman soldiers in 15:16-20, The notation "and spit upon him" of 10:34b (cf. 14:65a) is accounted for in 15:19b; 10:34c "and flog him" is covered in 15:19. The notation of 10:34d "and kill him" is accounted for in the reference to Jesus' crucifixion in 15:24 "And they crucified him" which is then followed by the death of Jesus in 15:37.

Second, the Simon episode is unrelated to things of the Passion setting that happen to fulfill scripture. For instance, while Judas and Peter are not especially singled out for their negative roles vis-à-vis Jesus' deliverance to death, it is quite clear that the betrayal associated with Judas and the denial with Peter in Mark 14 connect with what stands written in scripture: "You will all become deserters; for it is written, I will strike the shepherd and the sheep will be scattered" (Mark 14:27; cf. Zech 13:7).[28] Even the things which follow the Simon episode, e.g., the wine of Mark 15:23, the dividing of the garment of Mark 15:24, and so on, relate to particular Psalm passages or to other scriptures.[29] But the Simon episode does not.

Thus, if Dibelius and Bultmann are correct that the stress on scripture fulfillment in the Passion Narratives relates to early Christian problems with the death of Jesus, then it seems analogous that the role of Simon, albeit unrelated to "the shame and disgrace" of disciples and enemies, did not also find anchorage in scripture.[30] In any case, the Simon episode is neither governed by scripture fulfillment texts nor by Mark's prediction of things to take place in relation to Jesus' suffering and death in Mark 10:33-34. In view of these disjunctures for the Simon episode in Mark, closer inspection of its contents becomes necessary in both canonical and non-canonical sources given our initial concern regarding history or non-history in the Gospels in general and the Simon tradition in particular.

As to Mark 15:21 and its parallels, the first thing of note is that Mark does not present Simon as a willing crossbearer. The Greek verb Mark uses to describe the manner in which Simon becomes connected with the cross, *àggareũo*, suggests violence: Simon was forced to carry the cross against his will (cf. Matt 5:41).[31] However, in the later reports of Matthew and Luke, Mark's image of violence in relation to Simon's conscript status is tempered. For example, while Matthew keeps Mark's verb, he seems to alter its jolting character by use of *heuriskō*, "to find" (a favorite verb for Matthew) and so now the violence of the Roman soldiers in Mark 15:21 ("and they compelled a passer-by") is lessened in Matt 27:32: "As they went out, they came upon (found) a man from Cyrene . . . they compelled this man. . . ."[32]

Luke uses the verb *epilambánō*, which in Luke, depending on context, can have meanings which range from "the drawing of another to one's side for assistance" to "taking hold of or seizing."[33] In any case, the reader gets the impression in Luke's account that Simon is integral to the scene, not the stranger or "passer-by" who is violently forced to take up the cross in Mark. In short, the soldiers in Luke help Simon with what they want him to do—they take up the cross themselves and put it on Simon's shoulder (Luke 23:26c). Thus, from the editing of Mark's account by Luke and Matthew, it would seem that the latter found Mark's report of the episode a bit troubling and have sought to tone it down. Does this mean that Mark's account is closer to the state of things in the Roman world of the first century, particularly of things in Roman occupied Palestine at the time of the crucifixion?[34] Was Simon violently commandeered to take up the cross?

A second thing of note is the language Mark uses to describe Simon and scholarly interpretation of this description.[35] Language such as "coming in from the country" and "a passer-by" in Mark 15:21 seems to suggest an alien status for Simon vis-à-vis the city of Jerusalem. Yet some argue that Simon had come to Jerusalem to celebrate the Passover. Others make him a Jerusalem resident.[36] Still others venture that Simon might have been buried in the Kidron Valley on the basis of a grave site discovered there in 1941 which bore the names Alexander and Simon among others and exhibited characteristics of Jewish burial patterns of Cyrene.[37]

What one says about Simon's function or status by use of canonical sources must be controlled by Mark, Matthew, and Luke. Simply put,

Simon is a north African from the town of Cyrene. Without further details one moves beyond boundaries. Thus, the language "coming in from the country" and "passer-by" seems more appropriate for a stranger or alien than for a diaspora Jew who comes to Jerusalem to celebrate the Passover. In fact, a person with neither Jewish nor Greco-Roman status or interest could have found good reasons to be in Jerusalem, as Acts 8:26-40, the pericope of the Ethiopian official, demonstrates.

Because the Gospels are silent about Simon's reason for being in Jerusalem, as well as his identity, there has been a tendency among some to speculate that Simon of Mark 15:21 is Simeon or Symeon, called Niger (black) in Acts 13:1, who is listed by Luke with Lucius of Cyrene among the important teachers and prophets at Antioch, Syria.[38] Yet this is mere speculation and is largely due to the relationship of names, the appellation Niger and the reference to a Lucius of Cyrene.

However, what is beyond the realm of speculation is that, by the time of John's Gospel, the Simon we know from Mark 15:21 was no longer carried in the orthodox tradition. Where that Simon (Simon of Cyrene) continued was among African Christians whose ways and thoughts seemed "heretical" in the eyes of orthodox Christians. The second-century Christian Irenaeus of Lyons notes that the Egyptian Basilides had a different reading of Simon of Cyrene. Basilides taught that at the crucifixion Simon took on the appearance of Jesus and that it was Simon, not Jesus, who died on the cross. In fact, Jesus stood at a distance laughing at those who had supposedly crucified him (Irenaeus, *Adv. Haer.* I.24:3-7). Furthermore, what Irenaeus reports about Basilides' teachings regarding Simon is essentially restated in the Second Treatise of the Great Seth (VII.2.56), a document discovered among the Nag Hammadi materials of Upper Egypt in 1945.[39]

The fact that John's Gospel removes Simon the crossbearer from its tradition of the crucifixion is thought by many to mean that John was aware of the use being made of the Simon episode by the African Christians referred to by Irenaeus.[40] Yet the cause for Simon's removal could just as well reside in a serious reading of the Gospel of Mark by those so-called heretics. In Mark, Simon enters the narrative as crossbearer in 15:21. In 15:22, Mark notes "and they brought him to the place called Golgotha. . . ." This is contrary to the NRSV reading, which, though it notes the Greek uses "him," renders the verse "they brought Jesus to the placed called Golgotha." This statement is followed respectively in vv. 23 and 24 with "and they offered him wine mixed with myrrh . . ." and "they crucified him. . . ." The antecedent of the pronoun "him" in Mark 15:22 can only be Simon of Cyrene for close readers, since Simon is the subject of the previous verse, and thus the syntactical antecedent to the pronoun "him." In fact, the name of Jesus only returns to the Markan narrative in 15:34, i.e., in the verse which refers to the cry of dereliction from the cross, but even there the name of Jesus was a questionable reading from earliest times.[41] In a word, Mark leaves the reader uncertain as to whether Jesus was crucified at all.

This uncertainty regarding the identity of the cross victim in Mark seems to influence the way Matthew, Luke, and John treat Mark's cross inscription. Mark's inscription identifies the cross victim by title only: "The King of the Jews" (Mark 15:26). In Luke and Matthew, however, there is a more definite referent. "This is the King of the Jews" in Luke 23:38 is anchored in the earlier charge made against Jesus at the trial before Pilate, when Pilate asked Jesus if in fact he was the King of the Jews (Luke 23:3), as well as in Jesus' journey to the cross being followed by the crossbearer Simon and the weeping women (Luke 23:26, 27-31). The one that they follow is Jesus who is crucified on the cross between two thieves (Luke 23:33). "Jesus is the King of the Jews." The inscriptional reading in Matt 27:37, "This is Jesus, the King of the Jews," is no less definite, and that of John, "Jesus of Nazareth, the King of the Jews" (John 19:19), leaves no doubt in the reader's mind regarding the name and village of the cross victim.

Thus it seems that African Christians and others appeared not only less puzzled regarding how Mark's narrative was to be read regarding the identity of the crucified victim, but it was precisely the reading of Mark that caused the Simon episode to be excised by orthodoxy after the time of Matthew and Luke. Simon does return to the orthodoxy later, as we shall see, but only in a non-Marcan form and function.

Finally, the Gospel which first recorded the Simon episode is associated with African Christians. Egyptian Coptic Christians claim Mark (the writer of the Gospel of Mark) as founder of their church and its first patriarch. Their tradition states that Mark brought the Greek Gospel of Mark to Egypt from Rome; but as native Egyptian Christians were unable to read Greek, Mark produced a copy of his Gospel in the native Egyptian tongue. Coptic tradition also claims that Mark established Christian missions in Egypt, in Cyrenaica, and in other Libyan cities.[42]

I may summarize thus far: Simon's role as crossbearer in Mark is neither explained by the passion prediction of Mark 10:33-34 nor by scripture fulfillment texts in the context of the Simon episode. Simon cannot automatically be identified as a Jew just because he appears in a context where the Jewish Passover feast was being celebrated. The only sure thing the Gospels allow is that Simon was North African and thus an outsider to the matters surrounding Jesus' crucifixion. His outsider status seems indicated in Mark's ascription "a passer-by" and "coming in from the country". He appears to be a problem for the orthodox west but was promoted in the African world by groups considered a threat to "standard" Christianity. Yet such groups based their understanding of Simon on a close reading of the earliest Gospel, Mark. I propose then that the Simon episode should be taken seriously as a case of historic detail surrounding the death of the historical Jesus, because it stands outside of the theological mix of its contexts and seems more in accord with politics and issues of life in the Roman world.

The question now becomes: Is there a reasonable face for Simon in view of what the Gospels and ancient contemporary canons of the Gospels offer regarding persons of unclear ethnic designation, such as Simon of Cyrene?

A Reasonable Face for Simon the Cyrenian

What the Gospels offer (especially the earliest Gospel of Mark) toward the resolution of my query vis-à-vis Simon is the persona of a stranger. That is, Simon is not from Jerusalem, nor is he party to the rancor of Jesus' accusers, tormentors, and executioners. In Mark 15:21, his stranger status is particularly indicated in the language used— "coming in from the country" and "a passer-by"—and by the city from which he came. Since Mark, followed by Luke, has in a way linked together the soldiers' choice of him as crossbearer with details about his home and his coming in from the country, one can only wonder if Mark intends to say something further about Simon's stranger status, e.g., why the Roman soldiers selected him (and not a person more integral to the scene) to bear the cross. Otherwise, it is hard to see why all three recordings of the Simon episode (and Mark and Luke in particular) would offer details regarding geography (if not also ethnicity) that seem to detract from their crossbearing theme. In any case, Simon is a stranger in Mark 15:21.

What then do the Gospels intend to convey by a comment about a person whose is simply denoted as having a Cyrenian connection? In short, what were Mark's first readers to think, ethnologically speaking, when they came to the place in his manuscript which read: "And they forced a passer-by, a certain Simon, a Cyrenian coming from the field, the father of Alexander and Rufus, that he might take up his cross" (my translation)?

Significant help is offered for the determination of this issue in the work of Bruce J. Malina and Jerome H. Neyrey. Relying on the methods of social anthropology, they argue that first-century Mediterranean people thought in dyadic/interpersonal rather than individual/intrapersonal terms.[43] What they mean is that when one encounters individuals in the NT, one is not to think of them in individualistic terms.[44] That is, persons such as Simon of Cyrene were "primarily part of the group in which they found themselves inserted."[45] This means that Simon is not only viewed in corporate terms (Simon of Cyrene), but that "by the naming of a person's *éthnōs* or nation" (e.g., Simon's), readers, say of Mark, were expected to think a certain way about the nation or *éthnōs* that was attached to the person's name.[46] In the scenario of Malina and Neyrey, Simon of Cyrene would probably be a North African Jew; as they state, "In the Gospel (Luke), all people mentioned are presumed to be Jews unless specifically identified otherwise."[47]

But what follows will show the opposite. My contention is that all persons who are not specifically identified as Jews either by ethnic designation and/or narrative circumstance (e.g., by reference to religious affiliation or ancestral connections and customs) in the materials of Luke and Mark belong to non-Jewish groups or nations.

The writer of Luke-Acts offers many instances of this. Besides making it clear that the disciples (Luke 6:14-16) and the witnesses to pentecost (Acts 2:5-13) are unmistakenly Jews, Luke is careful to stress the Jewish identity of particular individuals. While an audience such as Mark's might have known that Joseph of Arimathea was a Jew by the position he held on the Sanhedrin Council, Luke, unlike Matthew and Mark, leaves the reader with no doubt by adding that the Joseph in question is "from the Jewish town of Arimathea" (Luke 23:51; cf. Mark 15:43; Matt 27:57).

Luke also lets his readers know to which priestly order or tribe certain characters belong, e.g., in the cases of Zechariah and Elizabeth of Luke 1:5 and Joseph of 1:27. Luke relates that Anna is the daughter of Phanuel and further notes that she was of the tribe of Asher (Luke 2:36), though it should have been quite clear to the reader from the temple context (Luke 2:21-38) that Anna was Jewish. Not only is one given a plethora of other characters which Luke identifies as Jews— e.g., Simon is identified as a Pharisee in Luke 7:37, 40 (cf. Matt 26:6-13; Mark 14:3-9); Zacchaeus the tax collector is a "son of Abraham" (Luke 19:9); the Rich Man and Lazarus are children of Abraham (Luke 16:24-25)—but in the book of Acts the pattern continues. In Acts 4:6, the names of the persons who belonged to the high priest family are given—Caiaphas, John and Alexander. Barnabas is identified as "a Levite, a native of Cyprus" (4:36); Gamaliel is a member of the Sanhedrin Council, a Pharisee and a teacher of the law; there is a Jewish false prophet whose name is Bar-Jesus (13:6); a disciple named Timothy whose mother is Jewish and whose father is Greek (16:1); "a Jew named Aquila, a native of Pontus" (18:2); "a Jew named Apollos, a native of Alexandria" (18:24); there is Paul in his own words, "I am a Jew, from Tarsus in Cilicia (21:39; 22:3); and then there is Drusilla, a Jewish woman (24:24).

What is especially significant about Luke's style is that he does not just identify his Jewish characters with additional details such as institutional relations and/or religious and tribal affiliations, but, if the character in question is a diaspora Jew, Luke is not shy about noting it. Paul says in Luke "I am a Jew, born in Tarsus in Cilicia" (Acts 22:3); Aquila is a Jew born in Pontus; and Apollos is a Jew born in Alexandria. Even Mark can identify the woman whose daughter was demon possessed: "a Greek of Syrophoenician birth" (Mark 7:26). Thus, it seems reasonable that if Mark and Luke (and especially given the evidence in Luke) wanted Simon to be thought of as a Jew by their readers, they would have noted it. If for Luke such was envisioned in the case of the Simon passage, Luke 23:36 would probably have read: "Having taken hold of a certain Simon, a Jew of Cyrene. . . ." Mark 15:21 also would have probably been penned in a similar manner by Mark, if the reference to the Syrophoenician woman is any measure of Mark's style. But they do not refer to Simon in that manner. Rather we have in both the designation "Simon the Cyrenian."

The fact that Mark (and both Luke and Matthew follow Mark in this case) has chosen to identify Simon by city and not by a specific ethnic designation (e.g., a Jew or Greek from a particular city or nation), when such was an option, suggests that Mark wants the reader to think of Simon in ethnic terms appropriate to his city or country. In the framework of Malina and Neyrey, Mark evidently wants the reader to see that Simon the Canaanaean whose name appears at the end of his list of the twelve disciples in 3:18 (cf. Matt 10:4) is to be ethnically distinguished from Jesus' Jewish disciples. Certainly Luke wants his readers to know of a Simeon who was called Niger (black), and of Lucius the Cyrenian, who are to be distinguished from other prophets and teachers in Acts 13:1, e.g., Saul the Jew of Tarsus and Barnabas the Jew of Cyprus. Luke also distinguishes the Samaritan from the Jewish priest and the Levite in the Good Samaritan story (Luke 10:30-37), and in the story of the lepers (Luke 17:11-19) the Samaritan leper is identified as a foreigner (v. 18). Mark also appears to resonate with Luke when he notes in Mark 15:21 that Simon was a passer-by coming in from the country, i.e., Simon was a stranger or of a foreign nation.

The issue now becomes: If the gospel writers can designate some of their characters by nation and ethnicity, e.g., Jews of a particular country, and others only by nations or cities within a nation, then what is the ethnic designation which Mark and Luke want their readers to envision regarding Simon the Cyrenian, given what has been noted already by Malina and Neyrey about the dyadic personality of first-century people? In the minds of Mark and Luke's first-century readers, Simon would have stood for the city or nation to which his name is connected. In this case, it is a North African city, and more especially a Libyan town. Since Mark and Luke do not offer that Simon is a Jew or Greek from Cyrene (there were Jewish and Greek settlers in Cyrene) and have no qualms about identifying characters in racial terms, then Simon's ethnicity is other for Mark and Luke. Simon for them is a person who comes from a Black nation. In the key of their contemporaries, when the term Cyrenian was uttered without further qualifications, e.g., a Jew or a Greek of Cyrene, it would have been more appropriate to think native than colonial. Thus, in their minds Simon is a native Black African of Cyrene.[48]

Hence I conclude that Simon of Cyrene is neither a Jew nor a disciple in Mark. He does not fit the mold of one who comes to the assistance of Jesus to help with a load that is too heavy for him to carry alone and so becomes his disciple. Rather in Mark, Simon not only bears the cross alone but does it unwillingly. The Romans' choice of him seems less arbitrary. They choose him because of his color, which was different from theirs and which Romans had come to associate not only with race and class but also with duties that native Africans performed in the Greco-Roman world.[49] Mark notes for his readers the Roman perception of Simon in the language "passer-by" and "coming in from the country"—terminology which shows that Simon was outside of Jewish and Roman canons of protection. In a word, Simon is from a different world. Thus, the poet Countee Cullen may have sensed correctly when he said in 1929 that the choice of Simon to carry the cross related to his black skin color.[50] If so, scholarly reasoning regarding his disappearance from "orthodox" usage after Matthew and Luke (John's Gospel does not have the Simon episode), i.e., Simon was being used by gnostic heretics, may merit another look because it was in the African world (and among Christians who had other ways of thinking) that original statements regarding Simon of Cyrene in the Gospel of Mark continued to survive.

63

CHAPTER 5

The Individual and the Group in Luke: A Study of Malina's Hypothesis of the Dyadic Personality in First-Century Mediterranean Society

H. Wayne Merritt

Bruce Malina's writings raise a number of challenging theses for contemporary NT studies.[1] As important as these theses are, however, Malina's approach to NT studies from the standpoint of cultural anthropology is, perhaps, the most significant aspect of his work. What Malina proposes to do is to provide biblical studies with a paradigm that fosters cross-cultural understanding and, at the same time, relativizes the normative dominance of Western European cultural and psychological models of interpretation. In a work which seeks to reclaim the Black presence in theological studies, and, to honor one who has kept this goal alive and at the forefront of the concerns of a significant number of North American scholars, it seems appropriate to take up one of Malina's hypotheses and examine in detail his thesis regarding the relation of the individual and group in first-century Mediterranean society.[2]

The particular concern of this essay, therefore, is the complex of interrelated issues pertaining to individualism, individuation, and dyadism in personality structure, formation, and interpretive consequences among persons in the Mediterranean world of the first century CE. It will first describe Malina's thesis concerning the dyadic personality in first-century Mediterranean culture, and then discuss the challenge of verification and its ground in relation to the Gospel of Luke.

Models of Personality and Dyadism

In his essay "The First Century Personality: The Individual and the Group,"[3] Malina employs two models of personality derived from the arena of cultural anthropology to describe the personality structure of persons living in the Mediterranean world contemporary with the rise of the NT. The first concerns "the non-individualistic, dyadic self-awareness that seems to have been typical of the first-century people in our New Testament."[4] The second, the "three zone model," sketches out "the conception of the makeup of the individual that seems to have been characteristic of the Semitic subculture of that period and earlier."[5] Of these two models, the first is of primary concern in this essay, although reference is made to the second at significant points.

The dyadic personality[6] that Malina hypothesizes for persons living in the first century and reflected in the NT writings is characterized by a different relation of the individual to the group, different personality dynamics, and different pivotal values than is typical of the dominant population group of North America and Western Europe. In Malina's definition:

> The dyadic personality is an individual who perceives himself [*sic*] and forms his self-image in terms of what others perceive and feed back to him. He feels a need of others for his very psychological existence, since the image he has of himself must agree with the image formulated and presented by significant others, by members of significant and person-sustaining groups like family, village, even city and nation.[7]

Thus, a person characterized by this structure

> internalizes and makes his [*sic*] own what others say, do, and think about him because he believes it is necessary, for being human, to live out the expectations of others. That person would conceive of himself as always interrelated to other persons while occupying a distinct social position both horizontally (with others sharing the same status, moving from center to periphery) and vertically (with others above and below in social rank). Such persons need to test this interrelatedness, with the focus of attention away from ego, on the demands and expectations of others who can grant or withhold reputation. Pivotal values for such persons would be honor and shame, not guilt.[8]

Hence, Malina is able to paraphrase a modern definition of the individual and describe and contrast the distinctive differences between the modern and first-century dyadic personality. An individual, according to Clifford Geertz, is perceived as a bounded, unique, more or less integrated motivational and cognitive universe, a dynamic center of awareness, emotion, judgment, and action organized into a distinctive whole and set contrastively both against other such wholes and against its social and natural background. . . .[9]

In Malina's paraphrase, however,

our first-century person would perceive himself [sic] as a distinctive whole *set in relation* to other such wholes and *set within* a given social and natural background. Every individual is perceived as embedded in some other, in a sequence of embeddedness, so to say. If our sort of individualism leads us to perceive ourselves as unique because we are set apart from other unique and set-apart beings, then the first-century person would perceive himself as unique because he was set within other like beings within unique and distinctive groups. . . .[10]

Group embeddedness and group distance, thus, appears to be a distinctive feature that differentiates the dyadic and modern personality. Further, for the modern biblical interpreter, it is significant to note that pivotal values for the two are not the same. The modern interpreter, therefore, either looks in vain for clues that stress unique, individual, psychological, personal information pertaining to behavior, motivation, self-awareness, or, simply reads these into texts where the clues that are there do not pertain to the interpreter's search. A final quotation from Malina makes this vividly clear:

In our culture, we tend to consider a person's psychological makeup or her personality development from infancy on, as well as his or her individuality and uniqueness (personal reasons), as perhaps the most important elements in understanding and explaining human behavior, both our own and others'. Yet if you carefully read the New Testament writings or any other writing from the same period and place, you will find an almost total absence of such information. One obvious reason for this state of affairs is that the people described in the New Testament, as well as those who described them, were not interested in or concerned about psychological or personality information. . . . Since this kind of information is lacking, you might conclude that the first-century Mediterranean person did not share or comprehend our idea of an "individual" at all. And I believe you would be right.[11]

Before leaving these observations, a word of caution pertaining to Malina's terminology and description is in order. It should be emphasized that the terminology and the description of the dyadic personality derives from the domain of cultural anthropology and not from psychological and, especially, not from contemporary psychoanalytic models and theories.[12] To be sure, this does not mean that the description of the modern and dyadic personality types are exempt from criticism or analysis by these domains, but, it is to stress that the model exists at a high level of abstraction that pertains to generalized observations relative to cultural groups and not specific individuals. Significant variation within groups, thus, is to be expected. On the other hand, it should not be overlooked that Malina's description of the two personality types are themselves socially located and, as a result, are described quite easily in terms of what is now traditional Freudian psychoanalytic theory. Indeed, Malina's (and Geertz's) definition of modern personality accords in all important respects with the role of the ego as the arbitrating and management center of the personality in dialogue with the demands and strains (frequently encountered as excessive) of the superego and other egos, while the dyadic personality appears to expend its greatest ego energy adjusting the personality to these demands. Hence, the one psychological term that is ventured in relation to dyadic personality derives from the discipline of family psychotherapy and relates to the dynamics of individuation within family groups. Here the degree and extent of group embeddedness encountered in the dyadic personality suggests a correlation with the phenomenon of "undifferentiated family ego-mass" encountered in the family therapy.[13]

Verification and Analysis

Malina's hypothesis of the dyadic personality in first-century Mediterranean society is regarded by him as just that—a hypothesis. It is up to the reader to test it. In issuing this challenge, suggestions as to how the model may be tested are offered as well as two important samples based on testing models. To test the dyadic model, Malina states:

> An easy way to do this is to look up the conjunctions "for" and "because" in a concordance, then look up the passages and collect those that provide explanation for some line of behavior. For example, . . . a sampling of statements containing the Greek conjunction *gar*, meaning "For, because" . . . normally sets out a reason for the previous statement. . . .[14]

Or, as an alternative, Malina suggests that one choose one NT writing and apply the analysis to that one writing. Following the latter alternative, he then sets out a sample from the Gospel of Matthew and 1 Corinthians and asks the following questions about the sample:

What did the sampling indicate? Are all the reasons stereotypical like proverbs, shared maxims, and/or external, outward, and culturally expected? Or did you find some reasons that are introspective, psychologically unique, extremely personal, and repeatable in terms of the culture?[15]

In my analysis I follow the alternative procedure and restrict my investigation to the appearances of the conjunction *gar* (for, because) in the Gospel of Luke.[16] Obviously, the data base could profit by taking account of the use of *gar* in Luke's second volume, Acts, as it could by extending the analysis beyond its present limitation to a single causative conjunction. Other causative conjunctions, or, motivational statements in general, are also relevant to the investigation whether the latter are introduced by these text markers or not. To do so, however, would extend the study beyond the limits of this article.[17] In turn, the rationale for the selection of the Gospel of Luke stems from the significance of this text for African American biblical hermeneutics and not merely because Malina did not provide a similar analysis. The relevant data for the investigation, thus, is comprised by the following passages in Luke: 1:15, 18, 30, 44, 48, 66, 76; 2:10; 3:8; 4:10; 5:9, 23, 39; 6:23, 26, 32, 33, 38, 43, 44, 45; 7:5, 6, 8, 33; 8:17, 18, 29, 46, 52; 9:14, 24, 25, 26, 44, 48, 50; 10:7, 24, 42; 11:4, 10, 30; 12:12, 23, 30, 34, 52, 58; 14:14, 24, 28; 16:2, 13, 28; 17:21, 24; 18:14, 16, 23, 25, 32; 19:5, 10, 21, 48; 20:6, 19, 33, 36, 38, 40, 42; 21:4, 8, 9, 15, 23, 26, 35; 22:2, 16, 18, 27, 37, 59, 71; 23:8, 12, 15, 22, 34, 41.[18]

In each of these texts, the conjunction *gar* appears, providing a basis for understanding behavior either presented earlier in the context or anticipated therein. It is not possible to discuss each of these texts individually nor is it possible to provide a detailed exegesis of the contexts in which this conjunction appears. My procedure is to classify and survey the texts first, giving concrete examples, according to the questions that Malina put to his own samples, and report the results. Then I will highlight a number of texts that strain Malina's model and suggest directions for future research.

Classification

Allowing for the possibility and eventuality that a given text could be classified in more than one way, the above cited texts in Luke may be divided among two broad general categories: (a) proverbs and maxims, and (b) cultural predictions (e.g., fulfillment of scripture) and obvious contextual generalities. In each text *gar* appears at least once (occasionally twice) and provides the ground or reason for understanding the behavior relevant to the context. The texts, consequently, may be subdivided into the following:

A. *Proverbs and Maxims*: 3:8; 5:39; 6:23, 26, 32, 33, 38, 43, 44, 45; 7:33; 8:17, 18; 9:24, 25, 26, 44, 48, 50; 10:7, 24, 42; 11:10, 30; 12:12, 23, 30, 34, 52; 14:14, 24, 28; 16:13; 17:21, 24; 18:14, 16, 25; 19:10; 20:38; 21:4, 9; 22:16, 18, 27.

B. *Cultural Predictions, Fulfillment of Scripture, Contextual Generalities*: 1:15, 18, 30, 44, 48, 66, 76; 2:10; 4:10; 5:9; 7:5, 6, 8; 8:29, 40, 46; 9:14; 11:4; 12:12; 16:2, 28; 18:23, 32; 19:5, 21, 48; 20:6, 19, 33, 36, 40, 42; 21:8, 15, 23, 26, 35; 22:2, 37, 59, 71; 23:8, 12, 15, 22, 34, 41.

Survey

The following texts are particularly useful or illuminating instances of the usage of the conjunction *gar* in Luke. I will throughout be using the RSV, which more clearly denotes this usage than other translations.

A. Proverbs and Maxims.

(1) Luke 9:24, 25, 26. This text is a particularly enlightening example in that the conjunction *gar* appears no less than three times in consecutive verses in a pericope (9:23-27) treating the theme of discipleship. In response to the exhortation that self-denial and taking up the cross daily is required of all who would follow Jesus, the conjunction provides the rationale in a maxim formulated chiastically in v. 24; "For [*gar*] whoever would save his life will lose it; and whoever loses his life for my sake, he will save it." *Gar* then appears in v. 25, as a proverbial question, which serves as a second justification for the theme of self-denial; "For [*gar*] what does it profit a man if he gains the whole world and loses or forfeits himself." In 9:26, the conjunction appears a third time in a Son of Man saying which functions as an eschatological warning. According to 9:26, "For [*gar*] whoever is ashamed of me and of my words of him will the Son of man be ashamed when he comes in his glory and the glory of the Father and of the holy angels." Thus, in 9:23-27, we find, formally at least, precisely what Malina predicts; namely, the conjunction *gar* pointing to behavior through exhortation and eschatological warning in proverbial form and in association with the values of honor and shame noted earlier as pivotal for the dyadic personality.

(2) Luke 10:24; 11:10. These texts may be considered together since the conjunction *gar* appears in both and both give evidence for the "three zone model." In his blessing over his disciples, Jesus states,

"Blessed are the eyes which see what you see!" and explicates this blessing with the statement "For [gar] many prophets and kings desired to see what you see, and did not see it, and to hear what you hear, and did not hear it." Similarly, in 11:9-10, Jesus' exhortation to prayer, "And I tell you, ' Ask and it will be given you; seek, and you will find; knock and it will be opened to you' . . ." is followed by the rationale, "For [gar] everyone who asks receives, and he who seeks finds, and to him who knocks it will be opened." In these texts the zones *eyes*, *mouth*, *ears*, and *hands* appear either at the surface level of the text, itself, or only thinly veiled below the surface.

B. Cultural Predictions and Contextual Generalities

(1) Luke 1:18, 66. In the birth narratives pertaining to John and Jesus the conjunction appears frequently as a means of describing present and future behavior. Luke 1:18 is illustrative of contextual generalities in that reference to Zachariah's and Elizabeth's ages appears here a second time in the course of the narrative (cf. Luke 1:7, 18). In response to the angel's announcement that he and Elizabeth will bear a child, Zechariah asks, "How shall I know this? For [gar] I am an old man, and my wife is advanced in years." In 1:66, at the naming ceremony, news of the events surrounding this miraculous birth spread throughout the hill country of Judea and of those who heard, it is said, "They laid them up in their hearts, saying, 'What then will this child be? For [gar] the hand of the Lord was with him.' " Here again, the "three zone model" (*hearts*, *hand*) is present with heart taking precedence over what a modern might assign to the agency of mind or memory.

(2) Luke 4:10; 5:39; 7:5; 9:14; 11:4; 18:23. These texts are significant in that they demonstrate the range of behavior from patently obvious and stereotypical to serious that is indicated by the conjunction. In 4:10, for example, Satan challenges Jesus to prove his status as Son of God by throwing himself off the pinnacle of the temple,

. . . for [gar] it is written,
    "He will give his angels charge of you,
        to guard you,"
and
    "On their hands they will bear you up,
    lest you strike your foot against a stone."

In the proverbial context of old and new wineskins, Jesus states that "no one after drinking old wine desires new; for [gar] he says 'The old is good' " (5:39). In 7:5, the elders of the people approach Jesus to intercede on behalf of a centurion whose slave is ill. According to the elders, the centurion is worthy of a miracle "for [*gar*] he loves our nation and he built us our synagogue." In 11:4, the principle of reciprocity is introduced as the rationale for the request for forgiveness in the Lord's Prayer: "and forgive us our sins for [*gar*] we ourselves forgive everyone who is indebted to us." Finally, after hearing the demands of discipleship imposed on him, the rich man goes away sad "for" (*gar*), as Luke adds, "he was very rich" (18:23).

Results and Analysis

On the basis of this brief survey, it is readily apparent that the texts introduced by the causal *gar* do in fact introduce behavior that is characteristically viewed from the standpoint of the conventional and culturally predictable and do not, as we might expect, include references and clues that point to the unique, the interpersonal, and the psychological. Without a detailed exegesis of the above texts, a number of observations concerning one particular text may aid in clarifying the results. In Luke 7:1-10, for example, several features in the narrative of the healing of the centurion's slave are adduced frequently as support for an interpretation other than the one argued here and above. The RSV translation of 7:2b, for instance, renders the word *éntimos* as "dear" and by that characterizes the centurion's attitude toward the sick slave. Further, in the entreaty of the elders on behalf of the centurion, they describe him as one who "loves" (*agapáō*) our nation and has built us a synagogue (7:5). There are further references in the text to the elders pleading the centurion's case "earnestly" (*spoudaíōs*, 7:4) and there are also references to "friends" (*philoí*, 7:6) and a statement of the centurion's "unworthiness" (7:6b-7a). Are not these markers in the text indicative of unique, personal, and psychological features even if the behavior indicated by *gar* in 1:5 is, itself, conventional and stereotypical? That they are not can be demonstrated quite sufficiently.

First, the RSV translation of *éntimos* (dear), which suggests "intimacy" between the centurion and the slave on the centurion's part, is misleading; *éntimos* is equally well, and perhaps best, translated by the economic term "valuable/expensive,"[19] as the RSV translation note acknowledges. Further, the reference to love, stated through the use of the verb *agapáō*, does *not* mean love in some unique and divine way as the scholarship of the past once argued,[20] and, as is still frequently heard in sermons. As this text indicates, the sentiments of past scholarship may have been in the right place, but the philology was flawed. The term *agapáō* does mean love, to be sure, but it designates human love also, and, one may add, love within the social structures of culture. What is striking here, however, is that the ground or basis of the love of the centurion for the nation is precisely what is *not* indicated in the context. The action of building a synagogue may well be related to this, but, the text presents these two features—loving the nation and building the synagogue—as two consecutives and not as a case of the latter originating out of the former. The *kai* (and) in the text is copulative.

Additionally, the text does not support the contention, frequently found in the commentaries, that is sometimes used to reconcile the tensions of the text and the modern interpreter's expectations of what should be there; namely, that the centurion loved the nation and built the synagogue "because" he, himself, was a god-fearer attracted to Judaism. The centurion is clearly a Gentile on the basis of 7:9, but the reference to "our nation" in the request of the elders in 7:5 mitigates against reading him as a proselyte. Moreover, the fact that a Gentile built a synagogue for the nation is not itself a unique event. An inscription from Egypt (second century BCE) memorializes a parallel case of a Gentile building a house of prayer for Jews.[21]

Finally, neither the intercession of the elders on behalf of the centurion nor the reference to friends in the text need indicate anything unique, personal, nor intimate, but they do, in fact, open up the text to the dynamics of life in Galilee in the first century. As the text demonstrates, the elders intercede for the centurion on the basis of the centurion's orders (7:3).[22] Authority to command the elders is implicit in 7:3 and it becomes explicit as a text dynamic in the interchange between the centurion's friends (themselves Gentiles) and Jesus in 7:6-8. In this exchange, the centurion's perception of himself is introduced also by a causal *gar*: "For (*gar*) I am a man set under authority (*exousía*),[23] with soldiers under me: and I say to one, 'Go', and he goes and to another, 'Come', and he comes; and to my slave, 'Do this', and he does it." The elders' dilemma, therefore, is not to convey the unique and surprising love of the centurion for the nation, but, rather, to provide a rationale for why a Jewish miracle-worker should come to the aid of a Gentile. The elders' arguments for the centurion's love of the nation and building the synagogue, consequently, are consecutive justifications of the "worthiness" (*hikanós*)[24] of the centurion and not markers of intimacy between Jew and Gentile. Further, the deference shown Jesus by the centurion, who confesses himself unworthy for Jesus to enter his house, more directly reflects social purity rules than it does unique, personal, psychological features. According to

M. Oholot 18:7, "The dwelling places of Gentiles are unclean."[25] In the culture, any Jew entering a Gentile house would be considered defiled. Instead of unique, personal, psychological features, the deference of the centurion—related through friends (*philoí*)—reveals the social hierarchy in which the dyadic personality attains self-awareness.

As previously stated, the dyadic personality perceives himself/herself, "as always interrelated to other persons while occupying a distinct social position both horizontally (with others sharing the same status, moving from center to periphery) and vertically (with others above and below in social rank)"[26] and this is precisely what occurs in the deference as well as in the unit at large. The centurion is a man set under authority (= vertical inferior)[27] with authority over subordinates (= vertical superior)[28] and he sends elders (vertical inferior)[29] and friends (= implied horizontal equals)[30] to intercede with a Jewish (= vertical inferior) miracle-worker (= vertical superior).[31] The text, therefore, does not present us with the cultural clues of modern individualistic Western society grounded in the unique, the personal, and the psychological, but, rather with the social mores, conventions, institutions and social organization and stratification of what Malina terms Mediterranean society in the first century. This becomes clear as soon as one reads the text with close attention to the cultural setting.

It is precisely in the act of a close reading of the text, however, that tensions in Malina's model first become evident. The pivotal value enunciated in the text is *not* honor and shame, even though honor and shame set the context as the focus on *worthiness—unworthiness* reveals.[32] The pivotal value of the text, rather, is stated in 7:9-10 in the statement "I tell you, not even in Israel have I found such faith" (*pistis*, RSV). Whether Bultmann understood the pericope correctly or not is one matter, but he was certainly correct in form-critically classifying the unit among the *apothegmmáta* (pronouncement stories) and not among the miracle stories despite its content and subject matter.[33] The climax of the unit, therefore, is none other than Jesus' pronouncement on the centurion's faith as the pivotal value of the unit and not the centurion's favorable attraction to Judaism, or, to Jesus' personality, nor to the miracle, itself. Hence, one almost has the sense that the interpretation of the unit is achieved when one states that here one encounters the Lukan thematic that through faith Gentiles enter the kingdom of heaven at the same time and on the same basis as Jews.[34] As soon as one states this, however, the close reading of the text refutes it. What the text states and what Jesus pronounces directly is not the equal status of Jews and Gentiles before God, but, that faith as the pivotal value is discovered in a *Gentile* army officer in the employ of the son of the despised Idumean king, Herod the Great, in a manner not found among the elders of the elect nation.[35]

To be sure, this observation does not overturn Malina's argument concerning the nature of the dyadic personality in the first-century Mediterranean world. Indeed, it could be taken, along with the above, as evidence that we have only identified the cultural embeddedness of Luke, a Gentile, in Greco-Roman culture as opposed to the Semitic subculture of Judaism. To follow through with this line of reasoning, however, contradicts the very thing we know of Luke. In his explication of Christian origins, Luke not only places Christianity in the context of Greco-Roman culture, but, simultaneously, locates that story in the context of the salvation history of Israel as well (cf. 3:16). Similarly, in Acts, to choose but an obvious example, Paul's literary, fictive journeys always start and end in Jerusalem, just as Paul characteristically initiates his missionary preaching in Jewish synagogues. If we may speak of cultural embeddedness in Luke, then, we must speak of the way in which Luke fuses these two cultures—Greco-Roman culture and the Semitic culture of early Christianity.

What Malina's typology does not clarify, therefore, is how a dyadic personality grounded in a dominant culture (politically!) can make the move toward identification with a subdominant culture (again politically!) and synthesize the two in such a way that he contributes materially to the formation of an individual and group identity that moves along the trajectory of sect to separate institution that is able to establish itself in competition with similar rivals (e.g., Isis, Mithra) as the official religion of an empire. Clearly, Malina's discussion of individuation and ego strength among dyadic personalities needs further clarification.[36] Instead of "an undifferentiated family ego-mass," one might argue that precisely the opposite is required in instances where the symbolic world of the dyadic personality undergoes radical transformation.[37]

Moreover, in a clarification of this type, our text and others in Luke may play a significant role. Reflect, for example, on the dyadic personality as Malina describes it and the words of John to those who came out for baptism:

> You brood of vipers! Who warned you to flee from the wrath to come? Bear fruits that befit repentance, and do not begin to say to yourselves, We have Abraham as our father; for I tell you, God is able from these stones to raise up children to Abraham. Even now the axe is laid to the root of the trees; every tree therefore that does not bear good fruit is cut down and thrown into the fire. (Luke 3:7-9)

Or, in the same vein, consider the social structure of the Mediterranean family[38] and the apocalyptic saying attributed to Jesus in Luke 12:51-53:

> Do you think that I have come to give peace on earth? No, I tell you, but rather division; for henceforth in one house there will be five divided, three against two and two against three; they will be divided, father against son and son against father, mother against daughter and daughter against her mother, mother-in-law against her daughter-in-law and daughter-in-law against her mother-in-law.[39]

Or, note the way in which Luke's positive acceptance of the socially marginal, the ethnically, linguistically, and geographically diverse, forces one to locate the social world of Luke's thought outside of ethnic groups that refuse to associate with the mixed population of the Greco-Roman world.[40]

What our text and others suggest, therefore, is that the alteration of pivotal values, e.g., faith versus nationalistic/ethnic religious identification, is a significant feature of Mediterranean life in the first century and this alteration has profound consequences relative to the process of individuation among dyadic personalities in this society as well. An analysis of individuation among dyadic personalities, consequently, is a mandate if we are to adequately understand and describe the relation of the individual and the group in Mediterranean society in the first century.

CHAPTER 6

Oppression and Identity
in the Gospel of John

David Rensberger

The work of Charles B. Copher might be appropriately characterized as "making the invisible visible." Copher has sought to bring
to the awareness of scholars and other students of the Bible the
significance of peoples whose very presence in the biblical text has
not always been recognized. The real problem, of course, does not lie
with the peoples in the text, but with the readers who fail to recognize
them. Perhaps, then, we might better characterize his accomplishment
as "making the blind to see"!

Copher's particular emphasis, of course, has been on the African
presence in the Bible, a task that the Gospel of John provides little
opportunity to carry forward. Simon of Cyrene, for example, who
appears in all three of the Synoptic Gospels, is not found in John,
where Jesus carries his own cross. I propose, however, to extend the
scope of the project somewhat, and to ask about the presence of
unrecognized people in general in this Gospel, specifically, the oppressed and their oppressors. If the oppressed are present in John, we
may then go on to inquire how the author relates them to the community of readers to which the Gospel is addressed.

It would be well, first of all, to clarify this reference to the
community of the Gospel's readers, and thereby to indicate the stance
within Johannine scholarship that this article presupposes. In recent
years it has become common to understand the Fourth Gospel as the
product of a struggle in which a group of Jewish Christians was
expelled from the synagogue community to which it had formerly
belonged.[1] This conflict was the crucible within which the distinctive
theology of John was formed. The presentation of Jesus in this Gospel
generally reflects this theology. In particular, the depiction of Jesus as
one who is not of this world but from above, and so is alienated from

77

a world that regards him with hostility, reflects the sectarian consciousness of the Johannine community.[2] Estranged from their social
and religious heritage, from the world of meaning and values that had
once been theirs, the community saw in Jesus a new source for the
validation and meaning they required. His alienation in the narrative
represents their own in history; his obedience to God represents their
own fidelity to what they have believed; and his fulfillment of traditional Jewish symbols, hopes, and customs offers them sustenance in
their isolated and threatened situation.

It will be perceived that the situation of this community bears
some of the marks of oppression and it is possible to evaluate the
theology of John as that of an oppressed group seeking liberation. I
have sought to make a beginning in this direction elsewhere.[3] What I
want to do here is to consider various characters in the Gospel's
narrative, from the point of view of their roles as oppressed, oppressor,
or something else. I shall examine what these roles might have meant
for the Johannine community, that is, for the author of the Gospel and
for its original intended readers. My aim will be to consider the way
in which figures in the Gospel who come from oppressed or powerless
groups relate to the identity of the Johannine community. Are oppressed groups and individuals in the story offered to the readers as
models with whom to identify? Are persons in power also presented
as such models, or do they appear as antithetical to the identity of the
Johannine readers?

To do this, I shall consider two sets of John's characters. A "character" in this sense can be an individual, or a group that functions
collectively in the narrative. In some cases, group "characters" are also
represented by individuals, through whom the author conveys a
conception of the group as a whole. A number of John's characters (the
women in the Gospel, for instance) have already been the subject of
thorough investigation in other studies. This will allow me simply to
summarize the results of those studies, and then consider their significance for my topic. The first and larger set that I shall examine consists
of characters who are in some sense oppressed, whether their oppression is due to gender, disability, social standing, or other factors. The
second set consists of oppressive characters, people in the story who
in some way carry out acts of oppression.

Particularly with group characters, important information will
often come from cultural and historical data outside of John. Generally,
though, the most important consideration will be the treatment of a
character within the story, both by the narrator and by other characters. This treatment can indicate oppressed status and how the author

regards the character. One important aspect of this, which will feature prominently in my discussion of most of the characters, is how Jesus, the central figure in John, relates to a character: how does Jesus respond to the character, and how does the character respond to him?

Three cautions must be mentioned before I begin. One is that I am considering these figures as characters in John's story, not as historical persons. The portrayal of some characters can only be understood by reference to historical data from outside the Gospel; but in characterizing people as oppressed or oppressors, I am not passing judgment on actual historical individuals. I am simply evaluating the portrayal of characters who appear in the narrative of the Fourth Gospel.

Second, the terminology of oppression itself can be problematic. Some may consider it prejudicial; if they prefer to think in more neutral terms, the point that is to be made will, I believe, emerge equally well.

Finally, one character is conspicuously absent from those considered here, namely Jesus himself. It is true that Jesus—alienated, rejected, and crucified—is the supreme figure in John who suffers and overcomes oppression. However, the discussion of Johannine Christology to which such an analysis of Jesus would inevitably lead would overwhelm the rest of the study.

As might be expected, the subject of oppression in John has not received a great deal of attention in the past. Aside from my own work previously alluded to, two studies—the first by Frederick Herzog, and the second the profound contribution of José Porfirio Miranda—have treated John in the light of liberation theology.[4] These books, however, do not consider concretely the presence of the oppressed in the Fourth Gospel. A recent study by Robert J. Karris, on the other hand, has done so in a very stimulating fashion.[5] Karris considers several categories of "marginalized" people who appear in John, including a number that I shall examine below in nearly the same order. It was Karris's book that caused me to begin thinking along these lines, and I shall have occasion both to draw on and to take issue with his work at a number of points in what follows.

Oppressed Characters

I begin with an examination of those characters in John whose origins are among the oppressed.

The "Crowd That Does Not Know the Law"

The first "character" to be considered is the group of those who are ignorant of the law, with specific reference to John 7:45-52. Here the Pharisees, disgusted with the temple police for failing to arrest Jesus, ask rhetorically, "Has any of the authorities or the Pharisees believed in him?", and then add, "But this crowd that does not know the law are accursed." Karris, along with most commentators, associates this attitude with that of later rabbinic texts toward the ʿammê haʾareṣ ("people of the land"), the ordinary people who were not learned in the law and were considered negligent in its practice.[6] He goes on to suggest that the Johannine community included people who came from this background.[7]

With all of this I might agree. I would not, of course, generalize from John 7:49 to suppose that all Pharisees in the first century had this attitude. Nevertheless, if one did not know what the Torah required, one could hardly hope to keep it faithfully, and that seems to be the condition of the "crowd" derided by the Pharisees here.

The "crowd" (óchlos) is mentioned several times in the course of John 7. Elsewhere in John, this is a neutral term referring to a large gathering of people (e.g., John 5:13; 6:1-5; 11:42; 12:9-18). In this chapter, however, it seems to refer to a specific group. They are not simply "a crowd," nor do they need to be defined as "the crowd standing there," or in some other way. They are *the* crowd, a group that Jesus is suspected of misleading (7:12). They are in a stir about him throughout the chapter, though their opinion of him varies. First they think he is possessed (7:20), but later many of them believe in him because of his signs (7:31). In the end, they remain divided (7:40-44). That this crowd, whose members are of course Jewish, should be afraid of "the Jews" (7:13) may seem surprising. We must bear in mind that "the Jews," here as elsewhere in John, are not the Jewish people as such, but the Jewish *authorities*, and represent opposition to Jesus (see below). The "crowd" is thus different from "the Jews," and different also from the somewhat ill-defined "people of Jerusalem," who appear in 7:25-30.[8] Of all these groups, it is only the crowd that has some members who believe in Jesus, and it is these who are characterized as "ignorant of the law" by the Pharisees.

To what extent should we regard this "crowd" as oppressed? There is no necessary connection between being an ʿam ʾhā-āreṣ and poverty. Yet the term does seem to designate the "commoners" in distinction from a religious elite, and it may well be that most such people were of lower social status.[9] There is no indication that the 'am 'hā-āreṣ as such were persecuted. However, the way in which the "crowd" is contrasted with "the authorities" does suggest that they were relatively powerless and without control, at least over their religious destiny.

Clearly the author of this Gospel expected its first readers to identify with those in the story who believe (cf. John 20:31). In the present instance, these believers are shown as condemned and disdained by the ruling authorities. Indeed, their very ignorance seems to be associated with their belief in Jesus. Thus by its treatment of the various characters in chapter 7, John draws the reader into identification with a despised group and into opposition to those in power. This suggests either that the real people for whom the book was written would have found such identification and opposition natural, or else that the author seriously proposed it as a change of social identity for them. I shall turn next to an individual character whose story exhibits this same quality.

The Blind Man

The story of the blind man in John 9 has been the subject of a number of studies, so that I can treat it in summary fashion here.[10] The blind man, who is healed by Jesus and then interrogated by the Pharisees, stands for the Johannine community itself. Like him, they have been "enlightened" by Jesus and thus have been brought into conflict with the synagogue authorities. He presents a model for their own response to those circumstances: under pressure from the Pharisees, he refuses to deny his experience for the sake of traditional concepts, and in this process of resistance comes to a deeper understanding of who Jesus is. Once he has been expelled, he encounters Jesus again and worships him as Son of Man. In the end, John has Jesus declare that it was not the blind man who was guilty of sin, but those who claimed they could see and yet failed to recognize what the coming of Jesus represented.

As Karris points out, the blind man may be regarded as marginalized in several ways.[11] As one who was physically disabled, he would have been religiously marginalized. Moreover, his disability left him in poverty: he was a beggar (John 9:8). It also caused people to regard him as being under God's judgment, whether for his own sin or that of his parents (9:2), as the Pharisees emphasize when they expel him: "You were born entirely in sins, and are you trying to teach us?" (9:34). Thus the blind man is the object of the same contempt as the crowd in chapter 7, and should most likely also be considered an 'am '*hā-āreṣ* like them. Of course, his defense of Jesus and his ejection by the authorities add yet another layer of marginalization, that of the Christian under persecution.

Thus the blind man belongs among the oppressed, an exemplar both of the crowd scorned by the Pharisees and of the Johannine Christians, whose open confession of Jesus had led to their own expulsion. It is surely significant that this Gospel symbolizes the community of faith to which its author belonged by means of such a man. He is pictured as someone without education or personal resources, invisible to other people except as an object of pity or a subject for abstract theological debate. Yet he makes a spirited plea on behalf of what he knows has happened to him, defying the learned and powerful men who question him. The Gospel writer seems to imply that the Christian community for which he writes can see itself both in the blind man's oppressed circumstances and in his courageous attitude.

The Lame Man

John 5 presents us with another victim of illness whom Jesus heals, this time a man disabled for thirty-eight years. As with the blind man, the Jewish authorities challenge his healing for a violation of the sabbath (5:10-12; cf. 9:13-16). When he attributes this violation to the instructions of the man who healed him, they desire to know who this is, evidently with hostile intent. Like the blind man, the lame man encounters Jesus for a second time; but unlike the blind man, instead of heeding what Jesus tells him, he goes off to betray Jesus to the authorities (5:13-16).

The lame man is as much a victim of oppression as the blind man. He too is on the fringes of society, poor and without resources, and ignorant enough of the law to pay no attention to sabbath regulations when Jesus tells him to pick up his mat and walk. We may surmise that he too is symbolic of people known to the Gospel writer. But rather than bravely challenging his interrogators, he goes looking for them and turns informer against Jesus. While it must be admitted that John does not characterize his actions as strongly as those of the blind man, it does seem likely that this is intended as a negative example.[12] It shows that not everyone who had experienced Jesus' life-giving power acted courageously, in the author's experience. It would be possible to claim that this man's oppression had left him still a victim even after his healing, unable to grasp his own empowerment and still obedient to the authorities who show themselves antagonistic to his healing and his healer. This goes rather beyond what John actually says, however, and though one may surmise that it is part of what the author intended, one cannot be certain.

Galileans

Karris and others have pointed out that Galilee is spoken of in a very distinctive way in John.[13] On the one hand, the territory and its inhabitants are an object of scorn. The Messiah cannot come from Galilee, nor can an eschatological prophet. Nicodemus is derided by the other Pharisees for even a mild defense of Jesus the Galilean (John 7:41, 52). On the other hand, Jesus' disciples are from Galilee (1:43-44; 12:21; 21:2). It is there that he first reveals his glory (2:11; 4:54), and he generally meets with a more believing reception in Galilee than in Jerusalem or Judea (4:43-45). It will not do to exaggerate this. John 4:43-45 seems either to identify Judea rather than Galilee as Jesus' homeland, or else to say that even in Galilee Jesus received no honor.[14] Similarly, the Galilean synagogue at Capernaum includes "Jews" who dispute Jesus' claims (6:41, 52, 59). Yet on the whole, Galileans seem more receptive to Jesus than Jews (or Judeans) in John.

Much later Talmudic sources suggest that Galilee was disparaged by the Pharisees' successors as being slow to take up rabbinic practices.[15] Whether or not this can be projected back into the first century, John clearly depicts Galilee as being looked down upon by the Jerusalem Pharisees (7:52). Thus here once again we see John inviting the reader to a greater affinity, at least, for members of a group disrespected by the authorities in Jerusalem. Once more the scorn of the Pharisees is in itself a kind of indicator of where John's attachments lie: their contempt for Galilee inevitably draws the reader's sympathy toward the region.

Finally, we may note in passing that even among Galileans there are attempts to draw distinctions. Nathanael, said to be from the Galilean town of Cana (21:2), is himself derisive of Jesus' home village of Nazareth (1:46). This provides another example of John's use of people and places that are objects of disdain to characterize Jesus and those who believe in him.

Samaritans

Karris also includes the Samaritans among those who were "geographically marginalized," alluding to the well-known Jewish antipathy toward Samaria.[16] This proposal, however, at least needs some further nuance. Samaria was not under Jewish control in the first century and never had been, apart from a brief period under the Hasmoneans c. 128–63 BCE. We cannot, therefore, think of the Jews as "oppressing" or "marginalizing" the Samaritans. However much or little mutual contact individual members of the two communities may have had, there was no way for either group to dominate the other. Samaritans were sometimes the victims of Jewish violence; sometimes Samaritans perpetrated violence against Jews (see Josephus, *Antiquities* 18.2.2, §30; 20.6.1-3, §§118-136, paralleled in *Jewish War* 2.12.3-7, §§232-246). We may imagine that the Samaritans *would have been* oppressed by the Jews if this had been possible; but it was not. Instead we have here a case of mutual hatred, in which both sides apparently despised one another equally.

Even so, it is significant that John, in Jesus' encounter with the Samaritan woman and her townspeople in 4:4-42, presents the Samaritans as far more open to Jesus than the Jews. Though Jesus himself restates the Jewish claim to superiority, this is entirely submerged in the assertion that from now on neither Jewish nor Samaritan worship matters but only the worship of God in Spirit and truth that Jesus himself mediates (4:21-23). Eventually the people of this Samaritan village accord Jesus one of the highest titles in the Fourth Gospel when they acknowledge him as Savior of the world (4:42). There is widespread agreement that this narrative represents an openness to Samaritans among the Johannine Christians, and indeed that Samaritans likely were present within their community.[17] This would require a dramatic shifting of traditional boundary lines for the Jewish members of the Johannine community, and suggests that, whatever may be the case with oppression, at least some barriers of longstanding ethnic hatred were being broken down within this group.

Women

Here again I may be brief, since there are several thorough studies of women's roles in John.[18] Certainly the parts played by women in John's narrative go beyond what might have been expected in that place and time. In the course of her conversation with Jesus, the Samaritan woman at the well, though she begins slowly, like most of Jesus' dialogue partners in John, gradually displays a far greater understanding than many others. Her forthright dialogue with the teacher and her increasingly insightful questions present quite an uncommon image for either the Judaism or the Samaritanism of the ancient world. Ultimately Jesus' words lead her to bear the news of his messiahship to her townspeople (John 4:4-42). Later in the Gospel Martha of Bethany makes precisely the confession of faith that it is John's purpose to evoke from the reader (11:25-27; cf. 20:31). Her sister, Mary, anticipates Jesus' glorification, i.e., his death and resurrection, by her anointing of him (12:1-8), an act that Raymond Brown calls "a culminating expression of loving faith."[19] In the most beautiful of all the Gospels' Easter stories, it is Mary Magdalene who meets the risen Lord, receives the good news of his resurrection, and brings the report to the other disciples (20:1-18).

All these women carry out the responsibilities of model disciples in John: they encounter Jesus and hear his word, they recognize him as the giver of life, they show their devotion to him, and they carry the message about him to others. The exercise of such autonomous roles by women in the Gospel of John suggests that their status in the Johannine community may have been an unconventional one as well. It also shows that the author does not hesitate to identify the highest aspirations of John's community of readers with people who belonged to oppressed segments of society. The community's identity is once again to be found among those who would elsewhere be anything but exemplary role models.

Oppressive Characters

I turn now to characters in John who, in one way or another, take part in oppression. I shall first of all consider perhaps the most obvious of these, the Roman governor of Judea, Pontius Pilate.

Pilate

As one might expect, Pilate represents the Roman state. At the time when John was written, the Jewish community was still recovering from the failure of the revolt against Rome and the destruction of the Temple in 70 CE. As some sought accommodation with the Romans, others continued to harbor hopes of redemption and restoration, including an end to Roman rule.[20] For either side there can be little doubt that the Roman authorities were still viewed as oppressors. It is against this background that John's depiction of Pilate must be understood.

For the sake of space, I shall simply summarize here conclusions concerning Pilate's role in John for which I have argued elsewhere.[21] In the trial narrative in chapters 18–19, John portrays Pilate as a ruthless and relentless opponent of both Jesus and "the Jews." If he is indifferent to Jesus and to truth (John 18:37-38), he is also scornful of Israel's hope of messianic redemption (19:13-15). He grants the Jewish authorities' desire to put Jesus to death, but only after wresting from them a heinous concession: by his ironic taunting he drives them at last to deny their God, in the declaration "We have no king but Caesar!" (19:15). By displaying the beaten and humiliated Jesus as "King of the Jews" (19:1-5, 13-15, 19-22), Pilate becomes one of a number of characters in John who bear witness to Jesus in terms that they themselves do not really understand (cf. 19:9-11).[22] Pilate is thus not a sympathetic character in John, but a hostile one. By this portrayal of Pilate, and by means of other components of the trial narrative, John displays his unwillingness to accept Caesar as legitimate king over God's people. For John, only Jesus can be Israel's king, even though his kingship is not of the sort established by the world's violent means.[23]

Thus the Roman governor Pilate is presented by John as one of the characters hostile to Jesus, and so implicitly to the Christian community. Since there is no evidence in this Gospel that the community was being persecuted by the Roman authorities, this enmity toward Rome may be a part of the group's Jewish inheritance. But it may also reflect John's conviction that any human system that requires allegiance and obedience for itself is inimical to the total demand expressed in the Johannine claims about Jesus. For John, all loyalty belongs to Jesus, Son of God and King of the Jews. Pilate, symbolizing the Roman oppression, is simply unable to assert any claim over the Johannine Christians that John is willing to acknowledge.[24] Thus in Pilate we have a character *against* whom the Johannine community seeks to establish its identity. He represents the opposition, or at least one facet of it. That is, he represents the world, which for John means, in the words of C. K. Barrett, "the whole organized state of human society, secular and religious."[25] We need only note further that he does so precisely in his character as oppressor, as one who claims (wrongly) to have power over Jesus to release him or to crucify him (19:10).

The Pharisees and "the Jews"

Of all the characters in the Gospel of John those who are most clearly oppressive are the Pharisees. Their role is so well known that I need only summarize it here. The Pharisees dispute with Jesus and are frustrated by their inability to check his popularity (4:1-3; 8:13; 9:40; 12:19). What may be most significant for us, however, is that the Pharisees appear as a hostile power group almost everywhere in John.

86

They send out priests and Levites to interrogate John the Baptist (1:24). They have the authority to question people suspected of violating the sabbath (9:13-17). As we shall see below, John presents the Jewish rulers as either associated with the Pharisees or intimidated by them (3:1; 7:47-48; 12:42). Alone among the Gospels, John associates the Pharisees with the chief priests in Jesus' persecution, arrest, and trial (7:32, 45; 11:46-57; 18:3). It is true that even some of the Pharisees do once entertain the possibility that Jesus is at least not a sinner, so that there is a division among them (9:16). But these sympathetic Pharisees never appear again in John and they in no way restrain the persecution of Jesus and those who believe in him by the Pharisees in general.

Since it is clear at certain points that "the Jews" in John are virtually identical with the Pharisees (1:19, 24; 8:13, 22; 9:13, 18), we must also consider the many instances of hostility by "the Jews" to fill out the Johannine picture of the Pharisees.[26] Like the Pharisees, "the Jews" dispute with Jesus, and are unable to understand him (2:18-20; 6:41-42, 52; 7:11-15, 35-36; 8:22-59). "The Jews" also investigate sabbath violations (5:10-16; cf. 9:18-34); persecute Jesus and seek to kill him (5:18; 7:1; 8:59; 10:31); and are involved in his trial and execution (18:31, 38-40; 19:7, 12-15). "The Jews" can be divided among themselves over Jesus' messiahship (10:19-39; 11:45-46; 12:9-11) but they remain essentially hostile to him. Indeed, Jesus' followers and would-be followers are often said to be "afraid of 'the Jews' " (7:13; 9:22; 19:38; 20:19), even though they are Jewish themselves. Based on this evidence, it has long been clear that the hostile use of the term "Jews" in John does not refer to the Jewish people as a whole, but specifically to the Jewish authorities, i.e., essentially the same body as the Pharisees.[27]

In sum, John portrays the Pharisees and "the Jews" as powerful opponents of Jesus, who not only refuse to believe that Jesus has come from God, but succeed in having him put to death and in ejecting those who do believe in him from the synagogue (9:22; 12:42). It is highly significant for John's attitude toward oppression that the major authoritative body in the story is presented in such a consistently negative way. The depiction of the Pharisees as ruling authorities is probably anachronistic in regard to the lifetime of Jesus, but it fits the circumstances of the Johannine Christian community exactly.[28] In the competition for dominance in Judaism after 70 CE, Pharisees were exercising authority in some manner to rid the local synagogue(s) of Christians. The Gospel of John was to a great extent written in response to this oppression, to encourage the Christian group to maintain and deepen their faith in the face of persecution. Needless to say, there is no evidence of any desire on the author's part for the readers to seek their identity with the Pharisees. Rather, the Johannine community understood itself as opponents and victims of the Pharisaic authorities.

The Jewish Rulers

Several times John refers to the *árchontes* of the Jewish community (singular *árchōn*; John 3:1; 7:26, 48; 12:42). This word is usually translated "authorities," or "rulers," though the New Revised Standard Version renders it "leader" in 3:1. These authorities stand in a dubious relationship to the Johannine believers. The disputed role played by Nicodemus, the one *árchōn* who is named, will be examined below. Here I shall consider the whole group that John calls *árchontes*.

Commentators often take these *árchontes* to be members of the Sanhedrin, the highest Jewish governing council in Jerusalem.[29] However, if any group represents the Sanhedrin in John, it is "the chief priests and the Pharisees" (7:32, 45; 11:47, 57; 18:3), who are not identical with the *árchontes*. We must bear in mind that John was written with an eye more to its own time than to that of Jesus. In the Johannine situation, after 70 CE and probably outside Palestine, the significant "rulers" would not have been the now-defunct Sanhedrin but the local Jewish community authorities. The designation *árchontes* was widely used for such rulers, whether of all Jews in a city (as in Alexandria and Cyrenaica) or of individual synagogues (as at Rome). Unfortunately, the exact duties of these officials are not clear. Nevertheless, the position was plainly one of high honor and responsibility, both within the Jewish community and as representing it to outside authorities. In some cases the office was elective or appointive, while in others it may have been hereditary, since even children are sometimes called *árchontes* or "future *árchontes*" in epitaphs.[30] This suggests also that the position of *árchōn* was connected to social class and status. Philo, for instance, complains that the Jewish *árchontes* and council members received degrading punishments during a crisis in Alexandria and "endured worse than their subjects, like the lowliest Egyptians guilty of the greatest misdeeds" (*In Flaccum* 80).

We should assume that when John speaks of *árchontes*, it is referring to such persons. It is striking that every mention of the *árchontes* in John has to do with their believing in Jesus. Nicodemus the *árchōn* comes to Jesus acknowledging him as a divinely sent teacher (John 3:1-2); the adequacy of his belief will be discussed in the next section. In 7:26, the people of Jerusalem wonder whether, since

Jesus is being allowed to speak openly, the rulers have decided that he is the Messiah. It is only a bit later that the Pharisees ask the temple police rhetorically whether any of the *árchontes* or the Pharisees have believed in him (7:48). Finally, we learn in 12:42 that many of the *árchontes* did indeed believe in him but failed to confess their faith for fear the Pharisees would put them out of the synagogue. On the basis of these passages, Martyn proposed that John uses the term *árchontes* to refer to a group of secret believers within the local governing body (the *gerousía* or council of elders).[31] Simply on linguistic grounds, this is unlikely. Moreover, the grammar of the questions in 7:26, 48 anticipates that the answers will be negative: the rulers do not think that Jesus is the Messiah, and (in the Pharisees' opinion) none of them believes in him. Even the rulers who do believe (12:42-43) are characterized quite negatively, as cowardly and preferring human glory to that which comes from God. This could imply that they feared a loss of class standing if they were expelled from the synagogue community and thus forfeited their status as *árchontes*.

In all this it must be recalled that the Gospel has in mind the Jewish *árchontes* of its own place and time, not those of Jesus' day. Some of these people are Pharisees, like Nicodemus; but the fact that the two groups can be named side by side shows that they are not identical, and 12:42 indicates that it was the Pharisees who held real power in the environs of the Johannine community. Even so, rulers are rulers, and it is precisely the contrast between them and the "crowd that does not know the law" that is significant in 7:48-49. Those of the ruling class who believe refuse to stand openly with the Christians among the common people by not letting their belief be known, and thus they sanction the oppression by their fellow *árchontes*. As we have seen, it is the ignorant crowd, cursed by the Pharisees and abandoned by the believing *árchontes*, with whom the Johannine reader will identify most strongly. It seems clear that John longs for the Christian *árchontes* to come forth, and is sharply critical of their failure to do so. Thus even though there are believers among them, the *árchontes* as a whole are not a group with which John desires the reader to identify. Even if they do not instigate oppression against the Johannine community, like the Pharisees, they remain an authority group associated with that oppression, and the Christians among them are virtually collaborators in it by their refusal to acknowledge their own belief in public.

Nicodemus

The final character I shall consider is Nicodemus, who is linked to each of the preceding two characters, being both a Pharisee and an *árchōn* (3:1). There is a tendency in Johannine scholarship to see Nicodemus as a "good Pharisee," one who seriously, if with some difficulty at first, believes in Jesus and even comes to his defense.[32] This impression, while not without its strengths, is in my view too charitable to Nicodemus as John presents him. To sum up a discussion that has been carried on in more detail elsewhere,[33] we should view Nicodemus as typical of the "secret Christians" who try to remain within the security of the synagogue community, and even to maintain their positions as Pharisees and rulers, while holding some form of belief in Jesus.

At his first appearance in John 3, Nicodemus addresses Jesus as "a teacher who has come from God," on the basis of the signs he has done (3:2). This aligns him with the people of unreliable faith just mentioned in 2:23-25. It also seems to place Jesus essentially on a level with Nicodemus himself, the "teacher of Israel" (3:10). Yet throughout their brief dialogue, Nicodemus seems totally unable to fathom what Jesus is saying. The reason is precisely that he has not yet been "born from above," of water and Spirit (3:3-8). That is, he represents would-be believers who have not taken the decisive step of baptism into the oppressed Johannine community, an open adherence that would set them apart from the world.

In John 7:50-52, Nicodemus responds to the rhetorical question whether any of the Pharisees or rulers have believed in Jesus. He does not make a forthright declaration of his own belief, but appeals instead to "our law"—i.e., to the law of "the Jews," Jesus' opponents (cf. 15:25; 18:31; 19:7). Though this is often seen as a courageous move, it is instructive to contrast his timid and quickly silenced remark with the vigorous challenge to "the Jews" offered by the blind man in chapter 9. Nicodemus, who is "one of them," one of the ruling group, is put to shame by comparison with the outspoken beggar.

To this point, Nicodemus seems to be one of the *árchontes* condemned in John 12:42-43 for their fear of confessing their belief in Jesus. His final appearance, in 19:38-42, does little to dispel this impression. Here he appears with Joseph of Arimathea, who is pointedly characterized as a secret disciple "for fear of the Jews." Their burial of Jesus, under no less than 75 pounds of spices, certainly suggests no expectation that he will rise again.[34]

Given the great diversity of opinions about Nicodemus noted above, we must at least say that he is an extraordinarily ambiguous figure in the gospel of John. Karris, who shares in the more optimistic view, regards him as a "marginalizer" who has by the end of the

Gospel's narrative joined the marginalized by becoming a disciple of Jesus.[35] I believe that this is what John is calling on "Nicodemus" to do, i.e., that the Gospel is urging the secret Christians among the ruling class to make themselves known and to take the risk of openly siding with those who are being expelled from the synagogue. But I cannot agree that the Gospel writer actually shows Nicodemus making this transition. In the highly dualistic worldview of John, ambiguity is not a particularly favorable trait.[36] John very much wants Nicodemus to cease being ambiguous, to take a stand on the side of the Johannine community. But even at the end, as the commentator Alfred Loisy remarked, Nicodemus has nothing to do with Jesus except with his corpse.[37]

Thus Nicodemus, precisely in his ambiguity, remains among the oppressors, not the oppressed. His membership in two groups that were oppressing the Johannine community, the Pharisees and the rulers, on the one hand, and his coming to Jesus with sincere, if somewhat dim, questions on the other hand, place him right at the crossroad of the issue of identity for John. His is the opportunity to decide whether he remains among the oppressive powers or sides wholeheartedly with the oppressed. There must surely have been some among John's intended readers who would have seen themselves in Nicodemus. His struggle, or lack of struggle, for identity will have mirrored their own. But for the Gospel's author, *endless* struggle and ambiguity do not represent an appropriate model. At some point, one must actually choose with which side one will identify.

Conclusions

The relationship between identity and oppression in John is clearly a complex one. One is tempted to say that that is the only clear thing about it. But in fact some fairly straightforward conclusions can be drawn from the foregoing study.

We have seen that most of the figures in John's Gospel with whom the Johannine readers would most closely identify come from groups or circumstances that should be identified as oppressed. By contrast, people from power groups tend to be hostile or at least dubious characters in the story, and to represent equally hostile or dubious figures in the environment of the Johannine community. This emerges most clearly when we observe confrontations within the Gospel narrative between people from different social levels. Given the choice between the ignorant "crowd" and the Pharisees who despise them in

John 7:49, the author's sympathies clearly lie with the crowd. Two characters in the Gospel may represent individualizations of this "crowd." One of them, the lame man who is healed in chapter 5, becomes dubious precisely when he identifies Jesus to "the Jews," i.e., to the Jewish authorities, as the healer who told him to violate the sabbath. The other character, the blind man in chapter 9, stands out in the Gospel as a hero who represents a kind of model for the Johannine readers. He resists the authorities' pressure to renounce Jesus, and instead stands by his own experience of healing. In this conflict, he not only grows in empowerment, but gains a deeper insight into who Jesus is. In all of these passages, by contrast, "the Jews," and specifically the Pharisees, are portrayed as those who persecute and oppress both Jesus and those who accept him as Messiah. These authorities consistently represent "the other side" for both the author and the Christian reader. Official religion is very much the enemy for John, precisely in its role as oppressor of the dissenting messianists. Even the rulers who believe in Jesus are characterized negatively, as failing to make the open profession of their belief that would identify them with the Christian "crowd" and so expose them to danger.

Other oppressed characters also show up in heroic, or at least highly positive, roles in John's narrative. The women in the Gospel are perhaps the most noticeable of these. Jesus interacts with them in the same way as with male disciples, and the women always come off in a positive light. Women in John confess Jesus' true identity and bear the news about him to others. They receive Jesus' teaching and understand it, fulfilling a discipleship role unusual in antiquity. It may take awhile for the Samaritan woman in chapter 4 to grasp who Jesus is, but unlike many others she does succeed in doing so. Her Samaritan compatriots then must come to a knowledge of Jesus based on their own experience of him; but they too do so with a promptness and profundity that contrasts sharply with the response of "the Jews" throughout the Gospel.

If we bear in mind that most members of the Johannine Christian community were probably of Jewish origin, this highly positive representation of women, Samaritans, and others who might have been regarded as inferiors or hostile outsiders becomes quite impressive. It suggests that the author had looked at his community's oppression and at that of others, and had taken a deliberate stand among the oppressed. To some extent, this reflects the fact that more of the community's members came from oppressed and outsider groups than from power groups. But it also reflects a willingness to affirm these connections, and a recognition that the coming of the Messiah had not elevated believers to the position of rulers, but instead required even the rulers among them to identify with the oppressed. That is the meaning of the ambiguous figure of Nicodemus. He represents those to whom the Johannine call to downward mobility is addressed, the Pharisaic rulers who, as a body, were the persecutors of the Christian community. If, as I believe, Nicodemus never fully accepts this call, then John must think of the Christian rulers as dubious and unreliable allies. But even if we regard Nicodemus as ultimately paying proper homage to Jesus at his burial, we must see in this a coming out of hiding and secrecy into open alignment with the ignominious "crowd." If Nicodemus is to be seen as courageous, his courage consists precisely in breaking with the actions of his colleagues and social equals.

It is true that not every oppressed character in John is presented as a positive model for identification, as seen in the case of the lame man in chapter 5. It is also true that not everyone to whom Jesus gives miraculous help in John comes from among the oppressed. Here we can only allude to several characters. There is no indication that the members of the wedding party at Cana were poor (John 2:1-11), and some hints that they were at least moderately well off. Lazarus's sisters Martha and Mary, though among the Gospel's women heroines, are in economic terms not oppressed (John 11:1–12:8). The royal official of Capernaum (John 4:46-54) would indeed have to be ranked nearer the oppressors than the oppressed. John, like the New Testament in general, may be conscious of class, but it does not pursue class warfare. That is also part of the point about Nicodemus: even those who have engaged in oppression are offered hope. But they are required to come to the source of eschatological hope, to the Messiah who inaugurates a kingdom based on truth and mutual love, not on manipulation and hierarchy. Unlike Pilate, who scorns truth and its messenger, the royal official comes to Jesus and begs him to grant life to his son; and, though it is not clear that John presents his faith as a model to be imitated, his petition is granted. The powerful man humbles himself before the son of Joseph from Nazareth and finds in the man from that unprepossessing village the divine source of life.

It is of the essence of the incarnational theology developed by John that when the divine Logos becomes flesh, the flesh it chooses is that of the oppressed. To be sure, one may question whether Jesus is pictured as among the economically oppressed in John, since he and his disciples have money themselves to care for the poor.[38] But there can be no doubt that the end of Jesus' life, in John as in the other Gospels, is that of a victim of oppression, executed by the Roman state for claiming to be king of a subject people. And it is here, in this nadir of defeat, that the Son of God cries out in triumph, "It is accomplished!" The purposes of God are achieved in the moment when oppression seems victorious, and the final revelation of divine Spirit takes place in this utter calamity of the flesh.

The revelation of Spirit, however, does not end even there. Those who believe in this dubious triumph are also "born of the Spirit," according to John, and their passage through the world is as mysterious to the world as that of the Logos itself (3:8). With them too the Spirit makes its home among the oppressed, among those too ignorant or female or foreign to be certified by authority as recipients of divine knowledge. Claiming such knowledge nonetheless, they are oppressed further for this very claim. The Gospel of John offers them hope by largely affirming their identity as oppressed, while transferring all those negative valuations—ignorance, weakness, alienation from God —to their oppressors. At the conclusion of the story of the blind man who overcomes his inquisitors even as they cast him out, we find this dialogue (John 9:39-41):

> Jesus said, "I came into this world for judgement so that those who do not see may see, and those who see may become blind." Some of the Pharisees near him heard this and said to him, "Surely we are not blind, are we?" Jesus said to them, "If you were blind, you would not have sin. But now that you say, 'We see,' your sin remains."[39]

CHAPTER 7

When the Vultures Are Finished, Can There Be Life? The Valley of Dry Bones and the Future of the Black Church

John W Waters

Despair is ever present. Depression appears on the faces of a somewhat hopeless people. Despondency describes the mood. Crime is rampant. The murder rate is given just as casually as one gives the recent baseball scores of the local teams. Life expectancy is decreasing. The birth of a young male child is noted with the cynical remark, "His chances of living into adulthood are only one in four." Drugs is the byword. They are the key to economic survival, assuring social and economic status. Everywhere houses are boarded up. Burglar bars and elaborate security systems are common place. Trash and debris are ever-present. Babies are unattended. Teenage girls and their mothers are pregnant, often by the same man. There is the blast of the boom box broken only occasionally by the quick firing of an automatic weapon. Young girls are seen with a hopelessness on their faces, void of feeling, of caring—no concern, no sense of a future, no understanding of the past.

Welcome to reality, Black America. This is life in the 1990s. We are at war. The empires of the world are crumbling. The "motherland" is wrought with violence. There is famine. There is greed. Tribe is against tribe. The wars, the fighting to determine what? Some say we are facing Armageddon (Rev 16:16). Is this the end time? Are we in the last days?

The United States and its cities are in a very real crisis. The issues are plain: economic, social, and moral survival. The issues are especially crucial for Black Americans. As a people, we often identify ourselves with the plight of the Hebrews/Israelites of the Old Testament tradition. From this perspective, an examination of one of the most familiar passages from the prophetic tradition will be undertaken. The foci of the examination are understanding the historical context of the text and its application for an understanding of the current plight of Black America with ramifications for theological education. The text, Ezekiel 37:1-14, the "Vision of the Valley of Dry Bones," lends itself to such an analysis.

Biography of the Prophet

Ezekiel is one of the most interesting, and most studied, books in the Bible. It is familiar to us for several reasons. The primary one has to do with the vivid symbolism employed by its writer. Ezekiel's name means "God make strong." He is an historical hero who emerges in Judah as an exile as a result of the political debacle of 597 BCE. His prophetic life span extends through the destruction of Jerusalem in 586 BCE, by Nebuchadnezzar II, King of Babylonia.[1]

The Setting of the Text

Ezekiel 37:1-14 is perhaps the most familiar of the Ezekian corpus. It can best be understood as reflecting the transition in the prophet's ministry. We first encounter Ezekiel as a prophet of doom. Here, he is a prophet of hope; a prophet of restoration. Ezekiel, in this regard, reflects the Deuteronomistic understanding of history. In any case, ours is a familiar passage, the "Valley of Dry Bones" vision. It is a somewhat brief, although vivid pericope which focuses on "the end of life." The imagery has provided the basis for countless sermons on "The Valley of Dry Bones." All too often the sermons misinterpret the vision.

Information about Ezekiel comes almost exclusively from the book which bears his name. By profession, he was a priest, and the son of a priest named Buzi. Joseph Blenkinsopp suggests that Ezekiel is of Arabian ancestry, citing Jer 25:23 and Job 32:2, 6 for support.[2] He was among the deportees, some three thousand leading Judean citizens, who were exiled in 598/7 BCE with King Jehoiachim. This was the first Babylonia deportation.

The prophetic ministry of Ezekiel spans slightly more than two decades, 593–571 BCE. His ministry can be divided into three distinct periods: 593/2–587, when he prophesies disaster and doom, in an attempt to free the exiles of their dependence on Jerusalem and the

Temple; 586–585, where he displays conditional optimism; and the last period is that of unconditional prophecies of salvation. Our text comes from this latter period.

The Structure of the Text

Old Testament scholars tend to agree that the book of Ezekiel is an edited work.[3] Within the material, there is a series of datable events which provide information about the process of its composition. There are four vision narratives in the book of Ezekiel: 1:2, the throne vision and call; 8:1, the vision of idolatry in the Temple; 37:1, the vision of dry bones; and 40:1, the vision of the restored temple. The third of the four visions begins rather abruptly. There is neither a heading or a date. Carley argues that this abrupt introduction to the vision and the unusual form of the verb used suggest that at one time there had been an opening statement which would have supplied sufficient data for dating. This is mere speculation on Carley's part.[4]

This vision begins with the same formula as the other three, "the hand of Yahweh was on me." Thus, the prophet was in a state of trance at the time of the experience. The location is the same as that of the vision experience in 3:22-27. That is, in a plain or valley near the Jewish settlement. This is identified as near Tel-Abid which has been identified with the Satt-en-Nil, a canal connected with the City of Nippur. In reality, the precise location is unknown. The Babylonian equivalent of the name is "the Hill of the Flood." This suggests that the Judean exiles had been located on a "ruin" or tell which the local tradition claimed a great flood had at one time destroyed.[5]

It is clear that Ezekiel is a visionary prophet. Our pericope comes from the section where the prophet's message is one of hope. Here, the priestly side of Ezekiel can be seen. Carley makes an interesting observation as it relates to an understanding of 37:1-10, as a visionary experience:

> The vision (verses 1-10) appears to have been of unusual intensity, for, like 11:1-13, it is not qualified as a visionary experience. Ezekiel seems to have felt himself involved bodily in the removal to the scene of events.[6]

On the other hand, Vawter describes the pericope as an "ecstatic vision." He points out that the imagery "is not as bizarre as are others in the book nor is its meaning difficult to determine." Of course, the meaning is supplied within the text.[7]

The pericope opens with the "Hand of Yahweh Revelationary

Formula."[8] Structurally, the text is simple, given the variety of "constructs" within the Ezekian corpus. There are two units: verses 1-10, comprise the vision proper; and verses 11-14, which provides an interpretation. One could argue that verses 11b-14 could stand on their own as a separate entity.[9] Such an argument does not posit justification to conclude that it is a secondary addition. Numerous scholars argue that verses 12 and 13 are later additions to the text.[10] Carley argues on text critical lines that verses 12 and 13 are absent from the Septuagint.[11] Similarly, Wevers sees them as secondary on the following form critical grounds:

> Formally, the interpretation has two conclusions, only one of which is original to Ezekiel, verses 13a and 14b contain recognition formula addressed to Israel, the latter ending with the conclusion formula. Verse 11 is unquestioned since it is pivotal to the entire section. Verse 12aα introduces the interpreting oracle both with the command to prophesy, as in verses 4, 9, and the introductory oracle formula. But the remainder of verse 12, together with verse 13, introduces a new figure, that of the grave, where as verse 14 properly applies the vision to the exilic situation as a prediction of divinely given life issuing in a return to the land. Verse 14 is thus the original interpreting oracle, whereas verses 12a, b, 13 are a double-accretion from a later traditionist.[12]

These arguments notwithstanding, I choose to follow the final form of the unit for this exegesis. Thus, there are at least four distinct literary structures to be found within the text of the Vision of the Valley of Dry Bones.

The significant question raised in our pericope is found in verse 3, "And he said to me, 'Mortal, can these bones live?'" Ezekiel believes that the punishment which has come was deserved because of the sinfulness of the people. He had condemned the City of Jerusalem. The people have lost the will to live. These are the dry bones.

Jeremiah uses the same imagery when he speaks of the bones of the unfaithful being brought out of the tombs exposed to the elements without any possibility of reburial (8:1-3). Ezekiel takes this same imagery and turns it into a prophecy of future hope by the revival of the bones.[13] It is clear that the intent is to demonstrate the power of God over death.[14]

To the question, "Can these bones live?" Ezekiel gives no answer. His response, "O Lord, God, you know," acknowledges that the power of God extends even into the realm of death. Here, Ezekiel moves into a deeper understanding of the role and power of God. God commands that the prophet is to proclaim a message to the dead, summoning the dead back to life. The prophet adheres to the command of God, and before his eyes, the dead come alive![15]

The Key Issues

Reading the text, it becomes clear that there are several key concerns. The large number of dry bones (verse 2) implies widespread death. The death is one of long duration. The bones had been stripped of all flesh and baked dry by the heat of the sun. The scene is one of desolation.

It is my contention that the meaning of the entire text hinges on the rhetorical question raised in verse 3: "Can these bones live?" The question calls attention to the hopelessness of the situation in view of the extent and finality of death. In verse 11, there is a response from the people, as quoted by God, suggesting they have come to accept their hopeless condition. They say, "Our bones are dried up, and our hope is lost; we are cut off completely," clearly meaning that they see no future for themselves as a nation.

Without question, the vision is applied to the situation in which Israel finds itself. Gone are the glorious days of David and Solomon, gone is the land. Now, Israel is broken in spirit, bereft of hope. The picture is one of death. It is interesting that Ezekiel does not demonstrate any resistance to being among the dead. The possibility of contamination by contact and the prohibition relating to contamination by contact by a priest with a corpse would seem to have no bearing.[16]

It is interesting to note that the text provides no apparent reason or motivation for the action God will take on behalf of Israel. This is a completely gratuitous act on God's part. "Restoration, when it comes, will be the result of a free decision of God. Israel (the dry bones) can only be passive recipients of God's power and benevolence."[17] The question has been put, "Can these bones live?" Blenkinsopp's comments are insightful:

> In responding, Ezekiel does not rule out the possibility of resuscitation or a reversal of the natural life-death sequence. He does not affirm it either, since belief in the post-mortem survival of the individual was not part of Israelite faith at that time; even considerably later the author of Job raises it as a possible solution only to discount it (Job 7:9-10, 21; 14:7-12). He leaves it up to God—"Lord Yahweh, thou knowest" . . . who is the living God, the source of life, he who kills and restores to life (Deut 32:39).[18]

Though it is not spelled out here, there is present in the tradition to which Ezekiel is heir, the notion of a "remnant." This idea and the belief in the "all-powerfulness" of Yahweh provide the foundation for a future hope. The restoration of Israel as a political, united entity is seen by Ezekiel as the equivalent of a "new creation." As Hals comments, this "new creation," suggested in chapter 37, is

> deliberately structured to correspond to the old creation in Gen. 2:7 by describing it as a two-phase event, in which infusion of the invisible life force ("breath" in Gen 2:7, "spirit" here, although elsewhere in this passage the word is used with the meaning of wind) takes place after the sharpening of the body. The analogy comes to enable the hearer trustingly to accept this promised new act because it follows the pattern of the old, and thus can be regarded as attesting to the same God who will do a similar thing one more time.[19]

This "new creation" motif will be used by the Prophet Deutero-Isaiah. Both Ezekiel and he understand that God is doing a "new work" in Israel. The "new work," the new beginning, is the basic element on which the theology of future hope is to rest. God never abandons his people; he has a covenant relationship with them, and he is faithful to the covenant.

Finally, as we look at the text, a word needs to be said about the vivid symbols used. As Blenkinsopp puts it, the bold metaphor of desiccated bones is

> expressive of physical and spiritual disability, [and] occurs frequently in poetry (e.g. Isa 66:14; Job 21:24). Taken up in a deliberately literal fashion it has been developed into a suggestive scenario of a field that had witnessed combat slaughter.[20]

The description provided by Ezekiel bears the imprint of Jeremiah (see Jer 8:1-2). This is often the case in Ezekiel. Klein's summary is apposite:

> What is to be concluded? Reading from the entire pericope, the prophecy is made sure by three words addressed to Ezekiel. These, Ezekiel passes on to the bones (37:5), to the life-giving wind itself (37:9), and to the exiles who have been lamenting disheartening words (37:12). Yahweh's word is enough to evoke faith in the future: "then you shall know that I, the Lord, have spoken and will act." All this is reinforced by the final words in the pericope: "An oracle of Yahweh."[21]

Exposition

Where can you find an adult Black Christian who has not heard a sermon entitled something like "The Valley of Dry Bones"? In the early 1940s, the late Reverend C. L. Franklin, the father of Aretha Franklin, recorded such a sermon. He, like so many, missed what I think is the essential message of the text. He focuses on the imagery and the symbolism of the connectedness of the various bones that hear the word of the Lord, rather than on the question posed in verse 3. Ezekiel's message of hope begins on the note of the prophet as "watchman," as a sentinel, who brings a message of life in the midst of death. The series of messages begins with 33:1. It is clear that one of the prophet's responsibilities is to warn his people, to call them back from their destructive behavior in order that they may live. God takes no pleasure in the death of a people or an individual (18:32; 33:11). The spokesperson for God is held responsible for providing the warning.

In our time, there are those who argue and/or believe that Black Americans should be on the endangered species list. Occasionally, we hear the cry of genocide by so-called prominent Black leaders. It is true, the statistics which relate to blacks are startling. Black on Black violence and crime is high. Teenage pregnancy is high. Drug abuse is high. There is no need to list all that is wrong. It is at this point when one can raise the rhetorical question of Ezekiel, "Mortal, preacher, given these conditions, can Black people survive in America? Is there any reason to hope?"

When the vultures are finished, can there be life? For Blacks, is now the apocalyptic moment? Let me attempt to determine who it is or what factors exist which contribute to the sad state of the Black community. In my view, the vultures are those things which prey on Black self-esteem, and Black self-confidence. A few of these are AIDS and other sexually transmitted diseases, promiscuity, federal and local entitlement programs. These are examples of the vultures hovering over the Black communities in America. The list is only a partial one. A vulture is a person or thing which preys ravenously; something or someone which is ruthless. Often the church, especially through its ministers, has and does act in a vulturous fashion, devouring that which is in its path.

Given the rip-offs, the con artists, the violations of trust which are all too common in the Black community, it is appropriate to raise the issue of hope. The Christian faith is founded on a principle of hope and prosperity. The essential message of the gospel of Jesus is, "And you can have life and have it more abundantly, if. . . ."

In light of the statistics, and the socio-economic conditions of Black Americans, can we justify a future hope? For me, the answer is an emphatic yes! The "yes" is conditioned by understanding the call of the gospel to repent, *metanoéō*, to have a change of mind. Life for Black Americans will be possible only if some essential changes take place. What can be done to enhance Black life from the context of the religious community? This is the essential question for the community of faith which has traditionally played a significant role in the community.

Ezekiel concerns himself, as prophet/priest, with the future of his people. Religion is significant in the lives of a people even when the people fail to be overly religious. Morals, concepts of right and wrong, and adherence to ethical and community-based principles are matters "at home" within the religious component of the community. Thus, what should be expected of those persons and institutions who are charged with preservation of the faith?

There is a great misconception about the role and influence of the church in the Black community. The influence is on a decline. It is now time for the church to take a proactive position within the community. Through its programs, emphasis should be placed on encouragement, support, and a genuine interest shown in the affairs of the community. Programs designed to help build self-confidence, to aid in skills development, and provide opportunities for economic development are essential for survival.

The church must be a church "in the world," not one reacting "to the world." The pulpit must become inhabited by those who are skilled in theological reflection and sensitive to the real needs of the people. Programs emphasizing the servant role of ministry should be the focus. There are too many churches pastored by "demigods"; and the people love to have it this way.

When the pastor expresses consistent interest in developing people, then the membership will become energized to begin productive work in the community. The key is knowing the strengths and weaknesses of both the church and the community. The pulpit should build on its strengths. There are all too many Black churches with no sense of real missions, no sense of direction. It would appear that they exist as entertainment houses with an open admission policy.

Some Black ministers have begun to renounce the notion that Blacks are entitled to government "handouts." Wanting such "handouts" reflects a plantation mentality which is still fostered by all too many who live in the Black community. This mentality has led to several generations of Blacks who will not work, who would rather accept welfare than assume personal responsibility. Such should be viewed as criminal behavior and not tolerated.

By the same token, the church, through its outreach programs, can become a provider of job opportunities, a vehicle for developing entrepreneurial skills. And some churches are doing this. Hartford Memorial Baptist Church in Detroit has a fast-food franchise. The Southern Baptists of Georgia, a predominantly White association, have their own hospital. Where are the Black church-related nursing homes, hospitals, and senior citizens' facilities? Can the Black church provide such? We need not say, "Only God knows." All things are possible.

Can this people live? To this, the church in all of its voice should begin by saying "yes." Contrary to the text, however, where the renewal is uncondititioned and communal, the "yes" should be conditioned to the degree that each is willing to assume personal responsibility. The key is personal responsibility.

In the area of cooperation, the church can affirm the survival of the Black community through demonstrating the value of churches cooperating with one another. Every church in a community does not need a day care program, a family life center, a food co-op, etc. The entire community could be better served with single-unit efforts. When church members observe the results of the cooperative endeavors coming from the pastors, they will begin to see and understand what results can be produced when people cooperate. Thus I sense a very real need for more ministers to demonstrate a willingness to be cooperative.

In the area of community support, pastors should encourage and practice support of Black enterprises. Too often, the Black church acquires its goods and services from non-Black vendors. Our dollars, our church monies, need to turn over more times in our own communities than is now the reality. In addition, we need to hold Black businesses to the same standards as we hold non-Black enterprises.

The pastor/preacher, if the race is to be revived, must begin to address those issues which affect the quality of life in the community. The preacher can ill afford not to address the issues of ecology, peace and justice, etc. It is clear that when the pastor/preacher calls attention to issues, the membership will begin to respond. The pastor/preacher should lead the demand for honesty and integrity among Black elected officials rather than yelling "racism" when someone is caught with his/her hand in the proverbial cookie jar. The church must demand a higher standard than what seems to be being accepted now.

Similarly, the pastor/preacher must begin to call into question the sources of financial support of agencies and programs in the Black

103

community. There is too much "tainted" money. Our people must come to understand how the "plantation" mentality works. It is difficult to attack the tobacco and alcohol industries whose products reduce the life-expectancy of Blacks while at the same time accepting large financial gifts which all too often go to enhance personal egos. The Black church must demonstrate an integrity which is not for sale. Need one pursue this further?

When the vultures are finished, can there be life? It may be appropriate to consider the role of theological education and its impact on the Black community. Emphasis will be on the place and role of the professional Black theological school within the Black community of faith.

The seminary should begin to take an active interest in the community. For example, several institutions around the Atlanta University Center have designed programs for assisting the public housing arena. The seminary needs to be in the midst of this attempt to reclaim positive life. There is an aspect of the theological curriculum which is known as practical theology. The emphasis is on the word "practical." It is necessary for the Black seminary to meet the requirements of the accreditation agencies. However, the seminary must also be responsive to the needs of its other constituencies, and this suggests a need to rethink its curriculum. Attention needs to be focused on teaching creative thought rather than molding students to fit a certain predesigned model. There is more to the Black church than preaching.

The seminary has both staff and facilities. Through creative use of both, it is in a position to determine the needs, desires, and wishes of the Black religious community. Through workshops, open forum, newsletters, and public debates, it can begin to hear the concerns of the people. We are in the information age. The seminary can gather and provide information to the local church. Where are the data provided by the seminary which are useful for ministry in these times under the existing circumstances?

Of major interest to note is the failure of the Black seminaries to provide adequate resources for the study of Black religions. The faculties must be encouraged to do basic research and publish materials useful at every level. Where are the books and publications about Black religions? Where are ITC, Virginia Union, and Howard Divinity School in their data gathering and information dissemination processes? Where are the history books which treat Black religions as a serious concern? Where does the Black seminary deal with techniques of motivation? Our young people are being "lost" because they lack motivation. Where are the "how to seminars" which teach students to do real Christian work in the community? It appears that fieldwork assignments tend to be given with little forethought and virtually no afterthought. Yet, there are countless churches in the Black community which could be helped by having the presence of one person who has some seminary based theological training. The biblical assertion that "the harvest is plentiful, but the laborers are few . . ." is true as applied to seminary-trained people found working within the Black church.

There is that cliché which speaks of the "ivory tower" educational syndrome. It would appear that the Black seminaries have accepted this as reality. What am I suggesting here? It is simple. The seminary which seeks to serve the Black community should train leaders for that community, providing the best training possible. The training must be functional. It must be practical. The curriculum should be multifaceted. There is no typical Black community. Since the church is to concern itself with all of life within the community, the institutions which train its leaders must provide as much practical knowledge as possible. The minimum requirement should be to teach people to think. Information is essential, but if one cannot use the information, then what?

The seminary, working with agencies such as the Atlanta Housing Authority, the Centers for Disease Control (CDC), the State Department of Public Health and neighborhood health units, could develop a model program for dealing with basic health concerns within the Black community. Similarly, a cooperative effort between the seminary and the various labor interest groups could provide a model for addressing realistically the problems of unemployment and underemployment among Black people.

My task has not been that of providing a detailed application of the text; it has been to examine the text as a biblical scholar, and then to suggest ways of application of the text. In its application possibilities, I write as a worker/minister in a Black community and as a former seminary professor. I see the needs daily as I wrestle with ways of providing creative ministry.

Much more could be said. It is clear that we as a people can survive the crises we face, but our survival depends on our willingness, as a people, to change our mind-set. We must assume responsibility for ourselves. Contrary to the text, no longer should we look for salvation only from beyond us. Our salvation rests with us and within us. We must begin to rise up against those who would keep us enslaved to welfare, regardless of their color, sex, or political agenda!

The response from the seminary and the church membership must be one which provides our people with the coping skills needed to endure the crises. It is necessary that we begin to stress to Blacks that it is death to adapt to a welfare mentality. This requires a fundamental change in our theology. What am I suggesting? Simply, White people are not our problem, or even our enemy. We are our own worst enemies. However, we also possess the ability to overcome.

Ezekiel 37 is a survival text. We are faced with the issue of surviving. We can survive if we want to survive. There will always be Black people in America. We will have a remnant. But the issue is, can Black Americans survive the current crises? Not just a few, but can the masses survive?

Ezekiel tells us only God knows! But God has given us the ability to think for ourselves. Is it not clear that we must do all we can to raise the level of self-esteem and self-confidence in our people? The key to survival is the will to survive. We must want to survive! It is just that simple. We must say "No!" to the vultures. We must say, "Though we may look dead, we are not dead!" Or, in the words of the Negro spiritual, "I'm so glad trouble don't last always."

Self-confidence, self-reliance, and interdependence are among the things we must teach our people. Our young men lack self-reliance. It is most unfortunate that we are not more self-reliant. Ezekiel 37 says to us, speak words of assurance to your people. There is power in the spoken word, especially when that word is infused with the spirit of God. When the church through its ministries speaks, it should speak in encouraging and helpful ways. Its programs should be spiritually based.

When the vultures are finished, can these bones live? We must say, "Yes. Yes, we can live." It is clear we cannot survive as separate individuals. However, working together, functioning together, growing together, we can overcome. There is an individual responsibility to overcome. To the degree we all believe, we can live.

The current crises which we face should be viewed as opportunities for growth and development. Now is the time for the minister/preacher, the seminary, and the community to assert what we have heard, the gospel, which is a gospel of hope. This gospel says it is a matter of choice to live or to die. He/she who chooses to live must be willing to fight, to push forward in spite of. . . . Those who wish to live must say "No!" to the easy solutions which are suggested. God has spoken a positive word: the dry bones *can* live again. God can make them strong.

CHAPTER 8

Toni Morrison's *Song of Solomon*: The Blues and the Bible

Abraham Smith

Toni Morrison's third novel, *Song of Solomon*,[1] brings together the blues and the Bible in an intriguing and penetrating mystery of undiminished aesthetic delight.[2] The novel virtually begins and ends with a blues song, and all throughout the blues lurk in the shadows, never quite absent even when not directly mentioned. The blues song "Sugarman" and the context in which it is sung haunt the reader from the very beginning. "What does the song mean?" the reader is nudged to ask. Of all the residents in the 1931 Detroit ghetto called "Southside," why does the narrator select a tall, unkempt woman—unnamed so far and not to be named until fifteen pages later—to sing the song at the suicide/flight of Mr. Robert Smith, the erstwhile ubiquitous and irksome insurance salesman? And how is it that the tall and uncouth woman can predict the time of birth for an urbanite woman's child? And how does the tall woman who sings about flight know that the child to be born will one day soar like a bird himself? Thus, only a few pages into the novel, the blues song already riddles the reader with perplexing questions, many of which cannot be answered until the novel draws to a close.

Biblical quotations, resonances, and names also surface in *Song of Solomon*—not in abundance, but occurring enough to cause a reader to ponder the purpose for their inclusion. Is there a relationship between the blues song sung by the tall woman and the title of the novel, *Song of Solomon*, a title which was also attributed to one of the books of the Hebrew Bible? Does the tall woman, later identified as Pilate, know the Bible well enough to use it as an authoritative source in a power transaction against the local police who have arrested her nephew and his friend? And does her nephew's friend understand it well enough to use it illustratively—to make his argument with the nephew seem more convincing?

These are some of the questions which Morrison's intriguing mystery induces the reader to ask. For a reader to answer these questions adequately, however, another issue must initially be resolved, namely, the overall purpose of Morrison's mystery as revealed by the text's own colors, canvas, paint, and spaces.[3] Once that purpose is explored, we may then return to the heart of our discussion, that is, the determination of the functions of the blues and the Bible within the novel's textual strategies and cues.

The "Heroic Quest" Interpretation

A common line of interpretation is that the story is about the western heroic quest for identity, about the trials of Macon Dead III, also known as Milkman, as he searches to unravel the mystery of his own life—as he seeks self-determination and autonomy.[4] Moreover at one level, perhaps it is possible to read Morrison's *Song of Solomon* as a heroic quest novel, for Morrison exploits the western hero archetype and other western literary allusions throughout the novel.

Any reader will find in *Song of Solomon* traces and resonances of familiar western lore—Rumpelstiltskin, the myth of Icarus, Hansel and Gretel, and Jack-and-the-Beanstalk, to name a few.[5] And Morrison certainly exploits the quest for identity myth in her character development of Milkman, for the narrator and the characters speak of the incoherence, partial knowledge, and backwardness beyond which Milkman must grow if he is to find himself.[6] Like the classic hero, moreover, Macon Dead III journeys to find himself. Initially, he takes an inward journey to awaken repressed and lurid memories about the origin of his nickname, Milkman. He is so named because Freddie, the born flunky, liar, town-crier, and busybody once caught his mother, Ruth, breast-feeding him even though the boy was tall enough to walk and to wear knickers. Later, Milkman also journeys physically to Danville, Pennsylvania, and to Shalimar, Virginia, to determine where his aunt, so his father alleges, has hidden an inheritance of gold. For Milkman, if he can solve the mystery of the gold, can gain his autonomy and self-determination.

While the "Heroic Quest" interpretation is possible, I think it neither accounts for Morrison's own ruminations about her novel's "classical" allusions nor for the text's portrait of Milkman as an anti-classical hero. Morrison has repeatedly insisted that "classical" allusions never fully illuminate African American culture.[7] In fact, Morrison notes that they often play a role in western art's programs of invisibility against African Americans.[8] And Milkman's "undeveloped [western] moral sense,"[9] his manipulative "Br'er Rabbit" character,[10] and his failure to return to his community[11] at the conclusion of the novel, all strain against the conventions of the classical western hero. Moreover, Milkman never finds the gold or an individualistic form of self-determination. Instead, he discovers a more important kind of inheritance, his family's origins and cultural heritage. Thus, the "Heroic Quest" perspective cannot resolve all of the issues of the novel. Rather, Morrison permits the western heroic conventions to emerge only to defamiliarize and unsettle the reader's conventional and rigid reading habits.[12]

The "Typological" Interpretation

A chorus of other voices, including Morrison's own, have rejected the "Heroic Quest" interpretation because it is too individualistic.[13] With a non-traditional interpretation, the chorus suggests that the novel, far from simply depicting the journey of a single individual, actually relates the journeys of a people or an ethnic community. With this interpretive perspective, then, Milkman is one typological representative of an ethnic community, but the novel has other representatives as well. From this "typological" perspective, moreover, all of the persons and events of the novel function as emblems, condensation symbols, registers, tropes or metaphors. As Dolan Hubbard says, "The Dead Family becomes a trope for those blacks who migrated to the North and Midwest in the wake of Reconstruction in order to escape from oppression and in the search for freedom."[14] Susan Willis invokes essentially the same line of interpretation when she calls Milkman's travels a "journey through geographic space in which the juxtaposition of the city and the countryside represents the relationship of the present to the past."[15]

Toni Morrison herself avers that the very first line of the novel holds within it the precise symbolic tension she wants to raise in the rest of the novel: "The North Carolina Life Insurance agent promised to fly from Mercy to the other side of Lake Superior at three o'clock" (3). For Morrison, this initial line "moves from North Carolina to Lake Superior—geographical locations, but with a sly implication that the move from North Carolina (the South) to Lake Superior (the North) might not actually involve progress to some 'superior state'—which, of course it does not."[16]

The novel itself bears witness that its story is not merely Milkman's quest, but actually a tale about a people and its struggles in maintaining its heritage after migrating to the North. A series of flashbacks interrupt the telling of Milkman's tale, thus allowing for the tales of other characters to be told.[17] And because the novel is replete with tales about other characters, including tales of *their* journeys,[18] it is ludicrous to see the novel as simply a quest story about Milkman.

Furthermore, the novel's repeated symbolic contrast between the North and the South bears witness to a distinction between types of individuals and not merely to the metamorphosis of a single individual.[19] Indeed, the contrast does not actually begin in the second part of the novel when Morrison narrates Milkman's journey to Pennsylvania and from there on to Virginia. Part I also accentuates the polarity with a series of antitheses—an early one between Ruth, who bears bourgeois trappings, and Pilate, whose garb is simple; another one between the individualistic values of Milkman and the communal values of his alter ego, Guitar;[20] and yet another between Pilate and her brother, Macon Dead II.

Through the third and more extensively developed contrast, moreover, Morrison underscores the problem for African Americans living in the North long before Milkman makes his journey to the South. It is the problem of the influence of commodity culture, and the problem is graphically dramatized in the competing value systems of Macon Dead II and his sister. Macon Dead II, a slumlord, is the richest Black in town, but he is also the coldest and the most detached. Willing to evict even penniless tenants, Macon's only concern is acquisition and the respect he can get from the White bankers. He treats his daughters like baby dolls for display purposes only. He only speaks to his son when he has a command to give him. For ten years, he abstains from conjugal relations with his wife, and once when he does so, it is only because of a roots spell his sister places on him. Then when his wife becomes pregnant, he unsuccessfully seeks the baby's termination. For the most part, he represses his orphaned past, speaking about it only when the past casts him in a favorable light or when it may add gold to his coffers.[21] Moreover, nothing really matters to him but the cold bunch of keys in his pocket, for the keys represent his property, his accomplishment, and his rugged individualism. For him, materialism is the way of progress.

By contrast, Pilate's life is uncomplicated and unencumbered. Her community-minded, anti-individualistic spirit is captured in her dying words: "I wish I'd a knowed more people. I would of loved 'em all. If I'd a knowed more, I would a loved more" (336). She never represses her past, but carries it with her—in a brass earring, in stories, and in the green bag of bones she called her inheritance. She also carries the past with her in an old blues song which she sings whenever she or others are troubled. The song, we later learn, is actually based on an early folk tune that depicts her family's origin. Her house lacks the external trappings possessing her brother. She has no comfortable furniture, electric lights, or inside plumbing. And though she sells wine, her business is never for surplus profit, but only for what her family needs to survive. In fact, in a poignant summary, the narrator tells us that *her* idea of progress is to go a little farther down the road (27).

The fact that Morrison stresses the contrast between the North and the South or between individualistic values and communal ones among so many of the novel's characters suggests again that *Song of Solomon* is not just about Milkman. Rather, his journey is emblematic of a problem facing African American families in the North who must struggle not to lose their cultural heritage of communal values. Indeed, the symbolic antithesis between the North and the South is a contrast between cultural uprootedness and cultural rootedness, a contrast between communities which may be losing their sense of heritage and those that are not. For Morrison, the problem of the ghettos of Detroit, Michigan is that African Americans in the North are heavily influenced by commodity culture, a pernicious force which generates distorted notions about progress and thus causes a community to forget its values, values once encoded in its music, humor, and folklore.[22] For Morrison, moreover, commodity culture also provides African Americans with a set of cultural symbols which either do not take African American identity as seriously as the cultural traditions do or perhaps not at all.

Thus, Morrison carefully crafts an anti-heroic story to expose the challenges of an entire community, especially when the community is exposed to insidious and isolationist influences which diminish their own cultural awareness and appreciation. The mystery is not really about Milkman; it is about a family's origins and how succeeding generations may come to terms with their heritage and roots. Morrison finds in Pilate, moreover, a character who retains her cultural rootedness. By northern standards, she may be regarded as strange and uncouth but she retains the values of generosity and community-mindedness and the revered traditions (stories of the past, the blues, and hoodoo) of her heritage, even as she lives in the North and is several generations removed from her African ancestors.

With the purpose of Morrison's mystery clarified, we may now consider the key questions: How do the blues function in *Song of*

Solomon? and How does the biblical imagery function in Morrison's third novel?

Morrison's Use of the Blues

Morrison uses the blues in two ways: (1) to absorb traditional values, and (2) to identify those characters with healthy cultural rootedness.[23] Accordingly, the song "Sugarman," perhaps like many blues songs, carried the cultural codes of an original folk tune about the plights of African people.[24] As Milkman learns, "Sugarman" was a reconstruction of an original folk tune about the flight of his great-grandfather, Shalimar, from slavery back to Africa. The folk tune also depicted the plight of Shalimar's family after his departure.

The blues song also functions to enhance the reader's identification with Pilate; her daughter, Reba; her granddaughter, Hagar; and Milkman—the only characters who sing the blues in the story. On the narrative stage,[25] Pilate sings the blues song "Sugarman" at least twice: once, as the insurance agent, Mr. Smith, gets ready to fly off the roof of Mercy Hospital; and later, in the presence of Milkman and his friend, Guitar, when she is joined by Reba and Hagar as all three women lament Hagar's hunger for love. When Pilate first sings the song, we hear only the part of the song relevant for the occasion:

> O Sugarman done fly away
> Sugarman done gone
> Sugarman across the sky
> Sugarman gone home (6).

Later, for Hagar, Pilate improvises[26] and sings:

> O Sugarman don't leave me here
> Cotton balls to choke me
> O Sugarman don't leave me here
> Buckra's arms to yoke me (49).[27]

Milkman sings the same blues song at the end of the story, improvising the lyrics as he sings the song to Pilate, who lies dead before him. As Joseph Skerrett suggests, "Here, in what may prove to be his last moments of life, Milkman has become an improvisational bluesman, denying the finality of death through the continuity of art."[28] He sings:

> Sugargirl don't leave me here
> Cotton balls to choke me here
> Sugargirl don't leave me here
> Buckra's arms to yoke me (340).

Whereas the reader learns early on that Pilate, along with Reba and Hagar, is culturally rooted, not until Milkman finally sings the blues is the reader assured that his cultural rootedness is complete. Now he can repeat the tradition, relish his family's past, and reclaim a part of his ethnic heritage, even while improvising the song to meet new occasions.

Morrison's Use of the Bible

As for the Bible, Morrison uses it in three ways: (1) to illustrate a touching plight; (2) to enhance the ironic victimization of certain characters; and (3) to issue a caveat, a warning of sorts, about traditions.

In an interview about *Song of Solomon*, Morrison admits that she used biblical names in the novel because Black people stand in awe of the Bible.[29] This awe may simply be respect for the Bible's powerfully illustrative pathos, for two characters in the novel allude to Jesus' suffering as an example of intense pathos. When Henry Porter longs for a woman, he speaks of his and Jesus' unrequited love—of a love that is too heavy to carry, a love that can get a person killed. Guitar calls Jesus a northerner whom the southerners think they own just because they had him strung up on a tree. The implication is that lynching is not tantamount to possession. For both Henry Porter and Guitar, then, the gospel lore's depiction of Jesus' suffering is a part of the repertoire of martyrdom, of the African American tradition of misery and travail. The two men do not exploit the paradigm of the cross as a testament to their ample biblical literacy; they are not concerned with issues of historicity—when Jesus actually died and whether he really arose. Rather, the cross allusion makes manifest the pathos and gravity of their plights.

In the characterization of the novel's dramatis personae, the Bible has another role: it aids in making unwitting characters the victims of irony. In securing the release of Milkman and Guitar from prison, Pilate has to explain to the local police why for fifty years she has kept a bag of bones, the same bag which the two young thieves took from her house. Pilate's explanation is that the bones belong to her dead husband whom she could not afford to bury. And to give authority to her accounting of the facts, she adds that she kept the bones because the Bible says "What so e'er the Lord hath brought together, let no man put asunder" (207). The hidden irony is that the chapter and verse she cites for the quotation, Matt 21:2, is not actually about the separation of a married man and woman; rather, the text refers to the loosing of two animals—an ass and a colt.[30] With a tongue-in-cheek irony, then, Pilate not only makes a wise-cracking comment about her nephew and his friend, i.e., they are *asses*. She also exerts a form of power over the police officers who hold the *asses* and to whom Pilate's story sounds convincing because she uses a text which they deem to be authoritative. Thus, with her knowledge of the biblical tradition (both of what it says and does not say), Pilate participates with the narrator in the ironic victimization of other characters. The greater victim, however, may be the reader if the reader does not know the biblical tradition as well as the narrator and Pilate know it.

Ideologically, Morrison's use of biblical names may be a caveat, a warning of sorts about the way in which we use tradition. To see this point, however, we must first note Morrison's "game of naming" in the novel. Early in the novel, Morrison dramatizes the importance of labeling by narrating the defiant authority of the Southside residents who insist on having the power to name the infrastructures of their community. They call Mercy Hospital "No Mercy" Hospital because up until 1931, the time that begins the novel's action, no "colored expectant mother was allowed to give birth inside its wards." And unlike the city legislators, the Southside residents call Mains Avenue "Not Doctor Street," for after the only Negro doctor on that block dies, the appellation "Not Doctor Street" best exemplifies their lived experience. Coming so early in the novel, this episode has a "primacy effect"; that is, it colors the reader's interpretation of any other act of naming. To put it crudely, the episode obliges the reader to adopt a hermeneutics of suspicion about all other naming acts. The reader is forced to ascertain the motivations behind labels, to see whether or not the labels are linked to the lived experiences of people.

Accordingly, when the reader discovers that all of the principal female characters in Southside have biblical names (Pilate, Ruth, Magdalene called Lena, Hagar, Rebecca called Reba and First Corinthians), the reader must question the impetus for the naming process. Interestingly, there is no correlation between the roles of the biblical characters and Southside's female characters. Hagar in the Bible has a child—not so in the novel. Pilate in the Bible is a male—not so in the novel. Mary Magdalene in the Bible once led a profligate life—not so in the novel. Ruth in the Bible is a strong character—not so in the novel. And the list goes on. And from what the novel suggests, the naming of the female characters with biblical names is so arbitrary as to be meaningless, a mere blind pointing of the finger to words in the Bible (or in a hymnbook).

114

The male character Shalimar is known as Solomon; yet Shalimar's character as a flying African is not correlated with the Solomon found in the biblical lore. In fact, the name is likely a slave designation. As Josie Campbell explains, "Propertyless and nameless slaves were often renamed by their masters and occasionally were designated eponyms."[31] Thus, the re-naming of Shalimar constitutes another instance of mindless naming and artificial symbolization for African Americans.

Before drawing conclusions about Morrison's caveat, another word is in order about the name "Pilate." While it is true that Pilate's father, Macon Dead I, simply extracted her name from the Bible, his selection of the name was not entirely meaningless, for the meaning deduced from the sound of the word—in his oral culture—was more important than any inscribed meaning. The word to him sounded like "pilot" (19). And in the course of the novel, Pilate takes on that role. She does not act as Pilate, the Christ-killer, but she "pilots" Milkman.[32] She teaches him how to fly free of his middle-class values.[33]

Perhaps, then, Morrison uses the Bible, a venerable tradition among African Americans, to call attention to the problem of adapting traditional values wholesale in our contemporary settings. Morrison's use of the Bible is not so much a condemnation of the Bible as it is a caveat to relate the Bible to the lived and true experiences of a people; otherwise the Bible becomes meaningless, empty, just rhetoric. Moreover, if Morrison's construal of the Bible is actually symbolic of an attitude to be taken toward all traditions, then Morrison's warning is that any tradition can become lifeless, and any use of a tradition can become a blind one, unless the tradition reflects the lived experiences of a people. Not to take the lived experiences seriously is to follow in the path of the drunken Yankee and Freedmen's Bureau clerk who mis-registered Milkman's grandfather with the name Macon Dead rather than Jake Solomon.

There is here an important lesson about hermeneutics. How can a people benefit from a tradition without becoming stymied by it, and without following it blindly and uncritically? Morrison's challenge affirms that we need traditions for a sense of who we are and how we came to be a family or an ethnic group or, for that matter, how we came to be a nation. At the same time, the tradition is vital only when it speaks a word to where we are now, even while it calls us to remember and celebrate the strength of our various and sundry pasts.

PART TWO

Theological Studies

CHAPTER 9

Slave Ideology and Biblical Interpretation

Katie Geneva Cannon

Scholars of stature within mainline Christian denominations have produced immense literature on the Bible and slavery with very little unanimity. Some have written about the various types of anti-slavery arguments found in the Old and New Testaments. Others have engaged in rigorous historical-critical exegesis of selected Scriptures used to condone slavery. What is interesting in the recent analyses by liberationists is the direct correlation between apologetic selectivity and the exegetes' political-social commitments. Thus, my particular concern as a liberation ethicist is to unmask the hermeneutical distortions of White Christians, North and South, who lived quite comfortably with the institution of chattel slavery for the better part of 150 years. Slaveholders knew that they needed religious legitimation within the White society, in addition to legal, economic, and political mechanisms, in order to keep racial slavery viable.

Apostles of slavery kept their eyes on the economic benefits and power relations at all times. Beneath their rhetoric and logic, the question of using the Bible to justify the subordination of Black people was fraught with their desire to maintain their dominance, to guarantee their continued social control. If the powerbrokers of the antebellum society were to continue benefiting from the privileges and opportunities the political economy provided, then the slaveholding aristocrats must, as a basic precondition, maintain their domination over the ideological sectors of society: religion, culture, education, and media.[1] The control of material, physical production required the control of the means of mental, symbolic production as well.

The practice of slaveholding was, therefore, largely unquestioned. The majority of White Christians engaged in a passive acceptance of the givenness of the main feature of slavocracy. Any questioning of the system or identification of contradictions to social practices within Christianity was undermined by the substratum of values and perceptions justified theologically by biblical hermeneutics determined from above. The rank and file of White church membership accepted the prevailing racist ideology; identifying with the slaveholders and copying their rationales, rituals, and values. They regarded slave ideology and Christian life as inseparable; they were integral parts of the same system. The defense of one appeared to require the defense of the other.

Admittedly, there were a few antislavery women and men in the mainline churches prior to the aggressive abolitionist movement of the 1830s, but as a whole the White church evaded responsibility and surrendered its prerogatives to slavocracy. For most of the years that chattel slavery existed, the mainline Protestant churches never legislated against slavery, seldom disciplined slaveholders, and at most gently apologized for the "peculiar institution."

Drawing principally upon socio-ethical sources of the late-eighteenth and early-nineteenth centuries, I investigate three intellectual, hierarchal constructs that lie at the center of the Christian antebellum society: (1) At what point and under what conditions did Americans of African descent lose their status as members of the moral universe? (2) What are the ethical grounds that make the formula for "heathen conversion" intrinsically wrong? and (3) What are the hermeneutical distortions that shaped the slavocracy's polemical patterns of biblical propaganda?

The Mythology of Black Inferiority

The first ideological myth legitimizing the hermeneutical assumption of Christian slave apologists was the charge that Black people were not members of the human race. Most church governing-boards, denominational missionary societies, local churches, and clergy held the position that human beings by nature were free and endowed with natural rights. Their basic concept of human relationships was equality of all people in the sight of God. No one was superior to another, none inferior. Black people had not forfeited their freedom nor relinquished their rights. This espoused oneness of humanity clashed directly with the perception that Black people must necessarily be possessed of low nature.[2]

To justify their enslavement, Black people had to be completely stripped of every privilege of humanity.[3] Their dignity and value as human beings born with natural rights had to be denied. Black Americans were divested so far as possible of all intellectual, cultural, and moral attributes. They had no socially recognized personhood.

The institution of chattel slavery and its corollary, White supremacy and racial bigotry, excluded Black people from every normal human consideration. The humanity of Black people had to be denied, or the evil of the slave system would be evident.

In other words, hereditary slavery was irreconcilable with doctrines of inalienable rights.[4] So as not to contradict their avowed principles, legislatures enacted laws designating Black people as property and as less than human.[5] Black people were assigned a fixed place as an inferior species of humanity. The intellectual legacy of slavocracy was the development of certain White preconceptions about the irredeemable nature of Black women and Black men as "beings of an inferior order," a sub-par species between animal and human. One of the many characterizations proposed was that Black people were irremediably different from Whites, as much as swine from dogs, "they are Baboons on two legs gifted with speech." [6]

Central to the whole hermeneutical approach was a rationalized biblical doctrine positing the innate and permanent inferiority of Blacks in the metonymical curse of Ham.[7] The Ham "curse" in Genesis 9:25-27 was not only used to legitimize slavery in general, but it was also used by proslavery, pro-White supremacists to justify the enslavement of Blacks in particular. Ham became widely identified as the progenitor of the Black race and the story of the curse, which Noah pronounced against Canaan, the son of his son Ham, was symbolically linked to the institution of racial slavery. In a book entitled *Bible Defense of Slavery*, Josiah Priest[8] took the position that the enslaving of Black people by the White race was a judicial act of God:

> The servitude of the race of Ham, to the latest era of mankind, is necessary to the veracity of God Himself, as by it is fulfilled one of the oldest of the decrees of the Scriptures, namely that of Noah, which placed the race as servants under other races.[9]

Christians caught in the obsessive duality of understanding Black people as property rather than as persons, concurred with both faulty exegesis and social pressure that depicted people with Black skin as demonic, unholy, infectious progenitors of sin, full of animality and matriarchal proclivities.

During the early part of the eighteenth century, state laws adopted the principle of *partus sequitur ventrem*—the child follows the condition of the mother regardless of the race of the father. Absolving all paternal responsibilities, this principle institutionalized and sanctioned sexual prerogatives of "stock breeding" with Black men and the rape of Black women by White men. What this means is that the Black woman's life was estimated in terms of money, property, and capital assets. She was a commodity to be bought and sold, traded for money, land, or other objects. Her monetary value was precisely calculated by her capacity to produce goods and services, combined with her capacity to reproduce "a herd of subhuman labor unit."[10] Hence, the Black woman as the carrier of the hereditary legal status, extended the status of slave to her children and her children's children, supposedly to the infinity of time. An entire race was condemned by the laws of a purportedly Christian people to perpetual, hereditary, unrequited servitude.[11]

The White antebellum church did not see the gross injustice of slavery. Outspoken supporters of slavery generally admitted that enslaved Blacks were mere property, a type of domesticated animal to serve as the White man's tool like any other beast of burden.[12] And as slaveholders, White Christian citizens must have the security that neither their property nor their privilege to own people as property would be taken from them. The church made every effort by admonition and legislation to see that the authority of slaveholders was not compromised. For them, the great truth written in law and God's decree was that subordination was the normal condition of African people and their descendants.[13]

Ideas and practices which favored equal rights of all people were classified as invalid and sinful because they conflicted with the divinely ordained structure which posited inequality between Whites and Blacks. The doctrine of biblical infallibility reinforced and was reinforced by the need for the social legitimation of slavery. Thus, racial slavery was accepted as the necessary fulfillment of the curse of Ham. This had the effect of placing the truthfulness of God's self-revelation on the same level of Black slavery and White supremacy.[14] The institutional framework that required Black men, women, and children to be treated as chattel, as possessions rather than as human beings, was understood as being consistent with the spirit, genius, and precepts of the Christian faith.

The Mythologizing of Enslavement

The second ideological process that legitimated Christian slave apology was a reconstruction of history and divine action in it. It was claimed that God sent the slave traders to the wilds of Africa, a so-called depraved, savage, heathen world, so as to free Africans of ignorance, superstition, and corruption.[15] It is more than passing significance that the proslavery writing portrayed Africa as the scene of unmitigated cannibalism, fetish worship and licentiousness. Using gross caricatures, slave apologists mounted an ideological offensive in justification of the ravishing of the entire continent of Africa.[16] They argued that Africans by nature were framed and designed for subjection and obedience. Their preoccupation was that people designated by nature as "bestial savages" and "heathens" were destined by providence for slavery.[17]

Embracing false dogma of inherent African inferiority, beneficiaries of White supremacy approximated African character as the most depraved humanity imaginable. Africans were depicted as the epitome of heathenism, "wild, naked . . . man-eating savages," and "the great ethnological clown." White Christians had to be enabled to consider it an unspeakable privilege for Africans to be brought to the Americas as slaves.[18] Repeatedly, they claimed that slavery saved poor, degraded, and wretched African peoples from spiritual darkness.

North American Christians credited themselves with weaning Africans of savage barbarity.[19] Their joy in converting Africans was that they were giving to "heathens" elements of Christian civilization. Being enslaved in a Christian country was considered advantageous to Africans' physical, intellectual, and moral development. Slavery exposed Africans to Christianity which made them better servants of God and better servants of men.

The popularity of "heathen conversion" was disclosed in the public reception of George Fitzhugh's *Cannibals All! or, Slaves Without Masters*,[20] in which he wrote that Africans, like wild horses, had to be "caught, tamed and civilized." Resting upon irrational antipathies, White Christians—prominent and common-bred alike—clearly distinguished their personhood from that of Africans. Many were convinced that African peoples were somehow irreparably inferior to and less worthy than Europeans. Fixated on the fetish of heathenism, they believed that the color of white skin proved sufficient justification to rob Africans by force and fraud of their liberty. The proper social hierarchy upon which the slave system rested—the putative inferiority of Africans and the alleged superiority of Europeans—had to remain safely intact.[21] Historian Winthrop Jordan declares:

> Heathenism was treated not so much as a specifically religious defect, but as one manifestation of a general refusal to measure up to proper standards, as a failure to be English or even civilized. . . . Being Christian was not merely a matter of subscribing to certain doctrines; it was a quality inherent in oneself and one's society. It was interconnected with all the other attributes of normal and proper men.[22]

Entirely under the power of Whites, against whom they dare not complain and whom they dare not resist, enslaved Africans were denied the right to possess property, deprived of the means of instruction, and barred from every personal, social, civil, political, and religious mode of agency. If they asserted their personhood in defiance of oppressive authority, slaveholders punished them severely.

Answerable with their bodies for all offenses, slaves were beaten with horsewhips, cowstraps, and a variety of blunt weapons. They suffered scalding, burning, rape, castration, sometimes dying from such infliction. The great cruelty exhibited toward enslaved Africans resulted in instances of eyes gouged, tongues slit, and limbs dismembered. The callous and brutal system of slavery required a considerable number of Africans to be marked off by brands, tattoos, wooden yokes, or iron collars with long extended spokes. The intent was to crush African people's spirit and will in order to transform an entire race of people, their lives and their labor, into basic commodities of production and reproduction. Never before U.S. chattel slavery was a people so systematically deprived of their human rights and submerged in abject misery.[23]

The prevailing sentiment of American Christians—the Presbyterians, the Congregationalists, the Roman Catholics, the Quakers, the Lutherans, the Baptists, the Methodists, and the Anglicans—was that African peoples deserved imperial domination and needed social control.[24] Many churches preached a gospel which declared that Black people were indebted to White Christians and bound to spend their lives in the service of Whites; any provision for food, clothes, shelter, medicine, or any other means of preservation was perceived not as a legal requirement but as an act of Christian charity. This "Christian feature" of Anglo-American enslavement was interpreted as an incalculable blessing to African peoples. Africans and their descendants were much better off bound in slavery with their souls free than vice versa.

These and similar judgments bolstered the belief that the Anglo-Saxons, Spaniards, Danes, Portuguese, and Dutch had a divine right to defend themselves against the intolerable suffering and absolute despotism that they imposed so heavily on others. As long as the image of Africans as "heathens" was irrevocable, then the church's attempt to Christianize via enslavement could continue indefinitely, the exploitation of Africa's natural resources could proceed without hindrance, and White Christians could persist in enjoying a position of moral superiority. Ruthlessly exploiting African people was justifiable Christian action.

Remythologizing Divine Will

The third ideological myth needed to legitimize the hermeneutical circle of Christian slave apologists was the understanding that the law of God and the law of the land gave them an extraordinary right to deprive Black people of liberty and to expose Blacks to sale in the market like any other articles of merchandise.

For almost two centuries, slave apologists maintained that slavery was constantly spoken of in the Bible without any direct prohibition; there was no special law against it. And, therefore, on the basis of the absence of condemnation, slavery could not be classified as sin. The presumptive evidence for many White Christians was that the absence of slaveholding from the catalogue of sins and disciplinary offenses in the Bible meant that slavery was not in violation of God's law.

Biblical scholars, along with distinguished scientists, lawyers, and politicians, produced a large quantity of exegetical data denying the arbitrariness of divinely ordained slavery.[25] The foundation of the scriptural case for slavery focused on an argument that neither Jesus of Nazareth, the apostles, nor the early church objected to the ownership of slaves. The fact that slavery was one of the cornerstones of the economic system of the Greco-Roman world was stressed and the conclusion reached that for the early church the only slavery that mattered was spiritual slavery to sin, to which all were bound. Physical slavery was spiritually meaningless under the all-embracing spiritualized hope of salvation. This line of reasoning was of central importance in reconciling the masses of White Christians to the existing social order. Instead of recognizing that slavery was ameliorated by early Christianity, slave apologists used their interpretative principle to characterize slavery as a sacred institution.[26]

So as to elicit White Christians' consent and approval of racial chattel slavery which, theologically, contradicted the liberation reading of the Christian gospel, some of the leading antebellum churchmen—such as Robert Lewis Dabney, a Presbyterian theologian; Augustine Verot, the Catholic bishop of Georgia and East Florida; and John Leadley Dagg, a Baptist layman who served as president of Mercer University—presented slavery as conforming to the divine principles revealed in the Bible. White clergy were trained to use the Bible to give credence to the legitimacy of racial chattelhood.[27] In other words, they adopted an implacable line of reasoning that made slavery an accepted fact of everyday life, not only in the entire Near East but also within normative biblical ethical teaching. Needless to say, the New Testament instruction that slaves should be obedient to their masters was interpreted as unqualified support for the modern institution of chattel slavery. The slave system was simply a part of the cosmos.[28]

Slave apologists such as George Fitzhugh, Thomas R. Dew, and William A. Smith used a hermeneutical principle that functioned so as to conceal and misrepresent the real conflicts of slave ideology and Christian life. Smith, as president of Randolph Macon College in Virginia, was quite candid:

> Slavery, *per se*, is right. . . . The great abstract principle of slavery is right, because it is a fundamental principle of the social state: and domestic slavery, as an *institution*, is fully justified by the condition and circumstances (essential and relative) of the African race in this country, and therefore equally right.[29]

Fitzhugh, a well-known essayist, and Dew, a prominent lawyer, concluded that since slavery was part of the natural order and hence in accord with the will of God, it could not be morally wrong.

Christian commentators, working largely to the advantage of wealthy aristocrats, used biblical and philosophical arguments to present slaveholders' interests and claims in the best possible light.[30] For example, scholars such as How, Ross, and Priest constructed "biblical facts" that permitted them to claim that the eradication of chattel slavery was inapplicable to Christian living. By using selective appeals to customary practices, they disseminated moral teachings so as to reinforce what counted as good Christian conduct. Clergy were condemned for preaching against slavery because abolition sermons were considered to be a part of a traitorous and diabolical scheme that would eventually lead to the denial of biblical authority, the unfolding of rationalism, deistic philanthropism, pantheism, atheism, socialism, or a Jacobinism akin to communism. Members of churches were warned against subscribing to antislavery books, pamphlets, and newspapers. The church condoned mob violence against anyone with abolitionist tendencies, which in turn, reassured that the existing social order would go unchallenged.

Having no desire to divorce themselves from the institution of slavery, church governing-boards and agencies issued denominational pronouncements on behalf of the official platitudes of slave ideology. Denominational assemblies reinforced publicly their compliance with the assumed principle of human chattelhood. Black people were classified as movable property, devoid of the minimum human rights society conferred to others.

The vast majority of White clergy and laity alike appropriated this ideology to convince themselves that the human beings whom they violated or whose well-being they did not protect were unworthy of anything better. White Christians seemed to have been imbued with the permissive view that the enslavement of Black people was not too great a price to pay for a stable, viable labor system.[31] In a political economy built on labor-intensive agriculture, slave labor seemed wholly "natural." The security and prosperity of slavocracy evidently enabled White Christians, slaveholders and non-slaveholders alike, to feel secure with the fruits of the system.

Through a close analysis of slave ideology and biblical interpretation we can discern the many ways that chattel slavery maintained itself even after it was no longer the most economically profitable method of utilizing natural and technological resources. The majority of White Christians had learned well not to accept the equal coexistence of Whites and Blacks in the same society.[32] They believed that giving Black people civil parity with the White population would threaten the ease and luxury of White happiness, and perhaps dissolve the Union. For the sake of the public welfare, people with ancestors born in Europe, and not in Africa, needed to be relieved of degrading menial labor so that they could be free to pursue the highest cultural attainment. Slavery, sanctioned not just by civil law but also by natural law as well, was considered the best foundation for a strong economy and for a superior society.

Concluding Ethical Reflections

In this paper I have sketched three mythologizing processes that served as the foundational underpinnings for slave ideology in relation to White Christian life. I believe that it is important for us to trace the origin and expansion of these myths because the same general schemes of oppression and patterns of enslavement remain prevalent today and because the biblical hermeneutics of oppressive praxis is far from being dead among contemporary exegetes. As life-affirming moral agents we have a responsibility to study the ideological hegemony of the past so that we do not remain doomed to the recurring cyclical patterns of hermeneutical distortions in the present—e.g., violence against women, condemnation of homosexuality, and the spiritualizing of Scripture to justify capitalism.

My analysis shows that slave apologists worked within an interpretative framework that represented the whole transcript of racial chattel slavery as ordained by God. They systematically blocked and refuted any discourse that presented contrary viewpoints. Using theo-ethical language, concepts, and categories, White superordinates pressed their claims of the supposedly inherent inferiority of Black people by appealing to the normative ethical system expressed by the dominant slaveholders. The political and economic context incorporated a structure of discourse wherein the Bible was authoritatively interpreted so as to support the existing patterns of exploitation of Black people.

Antebellum Christians, abiding by the developing racial and cultural conceptions, resisted any threat to slavocracy or any challenge to the peace and permanency of the order of their own domination. They conformed their ethics to the boundaries of slave management. It became their Christian duty to rule over African people who had been stricken from the human race and re-classified as sub-human species.

Not surprisingly, denominations sprang officially to the defense of slave-trading, slaveholding, and the Christianization of Africans with ingenious economic arguments. Wealthy slaveholders transmuted a portion of their disproportionate economic profit into modes of social control by public gestures that passed as generous voluntary acts of charity. They used revenue from slave labor to pay pastors, maintain church properties, support seminaries, and sustain overseas missionaries. Seduced by privilege and profit, White Christians of all economic strata were made, in effect, co-conspirators in the victimization of Black people. In other words, slave apologists were successful in convincing at least five generations of White citizens that slavery, an essential and constitutionally-protected institution, was consistent with the impulse of Christian charity.

CHAPTER 10

Womanist Jesus and the Mutual Struggle for Liberation

Jacquelyn Grant

I looked at my hands, to see if I was the same person now I was free. There was such a glory over everything, the sun came like gold through the trees, and over the fields, and I felt like I was in heaven.

I had crossed the line of which I had so long been dreaming. I was free; but there was no one to welcome me to the land of freedom, I was a stranger in a strange land, and my home after all was down in the old cabin quarter, with the old folks, and my brothers and sisters. But to this solemn resolution I came; I was free, and they should be free also; I would bring them all there. Oh, how I prayed then, lying all alone on the cold, damp ground; "Oh, dear Lord," I said, "I ain't got no friend but you. Come to my help, Lord, for I'm in trouble!"[1]

"I'm in trouble," Harriett Tubman said. What was the source of her trouble? She was finally free. Her prayers had been answered; her dream had come true. She had reached the "state" which she perceived to be like heaven—freedom—the long awaited reality. Freedom, in her understanding, was the essence of the good news of the gospel. What happens when we encounter the good news of the gospel? We are taught that the Christian response is to go forth in all the world and "spread the gospel" to others. Even from a Christian point of view, then, it is not difficult to understand the yearnings of Harriett Tubman. The gospel experienced, must be shared; freedom experienced, must be shared. However, it is not uncommon that the gospel, when encountered, creates dilemmas which are not easily resolved. The gospel keeps us in a perpetual cycle of decision making. We must say yes to the gospel, and that yes is manifested in life as lived daily; or we can say no even by our inactivity. The dilemma for Tubman meant trouble. Just as life in general for Black people was a perpetual state of "trouble," certainly for an escaped slave, the thought of going back into the den

129

of iniquity was a source for grave concern. For there were both political and social (negative) consequences, even possible death.

But for Tubman, the challenge was both a personal one and a religious one (though they are not necessarily mutually exclusive). The will for her family members and others to have the "heaven-like" experience was matched only by her Christian beliefs. The nature of her Christian belief was such that, as sung in the old time gospel song, she "just couldn't keep it to herself." Yes, freedom experienced is indeed freedom shared. What happens when the nature of the gospel and the nature of the existential situation render one in direct conflict with the "human principalities and powers that be"? Isn't that often what being a Christian means—challenging unjust and evil powers?

In the experiences of Black women, Jesus was ever-present; he has commonly been perceived and experienced as being present in "times of trouble." Ntozake Shange, in her choreopoem *For Colored Girls Who Have Considered Suicide When the Rainbow Is Enuf*, commented through one of her characters that to speak of Black women's existence as "colored and sorry" is to be redundant.[2] Sadness or sorrow (the pain, the sufferings) are perpetually a part of the African American woman's reality; so much so that, whatever else the consideration, these components are always present in the lives of Black women. Consequently, to be "colored and sorry" is to be redundant. In the same way, one could say that to speak of Black women's existence as being in trouble, or more to the point, having trouble, is to be redundant. The multidimensional nature of Black women's oppression means that "trouble" is always in the way. Contrary to another old gospel song, "Trouble in My Way, We Have to Hide Sometimes," it is literally impossible to hide. The pervasiveness and interconnectedness of racism, sexism, classism, and other forms of oppression which define a good portion of the lives of Black women, make "trouble" inescapable. Jesus, for many Black women, has been the consistent force which has enabled them not only to survive the "troubles" of the world, but to move beyond them and in spite of them. In essence, there is data to suggest that Jesus has served as the catalyst for the empowerment of Black women to continue to wave the banner of freedom and liberation.

In this essay, I will explore three sources of the troubles of African American women, with special reference to the problem of Christology.[3] This exploration enables us to understand the context which gives rise to the empowerment and the liberation efforts of Black women. Essentially, I argue that the central christological problem rests in the fact that Jesus Christ historically has been, and remains, imprisoned by the socio-political interests of those who have historically been the keepers of principalities and powers. This Jesus has been a primary tool for undergirding oppressive structures. I, therefore, wish to discuss the "troubles" of African American women by exploring three ways in which Jesus has been imprisoned: (1) The imprisonment of Jesus Christ by patriarchy; (2) The imprisonment of Jesus Christ by White supremacy; and (3) The imprisonment of Jesus Christ by the privileged class. Then, in conclusion, I wish to explore the implications for the liberation or the redemption of Jesus Christ based on the lived realities of African American women.

The Historical Imprisonment of Jesus Christ by Patriarchy

It is no accident that in the course of Christian history, men have defined Jesus Christ so as to undergird their own privileged positions in the church and society. This is evidenced by the fact that Jesus Christ is so often used to justify the subordination of women in the church. An understanding of the context in which this kind of interpretation emerges provides explications of the interpretation itself.

An aspect of the social context in which Christianity as we know it developed, and in which we now live, is "patriarchy." Defined in the male consciousness, patriarchy assumes male dominance and control, making normative the centrality of men and the marginality of women. The primary roles of men and the secondary roles of women, effectively insure a hierarchy in sex or gender roles. Moreover, patriarchy embraces "the whole complex of sentiments, the patterns of cognition and behavior, and the assumptions about human nature and the nature of the cosmos that have grown out of a culture in which men have dominated women."[4] That is to say, patriarchalism is a way of looking at reality so that role assignments are not arbitrarily given, but are a part of the rational and systematic structures of perceived reality itself. Patriarchy has been called a "conceptual trap" which ensnares its victims and keeps them in place through the constant reinforcements of society which cooperate to keep the male status quo in place. It's like being in a room, and unable to imagine anything in the world outside of it.[5] It becomes difficult then for either men or women to imagine themselves outside of their prescribed roles; and when this does happen, in the case of women, they are treated as "exceptions," as long as the system remains in place. "Exceptions" are always acceptable, for even when they are not controllable, or when they defy

131

oppressive structures, the masses are still held in check. They are then either treated as renegades, or coopted as "one of the boys."

Living within these parameters means living with dualisms which effectively keep men in superior and women in inferior positions, thus rendering men as authority figures over women. Just as Jesus has power and authority over men and women, men have power and authority over women and children. The christological import of these effects of patriarchy, of course, is that the divine is generally associated with what it means to be male in this society. In another place, I have explored the specific correlation between patriarchal assumptions about gender roles and the issue of women's leadership in the church.[6] However, suffice it to say here that the lingering controversies regarding leadership/ordination/placement of women in the church are overwhelmingly and distortedly christological.

Women have been denied humanity, personhood, leadership, and equality because of the church's history of negative Christology. This aspect of the negative Christology has resulted primarily from over-emphasis on the maleness of Jesus. The maleness, in actuality, has become idolatrous: the maleness of Jesus has been so central to our understanding of Jesus Christ that even the personality of Jesus, and interpretations of Christ have been consistently distorted. In effect, Jesus has been imprisoned by patriarchy's obsession with the supremacy of maleness.

Feminists have sought to break the prison of patriarchy. Using gender analysis, many of the historical, biblical, and theological interpretations have been challenged. Feminist theologians have been working diligently to overcome the sin of patriarchy. They have been able to break from the conceptual trap by taking seriously women's experiences as the context and one of the sources of biblical interpretations. Seeing reality through the eyes of women has lead to the rereading of biblical texts and the revising of biblical and theological interpretations. In other words, feminists have uncovered the fact that the presence of women in the Bible was important, and that Jesus was not only not anti-woman, but in fact was always affirming of women. In many instances of biblical interpretations, feminists have tried either to reform Jesus or to liberate Jesus and women by suggesting that though Jesus can be seen in relation to the male physical reality, Christ transforms maleness and may take on female or feminine forms. Other feminists have argued the uselessness of these revisionist approaches, for in their views, to speak of Christianity and patriarchy is to be redundant. What is being said here simply is that whereas men have, heretofore, defined religion, Christianity, Christ, and so forth,

132

women must now be empowered to become participant definers of these matters.

As victims of sexism, African American women, along with other women, are once removed from the image of God.

The Historical Imprisonment of Jesus Christ by White Supremacy Ideology

As I explore the problem of Christology from the perspective of an African American woman, the question of sexism and its function in the historic oppression of women must be adequately addressed. Feminists have provided some significant analyses that have helped in breaking the prison of patriarchy, pointing directions for eliminating the sin of sexism from our lives, our churches, and our societies. For African American women, however, the question is much broader than the sin of sexism. Racism, in the view of many, has been the basic defining character in the lives of African American women in North America. Recent publications continue to document the contemporary manifestations of racism in our everyday lives.

Unfortunately, the church has not escaped this sinful reality. On the contrary, the church has been a bastion of the sin of racism. This is reflected not only in the practice of much of its populace, but in the structures and in the theologies of the churches. Studies on church leadership (including present patterns), religious and educational institutions, and the history of theology would confirm this. For example, even though "open itineracy"[7] is claimed in the church, it is more likely that White men would be placed in leadership in Black and integrated churches, than that others, especially Black men and Black women, would be so placed. In university and seminary settings, though the claim of being an equal opportunity employer is made, minorities are consistently underrepresented in the administrations, faculties, and staff of predominantly White institutions in North America. And when the minority presence is there, it is overwhelmingly located in service/servant positions.

Theologically, this is perhaps nowhere more apparent than in the christological issue, wherein negative color symbolism has been institutionalized in Christian theology. The constant battle between light and dark, good and evil (God and the devil), white and black, is played out daily in racial politics of the dominant culture (Euro-Americans), and at the same time, theologically legitimated and institutionalized in the racial imageries of the divine. The racism is reflected in the fact that the white imagery is presented as normative and to the exclusion of any other possible imagery of Jesus or God.

These oppressive ideologies and theologies have been developed in the context of racial/White supremacy. The ideology of White supremacy produces the kind of racism with which we have been afflicted throughout most of the history of this continent as we know it. Racism, according to Joel Kovel, "is the tendency of a society to degrade and do violence to people on the basis of race, and by whatever mediations may exist for this purpose."[8] These mediations are manifested in different forms, and are carried on through various disciplines: psychology, sociology, history, economics, art, and symbolism of the dominant (White) group. Racism is the domination of a people which is justified by the dominant group on the basis of racial distinctions. It is not only individual acts, but a collective, institutionalized activity. As C. Eric Lincoln observed:

> For racism to flourish with the vigor it enjoys in America, there must be an extensive climate of acceptance and participation by large numbers of people who constitute its power base. It is the consensus of private persons that gives racism its derivative power. . . . The power of racism is the power conceded by those respectable citizens who by their actions or inaction communicate the consensus which directs and empowers the overt bigot to act on their behalf.[9]

Racism, then, is not only measurable by individual actions, but by institutional structures, and theoretical precepts. Its presence is guaranteed even in the absence of any particular human carriers.

Now, theological and specifically, christological expressions of this racism are represented in our common imaging of Jesus Christ and of God. The irrationality used here is similar to that used in the sin of sexism. For example, even though we insist that God is a spirit and Jesus died for us all, we persist in deifying the maleness of both God and Jesus, certainly giving men a social, political, and theological advantage over women. With regard to the sin of racism, though we claim God as spirit and Jesus as being for all, we have consistently and historically represented God and Jesus as White. We have in fact deified "Whiteness."

Even in popular culture, God, as reflected in Hollywood (for example, in the movie *Oh God!*), has been given to us as residing in the midst of pure Whiteness, and being represented by "an old White man" (perhaps the only thing approximating accuracy in the image of God presented here is "old"; if eternity implies anything, perhaps it implies old, even though the concept of "eternity" defies all such

134

human categorizations, and the "eternal nowness" of God should be perceived to be ageless). In other words, Christian consensus, based upon and grounded in the history of theology, enables "respectable Christians" to accept without question the destructive negative color symbolism of Christian theology. No wonder some Black folks are still singing and praying "Lord, wash me whiter than snow," in spite of the problematic (at best) nature of related Scriptures.[10]

In the White church tradition, Jesus Christ has functioned as a status quo figure. Because, historically speaking, Christology was constructed in the context of White supremacy ideology and domination, Christ has functioned to legitimate these social and political realities. Essentially, Christ has been White. This is evidenced not only in the theological imagery, but also in the physical imagery of Jesus himself. In a society in which "white is right and black stays back," and white is symbolized as good and black as evil, certainly there would be socio-political ramifications of color with respect to Jesus. The implication that white/light is good and black/dark is evil functions, not only with respect to humanity, but also with respect to humanity's concept of their deity. The late Bishop Joseph Johnson put the point strongly this way:

> Jesus Christ has become for the white church establishment the "white Christ," blue eyes, sharp nose, straight hair, and in the image of the Black [person's] oppressor. The tragedy of this presentation of Jesus Christ by the white church establishment is that he has been too often identified with the repressive and oppressive forces of prevailing society. The teachings of the "white Christ" have been used to justify wars, discrimination, segregation, prejudice, and the exploitation of the poor and the oppressed people of the world. In the name of this "white Christ" the most vicious form of racism has been condoned and supported.[11]

To counteract this historical and theological trend, Black theologians have called not only for a new departure in theology but even more specifically for a new christological interpretation. The White Christ must be eliminated from the Black experience and the concept of a Black Christ must emerge. Theologians like Cone, Wilmore, Cleage, and others have argued this point from various perspectives. Some argue for literal blackness; some for symbolic blackness. The point is to uplift the oppressive ways in which the negative images have functioned for Black and White people; it is a question of images in relation to human beings. We have been given to believe that Blacks are not in the image of God. For this reason, many still harbor beliefs, strong feelings, and attitudes about the inferiority of Blacks even when our intellect tells us otherwise.

African American women, as women and as Black persons, are thus twice removed from the image of God.

The Historical Imprisonment of Jesus Christ by the Privileged Class

What for some have been called theological paradoxes and dialectical tensions have been for others in actuality historical contradictions which have led to social, economic, and political imprisonment. Take, for example, the notion of "servanthood," both in the Christian and the secular contexts. Explorations into the area of domestic servanthood illustrate my point. In particular, a look at the relationship between Whites and Blacks vis-à-vis slavery and domestic service demonstrates that the Christian notion of servanthood has historically been used to reinforce a servant, subservient, and obedient mentality in politically oppressed people.[12] The catechisms which were taught to slaves were designed to clearly identify the earthly slavemaster as the god of the slave. One such catechism, Jones's Catechism, admonished the slave to respond to the master

> 'with all fear,' they are to be 'subject to them' and obey them in all things, possible and lawful, with good will and endeavour to please them well, . . . God is present to see, if their masters are not.[13]

Even after slavery it appears that the attitude survived, for Black people in general and Black women in particular have always been disproportionately relegated to being servants of White people. Still, they were given to believe that it was not only their civil duty, but their Christian or heavenly duty to obey. In other words, Christian servanthood and socio-political servanthood were taught to be the same.

In spite of this, however, Black people recognized the contradictions. So they sang:

> I got-a shoes
> You got-a shoes
> All o' God's chillun got-a shoes.
> When I get to heab'n,
> goin' to put on my shoes,
> I'm goin' to walk all ovah God's heab'n.

Even though people outside of the culture may interpret this message as mere concern for shouting, or the ecstasy that comes with various

136

forms of spirituality, it in fact was a challenge to the contradictions under which they lived. The refrain took an interesting twist:

> Heab'n, heab'n,
> Everybody talkin' 'bout heab'n ain't goin' dere;
> Heab'n, heab'n,
> I'm goin' to walk all ovah God's heab'n.[14]

Those Christian servants who have (had) the power to define the politically oppressed servants ought not to assume that their earthly political and social powers controlled divine things. They may be forced into dehumanized forms of servanthood, but divine retribution was to come.

Interestingly, even though we use the servanthood language with respect to Jesus, we have in effect made him a part of the bourgeoisie. He has been made a privileged person, not unlike the so-called Christian servants of the culture of oppressors. They specialize in maintaining their privileged positions in the church and society, while the real "servants" of the world are structurally and systematically disenfranchised. The real servants are the economically deprived, the socially ill, the politically impotent, and the spiritually irrelevant, if in fact not spiritually empty, according to those in the culture of oppressors.

Jesus has been made to escape all of these realities. Though he was born in a stable, he has been made royal—he's King of Kings; though he was a Jew, all traces of his Jewishness have effectively been erased; though he died the common death of a criminal, we've erased the agony, suffering, and pain, in the interest of creating a "comfortable Jesus." In an interview in which he interpreted the images on the stained glass windows just recently installed in his church, a Black pastor commented:

> The White church has erased the pain from the face of Jesus. He does not suffer. The crucifixion is a painful experience. We show the pain, the agony, the suffering. It's the face of the Black man—the face of Black people.[15]

It's the face of the real servants of the world.

I am arguing that our servanthood language existentially functions as a deceptive tactic for keeping complacent non-dominant culture peoples and the non-privileged of the dominant culture. Thus, the White Jesus, the Jesus of the dominant culture, escapes the real tragedy of servanthood, but oppressed peoples do not. Christian theology and history have ensured the "embourgeoisment" of this Jesus. I am argu- ing (as others have done) that Jesus has been conveniently made into the image of White oppressors. William Jones some years ago asked the question, "Is God a White racist?" Feminists have asked, "Is God/Jesus a male chauvinist pig?" When poor people ask, "Why, Lord?" one could interpret this question to be, "Is God/Jesus for the rich and against the poor?" All of these oppressive conceptions about God/Jesus are reinforced by the imagery, symbols, and language of the dominant culture. What is needed is a challenging of Christian theology at the points of its racist, sexist, and servant languages, all of which are contrary to the real message of Jesus Christ.

Being among neither the dominant culture nor the privileged class, again, Black women and other non-White women, because of their triple jeopardy, are three times removed from the image of God.

Womanist Jesus: The Mutual Struggle for Liberation

African American women's understandings of Jesus help us to see how Black women are empowered in appropriating Jesus, even in spite of the historical oppressive presentations of him. What we find in the experiences of African American women is a process of mutual liberation: Jesus was liberating or redeeming African American women, as African American women were liberating or redeeming Jesus. The Jesus of African American women has suffered a triple bondage or imprisonment as well. Jesus has been held captive to the sin of patriarchy (sexism), the sin of White supremacy (racism), and the sin of privilege (classism). As such, Jesus has been used to keep women in their "proper place"; to keep Blacks meek, mild, and docile in the face of brutal forms of dehumanization; and to ensure the servility of servants. African American women heard twice (and sometimes three times) the mandate "Be subject . . . for it is sanctioned by Jesus and ordained by God. . . ." Consequently, both African American women and Jesus have suffered from the sins of racism, sexism, and classism.

However, in spite of this oppressive indoctrination, Jesus Christ has been a central figure in the lives of African American women. They obviously experienced Jesus in ways different from what was intended by the teachings and preachings by White oppressors (and other oppressors). Five experiences demonstrate how African American women were able to liberate Jesus as Jesus liberated them: (1) Jesus as Co-Sufferer; (2) Jesus as Equalizer; (3) Jesus as Freedom; (4) Jesus as Sustainer; and (5) Jesus as Liberator.

Jesus as Co-Sufferer

Chief among Black people's experiences of Jesus was that he was a divine co-sufferer, who empowered them in situations of oppression. For Christian African American women of the past, Jesus was a central point of reference. For in spite of what was taught them, they were able to identify with Jesus, because they felt that Jesus identified with them in their sufferings. There were mutual sufferings. Just like them, Jesus suffered and was persecuted undeservedly. Jesus' sufferings culminated on the cross. African American women's cross experiences were constant in their daily lives—the abuses, physical and verbal, the acts of dehumanization, the pains, the sufferings, the loss of families and friends and the disruption of communities. But because Jesus Christ was not a mere man, but God incarnate, they, in fact, connected with the Divine. This connection was maintained through their religious life—their prayer tradition and their song tradition. Their prayers were conversations with one who "walked dat hard walk up Calvary and ain't weary but to tink about we all dat way."[16] The connection was also evidenced by the song tradition in which one could lament, "Nobody knows the trouble I see . . . but Jesus. . . ."

Jesus as Equalizer

African American women had been told twice that their inferiority and inequality were a part of the nature of things. They, along with African American men, were taught that they were created to be the servant class for those in control. They were not to preach (in the case of women, and Black men in some traditions), and they were to acknowledge their place as a part of God's providence. But African American women experienced Jesus as a great equalizer, not only in the White world, but in the Black world as well. And so they would argue that the crucifixion was for universal salvation in its truest sense, not just for male salvation, or for White salvation. Because of this, Jesus came and died, no less for the woman as for the man, no less for Blacks as for Whites. Jarena Lee, in the last century said:

> If the man may preach, because the Saviour died for him, why not the woman? Seeing he died for her also. Is he not a whole saviour, instead of a half one? as those who hold it wrong for a woman to preach, would seem to make it appear.[17]

Because Jesus Christ was for all, he in fact equalizes them and renders human oppressive limitations invalid.

Jesus as Freedom

Fannie Lou Hamer articulates, perhaps better than anyone, Black women's understanding of Jesus in relation to freedom. She takes us a bit further than the equality language by challenging our understanding of and desire for mere equality:

> I couldn't tell nobody with my head up I'm fighting for equal right[s] with a white man, because I don't want it. Because if what I get, got to come through lynching, mobbing, raping, murdering, stealing, and killing, I didn't want it, because it was a shocking thing to me, I couldn't hardly sit down.[18]

We are challenged here to move beyond mere equality to freedom. Hamer inspires us to raise the question, "Equal to whom?" Do we merely seek to be equal with those who practice oppression against others? Is the goal simply that we not be among the oppressed? Freedom is the central message of Jesus Christ and the gospel, and is concisely summarized in Luke 4:18. Based upon her reading of this text, Hamer's consistent challenge to the American public was that to be a follower of Jesus Christ was to be committed to the struggle for freedom.

Jesus as Sustainer

The oppression under which the masses of Black people have lived has provided them with few support systems. Even in the aftermath of slavery continuing still today, Blacks have had to depend on alternative ways of getting their needs met. In addition to the various social service agencies, organizations, and clubs established, churches and religion provided a significant sustaining support for them. This was reflected in and through the song and preaching traditions of Black people. In those contexts one would (and still does) hear the refrain exclaiming Jesus (Lord) "as a shelter in times of storm, a doctor in the sick room, a lawyer in the court house, and one who in fact makes a way out of no way. . . ." The notion of Jesus functioning as family is significant in contexts in which the family system has been thoroughly assaulted and insulted. So they proclaimed—"you're my father when I'm fatherless, my mother when I'm motherless, my sister when I'm sisterless, my brother when I'm brotherless, and my friend when I'm friendless." One could argue that the Divine could function in anyone's life in these ways, for people often find themselves in situations in which they are without family members. However, in regard to Black people, the family system has been systematically violated and sometimes rendered unstable. The fact that they experienced Jesus in this way then meant that Jesus was not only a sustainer in the normal vicissitudes of life, but also during times of greatest crisis.

Jesus as Liberator

The liberation activities of Jesus empowers African American women to be significantly engaged in the process of liberation. Sojourner Truth was empowered, so much so that when she was asked by a preacher if the source of her preaching was the Bible, she responded, "No honey, can't preach from de Bible—can't read a letter." Then she explained, "When I preaches, I has jest one text to preach from, an' I always preaches from this one. My text is, 'When I found Jesus!' " In this sermon Sojourner Truth talks about her life, from the time her parents were brought from Africa and sold, to the time that she met Jesus within the context of her struggles for dignity and liberation for Black people and women. The liberation message of Jesus provided grounding for the liberation and protest activities of such persons as Sojourner Truth and many other women activists.

Looking Ahead

As we move toward the turn of the century, the issues raised in this essay will have to be addressed. Do our images and languages continue to undergird oppressive attitudes and structures? Can we concede that to continue to speak exclusively of a male God is problematic, to say the least? Can we understand that the claim of so-called generic language (in English) is another way of perpetuating the misguided belief that the male experience is universal, and therefore normative? Can we not acknowledge a relationship between the dominant culture and the creation of God in the image of White male oppressors, and the detrimental oppressive effects on the vast majority of the peoples on the earth? Ought we not at least raise the question, why are some people always more servant than others? How do we empower Black women to continue the womanist tradition of liberating Jesus and themselves?

Womanist Theology calls for a minimally tri-dimensional analysis, but more accurately pushes us toward a multi-dimensional analysis, as we move toward liberation. In other words, we must construct a world which is free of oppression in whatever form(s). Martin Luther King, Jr., was fond of reminding us that "injustice anywhere is a threat to justice every where." The embodiment of Black womanhood challenges us to move beyond single issue analyses which leaves many faces of injustice unchallenged. A holistic analysis is needed which paves the way for the ushering in of a liberating and liberated society. Black women cannot be asked to split their being. To do so would be ontologically impossible, existentially catastrophic, psychologically depressing, politically unwise, socially alienating (even from the self), and spiritually devastatingly dichotomous. King's "beloved community" certainly will never become a reality as long as Black women remain on the underside of "herstory" and under the underside of history. The various prisons which have been built for us and which are perpetuated to hold us must be destroyed. Womanist theology points us in that direction.

Both White women and Black women have re-thought their understandings of Jesus Christ. They have done so against all odds. For they both live in the context of patriarchy, which has enabled men to dominate theological thinking and church leadership. Black women continue to suffer from the sin of White supremacy, wherein it is believed that the theological task belongs to Whites. Black and other minority women must continue to struggle against the conditions of racism, sexism, and classism which persist in rendering them "servants of the servants of servants," and to insist that the experiences of *all* women—African American women, Native American women, Hispanic women, Asian women, and White women—must be taken seriously.

CHAPTER 11

Symbols of Revelation:
The Darkness of the Hebrew Yahweh
and the Light of the Greek Logos

Octavius A. Gaba

One of the foes of early Christianity was a movement called Gnosticism. Paul and the great Augustine each battled Gnosticism of one kind or another. Augustine took great pains to refute the error of Manichaeanism. Paul went to great lengths to dispel Gnostic heresies in his propagation of the gospel. Would that the pens of these two great theologians had been enough to dispel Gnosticism forever. But Gnosticism never went away; it simply changed form. Today Gnosticism is alive and well in Protestant Christianity. It hides under the rubric of Christian dualism and permeates human relations as racial dualism. Human being and worth are still determined by proximity to light and darkness.

Protestant theology has maintained a Gnostic dualist tendency to the extent that it has affirmed for the symbol of light and denied for the symbol of darkness any participation in the being of God. Some recent responses to this prevailing tendency have been reactionary, choosing simply to emphasize the darkness of God. Both approaches see darkness and light as mutually exclusive and fail to do justice to the being of God which positively includes both darkness and light. A revelational doctrine of God which cannot accomplish this task remains not only latently Gnostic but also idolatrous because it fails to adequately represent the revelation of God.

The task of this essay is to present the biblical basis for a systematic theology which affirms both darkness and light in the revelation of God.

143

Darkness and Light in Christian Theology

Three approaches epitomize recent treatments of darkness in Protestant theology. The first is the reformed approach representative of the theology of Karl Barth. The second is existentialism as depicted in the theology of Paul Tillich. The third is liberationist thought as espoused by James Cone.

Genesis 1–3 helps form the basis of Karl Barth's understanding of the relationship of darkness and light. Barth interprets darkness as "that which is absolutely without basis or future."[1] According to Barth, in darkness "there is no knowledge, and therefore no objectivity."[2] In it man cannot be human, only sleeping, intoxicated, dreaming human.[3] Continuing his line of hermeneutics against darkness, Barth writes of the biblical saga:

> The obscurity in which its God dwells is "the light which no [one] can approach unto" (I Timothy 6:16), and not darkness. "Yea, the darkness hideth not from thee; but the night shineth as the day: the darkness and the light are both alike to thee" (Psalm 139). God's relation to this magnitude is one of victory over darkness. Hence darkness—even in its connection with tehom in v. 2, to which it is obviously related as heaven is related to earth in the world created by God—cannot possibly be regarded even as a positive magnitude. Just as nothing good can come out of tehom, nothing good can come out of darkness.[4]

Creation for Barth is therefore an event of election and rejection. In creation God elects light and rejects darkness. Darkness becomes for Barth that which seeks to be, but is denied being by God. Darkness is the impossible possibility: "Creation means the irruption and revelation of the divine compassion. Once and for all the word of God went out against the rejected and vanished reality of an alien and hostile creature."[5]

Barth consequently not only sees darkness as separated from God but also as separated from light in creation. And since for Barth creation means separation as in election and rejection, he views darkness and light as mutually exclusive. "The one confronts the other; light darkness, and darkness light. There is no question here of symmetry or equilibrium between the two." They confront each other as good versus bad.[6]

Barth's language of separation, of election and rejection, is hardly a language capable of overcoming ultimate dualism. Barth's analogy of relation (*analogia relationis*) does not fully grasp the meaning of the Hebrew that the earth was *tohû* and *bohû*.[7] The intention of Genesis

1:2 is not to give an explanation of the origin of the earth. It makes only the positive observation that in the beginning when God created the heavens and earth, the earth was without form and void.

That the earth was without form and void is a positive statement. That the darkness covered the face of the earth is also a positive statement. It is only as God speaks the creative word that light comes into being. For a child of the enlightenment as Barth, this creation of light means the election of light and the rejection of darkness. That which was positive prior to light is now negated by light itself. Light becomes good and darkness evil. This is Gnosticism.

There are two traditions within the Old Testament, the Priestly (P) and the Yahwist (J), with opposite interpretations of the meanings of water, flood, and the darkness. Barth is content to argue the Priestly interpretation of the darkness and the water as abysmal and chaotic. The brilliant Barth is susceptible to the same kind of Enlightenment rationalization which branded the African rain forest a "jungle"—an unintelligible chaotic maze without rhyme and reason, inhabited by dark beings void of reason and intellect. Nothing good could come out of the jungle. For hundreds of years its destruction was encouraged. Only recently was it discovered to be indispensable to the "survival" of the human species. Now there is a loud cry to preserve the rain forest. That which was rejected is now embraced.

Despite the power of Barth's language of election and rejection, one must question the omnipotence of a God who creates by creating what he does not will and then rejecting it. How omnipotent is a God who in the beginning cannot create what he wills and must reject it? Barth's analogical language tends towards dualism because in construing darkness and water, as posited "realities" which are rejected as chaotic, even evil, Barth ontologizes evil and rejects part of "created being". Instead of explaining evil relationally, Barth explains it substantially as darkness, that which is rejected. That darkness is nonbeing contradicts several passages in the Old Testament in which darkness is used as a symbol which both participates and points to the being of God. Barth, of course, ignores all of these Old Testament witnesses to the being and positivity of darkness relative to the Godhead. Barth uses a host of New Testament sources to buttress his hermeneutic which follows the Priestly tradition.[8]

Paul Tillich takes quite a different theological approach from Barth. Where Barth's theological method is *analogia relationis* (analogy of relation), Tillich's method is *correlation*, and his language is *existential*. Tillich interprets God as the creative and abysmal ground of being. The symbol "ground" is synonymous with other symbols such as "soil," "earth," "dirt." Implicit in this symbol of God as ground is the participation of darkness in being-itself. Following this herme-neutic, one could say that humans who treat dark humans as "dirt" are merely disregarding the "ground" of all being which includes them (God). In the participation of darkness in being-itself, Tillich's doc-trines of God and creation escape the dualism to which Barth's language of election and rejection is prone; a tendency Barth himself recognizes and sought to overcome.[9]

In discussing the "reality of God," Tillich states that theological language about God must begin with a non-symbolic statement about God, namely that God is being itself.[10] In Tillich's words, "after this has been said, nothing else can be said about God which is not symbolic."[11] A symbol points to and participates in that to which it points:

> A symbolic expression is one whose proper meaning is negated by that to which it points. And yet it also is affirmed by it, and this affirmation gives the symbolic expression an adequate basis for pointing beyond itself.[12]

It is this dialectical nature of the symbol that allows Tillich to overcome the dualism to which Barth's rationalistic theism is suscep-tible. Thus Tillich describes the reality of God symbolically as the creative and abysmal ground of being. In this abysmal, creative or divine ground, Tillich identifies three ontological or trinitarian ele-ments which participate in the darkness and light of this ground: spirit, power and meaning. Tillich writes:

> The statement that God is spirit means that life as spirit is the inclusive symbol for the divine life. It contains all the ontological elements. God is not nearer to one "part" of being or to a special function of being than [God] is to another. As Spirit [God] is as near to the *creative darkness* of the *unconscious* as [God] is to the *critical light* of *cognitive reason*. Spirit is the power through which meaning lives, and it is the meaning which gives direction to power.[13]

Tillich argues that the *darkness* of the divine ground or the *abyss* (the element of power) and the *light* or fullness of its content (the element of meaning) have always been distinguished in human intui-tion. *Darkness*, "the first principle, is the basis of Godhead, that which makes God God. It is the root of [God's] majesty, the unapproachable intensity of [God's] being, the inexhaustible ground of being in which everything has its origin. It is power of being infinitely resisting nonbeing, giving the power of being to everything that is."[14] Tillich contends that "during the past centuries theological and philosophical rationalism have deprived the idea of God of this first principle, and by doing so they have robbed God of [God's] divinity."[15] This is clearly a call for Protestant theology to demolish the "idol" that now masquerades as God.

The second ontological element of the divine ground is the *logos*. *Logos* is identified with meaning and structure. Tillich writes: "The *logos* opens the divine ground, its infinity and its *darkness*, and it makes its fullness distinguishable, definite, finite. The logos has been called the mirror of the divine *depth*, the principle of God's self-objectification. In the logos, God speaks God's "word" both in [God's] self and beyond [God]."[16] Tillich holds that without this second principle, the first principle would be "chaos, burning fire, but it would not be the creative ground."[17] That which holds together the first principle (*darkness*) and the second principle (*light*) is the third principle, *spirit*. Power and meaning as the elements of the divine ground are united and made creative by the spirit.

Tillich raises significant questions about the relation of symbolic language to the revelation of God. He attempts to overcome the Gnostic dualistic tendencies which remain in Protestant theology. He has framed and existentially posed the question of being and non-being as it relates to the principles of darkness and light as symbols of Being Itself (God). But even Tillich's existential language is also a product of the Enlightenment. Tillich, therefore, identifies *darkness* with power and *light* with meaning. Light is the mirror of the divine depth or that which makes the power of darkness intelligible. Tillich views the *spirit* as that which unites *power* (darkness) and *meaning* (light) in the ground of being. Yet in order for this triad of symbols to be fully trinitarian, each principle must be *perichoretic*. That is, all three principles *power*, *meaning*, and *spirit* must participate and be integrated in the other without ceasing to be what they are. A strong argument can be made for darkness as meaning and light as power.

Tillich makes a worthwhile contribution in emphasizing that darkness and light belong together in the Godhead. His correlation of God as being-itself affirms the Christian doctrine of *creatio ex nihilo* as "Christianity's protection against any type of ultimate dualism."[18] He contends that *ex nihilo* not only rejects dualism, but also cannot be (*ouk ōn*)—the absolute negation of being, nor (*me ōn*)—the relative negation of being.[19] This is because "creatureliness implies nonbeing, but creatureliness is more than nonbeing."[20]

The intent of the doctrine *ex nihilo* is to safeguard the doctrine of God from duality, causality, even pantheism. *Ex nihilo* means out of no-thing. Its purpose is purely descriptive. It therefore not only describes the creative act, but also reveals something definitive about the being of the Creator in relation to the creature. It does not refer to non-being or a negation of being. It is the negation of no-thing and hence the affirmation of one being-God. Neither does *ex nihilo* refer to abyss or should it be construed as darkness. Once *ex nihilo* is misconstrued as the negation of being, and the negation of being symbolized as darkness and chaos, a dualism emerges which splits off darkness from the ground of being or being-itself. Darkness is pure symbol and as such it is transparent to God's power, the first principle of the Godhead. But darkness is more than power and potentiality, much more. Any attempt to turn it into a principle of negation (non-being, abyss, chaos) introduces the elements of causality and duality into the concept of God—the very thing *ex nihilo* seeks to avoid. Darkness is also meaning. Darkness speaks; darkness is intelligible.

Tillich's existential language, while attempting to avoid dualism and causality in God-talk, becomes increasingly pantheistic and in the process loses the trinitarian concept of God as person (*persona*), relativizes the special revelation of God in the man Jesus Christ, and makes God the origin of evil.

James Cone addresses the light-darkness ontological problem by focusing on blackness and its oppression in White America. Cone emphasizes the positivity of "blackness" and the identification of God with the oppressed, i.e., those who are existentially "black." In the beginning pages of *A Black Theology of Liberation*, Cone refers to Black theology as survival theology. This is so because central to the theological agenda of Black theology is the ontological question: "How are we going to survive in a world which deems Black humanity as an illegitimate form of human existence?"[21] Cone continues: "By white definitions whiteness is 'being' and blackness is 'nonbeing.' For Black people to affirm their being in this situation is to live under the sentence of death."[22]

Cone attempts to answer the ontological question that confronts Black being by making Black existence the theological point of departure. Consequently he outlines the sources which provide answers to this question as follows: Black experience, Black history, Black culture, revelation, Scripture, and tradition.[23] For all these sources, Jesus, as the Black Christ, is the theological norm. Cone views the ontological problem of theology in relation to the history of Black being. He writes of the Black man [*sic*]: "his blackness, which society despises, is a special creation of God himself. He has worth because God imparts value through loving."[24]

In choosing history as the theological point of departure versus revelation, Cone runs the risk of particularizing the being of God to the exclusion of White being. In his passion for liberation, a god in which there was no room for "Blacks" becomes a god in which there is no room for "Whites." Just as Black being was offered full being through *integration* into White being, now White being is offered full being through *liberation* from being White. The impossible possibility, the requirement that Black being become White being through integration, now is reversed in the requirement that White being become Black being through liberation.

Cone's passion for liberation, undeniably right, leads him to ignore the content of divine being; that is divine symbols which identify the being of God with all created being in such a way as to be both creator and judge of being. Therefore Cone's argumentation leads to the identification of White being with the satanic[25] and the rejection of a "God who loves whites the same as blacks."[26] Cone sees and identifies God with blackness:

> God as creator means that [God] is the ground of my blackness (being), the point of reference for meaning and purpose in the universe.[27]

> The system is based on whiteness, and what is necessary is a replacement of whiteness with blackness.[28]

> It is incumbent upon me by the freedom granted in the creator to deny whiteness and affirm blackness as the essence of God.[29]

In the end, the magnificence of Cone's answer to the ontological question becomes muted by liberation passion and obscured by existential language which envisages the emergence of Black being only in the demise on White being and the definition of God as Black:

> Whites will be free only when they become new persons—when their white being has passed away and they are created anew in black being. When this happens, they are no longer white but free and thus capable of making decisions about the destiny of the Black Community.[30]

If the words *black* and *white* are interchanged in this last quotation, it becomes obvious that Cone's response does not answer the ontological question completely. It identifies with Black being. It rejects and denies White being insofar as it dehumanizes Black being. Theology must not reject being, but affirm it, because God affirms all being. Theology must reject sin, because God loves the human but rejects its sin.

Sin is a relational symbol, not an ontological symbol. Theology must define sin in *relation* to all being, affirm the *judgment* of the human tendency to sin, without equating sin to being (*ontologizing sin*). No part of being must be equated to sin, evil, or chaos so that it ceases to participate and point to the being of God, except by *being deontologized*, by becoming what it cannot become, Black becoming White or vice versa. The problem of sin has to do with the relationship of being and act. The tendency of certain theologians to equate act and being ultimately results in the identification of being and sin. Cone does not view White being in relation to its sin. He views White being and act as synonymous and rejects them both.

When Cone writes that the "goal of Black Theology is the destruction of everything *white* so that Black people can be liberated from alien gods,"[31] one must warn against the danger of the "golden calf," lest the "people" be liberated only to fall prey to an idol, a god after their liking and in their image, but nevertheless false, because it denies being to others and forces them to fall down before it or sink into non-being.

The interpretations of light and darkness in Barth, Tillich, and Cone leave something to be desired. An examination of the presentation of light and darkness in the Bible will provide insights into the interconnectedness of the two.

Darkness and Light in the Old Testament

The positivity of darkness in relation to the Hebrew Yahweh occurs in several passages in the Old Testament. In the Creation event (Genesis), the Exodus event (Exodus, Deuteronomy, Numbers), the words of the Prophets (2 Samuel, Job, Isaiah, Jeremiah, Ezekiel, Daniel, Amos), and the words of the Psalmist we have indications of the positive participation of darkness in the being of Yahweh.

The Creation event in Genesis 1–3 begins with the primacy and proximity of darkness relative to God. Two traditions, the Yahwist (J) and the Priestly (P), have differing perspectives of this event. The Yahwist apparently views darkness as positive, for darkness (*hošek*) is where God is when the spirit of God moves over the waters prior to the creation of light. God creates light for creation, and in this creation of light for that which is to follow, God saw that the light was good. But many interpreters of the Creation event seize upon the statement about the goodness of light to imply that darkness is evil rejected by God. The differentiation which God makes between light and darkness for the sake of creation is read back into the God-head to imply that

150

God is light and rejects darkness. This interpretation is of course rejected by the Yahwist tradition, as becomes apparent in the Exodus event.

In Exod 13:21ff we read: "The Lord went in front of them in a pillar of cloud ['anan] by day, to lead them along the way, and in a pillar of fire ['eš] by night, to give them light, so that they might travel by day and by night." Here the Hebrew points to both darkness and light in the revelation of God. Darkness ('anan and ḥošek) as a symbol of the Hebrew Yahweh emerges again in Exod 14:19-25 and in Exod 19:9 when "the Lord said to Moses, 'I am going to come to you in a dense cloud, in order that the people may hear when I speak with you and so trust you ever after.' " Yahweh again speaks Yahweh's Word out of darkness in Exod 20:21-23:

> Then the people stood at a distance, while Moses drew near to the thick darkness ['arapel] where God was. And the Lord said to Moses, "Thus you shall say to the Israelites: You have seen for yourselves that I have spoken with you from heaven. You shall not make gods of silver alongside me, nor shall you make for yourselves gods of gold.

Numbers also describes the being of Yahweh in relation to darkness and light. Num 9:15-23 describes the cloud which covered the tabernacle by day and the appearance of fire over it at night. In Num 11:24-25, Yahweh came down in a cloud ['anan] and spoke to Moses, and "took some of the spirit that was on him and put it on the seventy elders."

In Deuteronomy, Yahweh appears at Horeb in the midst of darkness and fire. God speaks out of the midst of the fire, but there is no form, only a voice (Deut 4:11-13). The words for darkness and fire in this passage are ḥošek and 'eš. Deut 4:15-20 warns therefore of making an image of Yahweh, since in the revelation at Horeb no form was seen. The only images were darkness, fire, and a voice emanating from the fire. Here Deuteronomy indicates that the fire, the light of God, is equally intelligible as the darkness of God. It speaks. Deut 5:23-24 speaks both of God's "voice out of the darkness [ḥošek]" and "his voice out of the fire ['eš]".

The prophets also have something to say about the being of Yahweh in darkness. Second Samuel writes of calling the Lord in his distress: "Smoke went up from his nostrils, and devouring fire from his mouth; glowing coals flamed forth from him. He bowed the heavens and came down; thick darkness ('arapel) was under his feet" (2 Sam 22:8-9). Job writes of the day on which he was born: "Let that day be darkness! May God above not seek it, or light shine upon it. Let gloom and deep darkness claim it" (Job 3:4-6). Here *'opel* and *hošek* are the Hebrew words for darkness. Do they mean darkness or "dark-lessness"—the absence of darkness or light, that which points to God? Isaiah writes of the darkness and light of God:

> Then the Lord shall create over the whole site of Mount Zion and over its places of assembly a *cloud* by day and *smoke* and the shining of a *flaming fire* by night. Indeed over all the *glory* there will be a *canopy*. It will serve as a pavilion, a *shade* by day from the heat, and for a *refuge* and a *shelter* from the storm and rain. (Isa 4:5-6, italics added)

Isaiah 5:20 condemns the confusion of darkness and light: "Ah, you who call evil good and good evil, who put darkness for light and light for darkness." This statement of woe condemns those who confuse the goodness of darkness and light with evil or identifies either with evil—a very Gnostic tendency. Isaiah has two profound insights into the attempt to be without God either through "darklessness"—being without darkness or "enlightenment"—being with a light that is anti-darkness and hence anti-God. Of those who attempted to live without God, Isaiah writes in 9:2: "The people who walked in darkness have seen a great light; those who lived in a land of deep darkness—on them light has shined." Of those who have fashioned their own light, Isa 50:10-11 says this:

> Who among you fears the Lord and obeys the voice of his servant, who walks in darkness, and has no light, yet trusts in the name of the Lord and relies upon his God? But all of you are kindlers of fire, lighters of firebrands. Walk in the flame of your fire, and among the brands that you have kindled! This is what you shall have from my hand: you shall lie down in torment.

Ezekiel describes the hand of the Lord upon him in Ezek 1:4: "As I looked, a stormy wind came out of the north: a great cloud with brightness around it and fire flashing forth continually, and in the middle of the fire, something like gleaming amber." This testimony is consistent with the Exodus revelation of God. The prophet Daniel confirms Ezekiel's testimony in Dan 10:5-9.

When the Psalmist speaks of God in Ps 18:9-12, he writes: "He bowed the heavens and came down; thick darkness [*'arapel*] was under his feet . . . He made darkness [*hošek*] his covering around him, his canopy thick clouds dark with water. Out of the brightness before

152

him there broke through his clouds hailstones and coals of fire." Here the image of God is one inclusive of darkness and light. The Psalmist goes on to describe the providence of God in Ps 91:1-2: "You who live in the shelter of the Most High, who abide in the shadow of the Almighty, will say to the Lord, 'My refuge and my fortress; My God, in whom I trust.' " The insight of the Psalmist that darkness and light both participate in the being of God is summed up in Ps 139:11-12: "If I say, 'Surely the darkness shall cover me, and the light around me become night,' even the darkness is not dark to you; the night is as bright as the day, for darkness is as light to you."

The relation of darkness and light to the revelation of God in the Old Testament discloses many insights. One of these is that when God creates humanity as male and female, humanity is created to reflect the very image of the triune God. Humanity is therefore created to reflect the images of darkness and light evidenced in the revelation of God. In the revelation of God there is no anti-darkness or anti-light bias. Both darkness and light point to and participate equally in the being of God. Both dark humans and light humans point equally to one image of God. Both images of God are equal. Both are positive. It is time that theology stopped construing one as negative or defining them as opposites. The paradox of darkness and light in God must not become dualist or Gnostic.

The revelation of God as presented in the Old Testament consistently presents an event in which both darkness and light both participate and point to the being of God. Several definitive Hebrew words appear in this presentation of revelation. They are: *ḥošek* (darkness), *'anan* (cloud), *'eš* (fire), *'arapel* (thick darkness), *'opel* (gloom), *makaseh* (refuge or shelter), *ḥuppah* (canopy), *maktîr* (shelter). *Ḥošek* (darkness) is predominant and appears in almost every revelatory event. *Ḥošek* is sometimes replaced in the literature by *'arapel* (thick darkness), e.g. Exod 19:9. *Ḥošek* is used interchangeably with *'anan* (cloud). This is significant because later on in the Greek New Testament, with its latent Greek anti-material and anti-darkness bias, the word *nephélē* (cloud) is used in the transfiguration event, without explicitly conveying the intent of the Hebrew *'anan* as a metaphor for *ḥošek* (darkness).

Contrary to popular theology, darkness does not necessarily hide and light does not necessarily reveal. Both darkness and light can hide and reveal. Both darkness and light can blind as well as disclose. Both darkness and light are intelligent and intelligible. God speaks out of both darkness and light (Deut 5:23-24). Both darkness and light are pregnant with meaning and power.

153

Darkness and Light in the New Testament

When the linguistic medium of the word of God shifts from the Hebrew of the Old Testament to the Greek of the New Testament, the dialectical texture of divine revelation in which both darkness and light have equal participation becomes obscured by a dualistic Greek idealistic materialism that tends to conceive of revelation predominantly in terms of light. The Synoptic Gospels tend to present the revelation of the Word and conformity to the Word in terms of *light* (*phōs*).

Matthew ignores the darkness motif in the revelation of God as presented by Isaiah and chooses to focus on the light motif. Therefore he repeats the passage from Isaiah: "the people who sat in darkness have seen a great light" (Matt 4:16). Matthew goes on to conceive of being in terms of light: "The eye is the lamp of the body. So if your eye is healthy, your whole body will be full of light; but if your eye is unhealthy, your whole body will be full of darkness" (Matt 6:22-23). Modern physics and hermeneutics reveal what the eye perceives as light is relative. And it is precisely this relative nature or relatedness of light and darkness that renders absolute dualism between darkness and light revelationally naive and false.

The Gospel of Mark, like Matthew, tends to construe being in terms of its relatedness to light. Mark 4:22 contends "there is nothing hidden, except to be disclosed; nor is anything secret; except to come to light." Mark and Luke share a dramatic event—the transfiguration—which Matthew does not report. Mark attempts to present the transfiguration as being identical to the revelation of God which occurred in the Exodus event, but Koine Greek does not lend itself to presenting darkness in a positive "light." The best that Mark can do is to say that God spoke from a cloud (*nephélē*): "Then a *cloud* overshadowed them, and from the *cloud* came a voice, "This is my Son, the Beloved; listen to him" (Mark 9:7). The Greek *nephélē*, however, does not do justice to the Hebrew *hošek*, nor is it transparent to darkness as the Hebrew *'anan*. Many exegetes who seek to banish *darkness* from the being of God interpret *nephélē* in such a way that it is neuter and cannot symbolize darkness.

Luke contains the usual Koine Greek perceptions of being in terms of light (Luke 11:33-36, 8:16-18), and the transfiguration event (Luke 9:28-36) is described in terms of the intelligible voice of God that emanates from a cloud (*nephélē*). Luke also presents a view of the demonic or satanic that is often masked by interpreters due to enlightenment reasoning and Greek idealism. The predominant tendency in the history of Protestant theology has been to conceive of Satan as the "prince of darkness." But Satan, in his distortion of being, projects not only darkness but also light. Satan is equally satanic as Lucifer, the prince of light, or as Beelzebub, the prince of darkness. Luke describes his fall as like lightning. The white mounds of cocaine under which millions are suffocating today and the black mounds of smoldering earth under which millions of Jews and Africans of the Nazi and slavery holocausts lie all belong to one Satan.

The Gospel of John deservedly stands apart from the Synoptic Gospels. It presents the best and the worst of what Greek idealism has to offer. John takes us into the divine life of God. Using Greek idealism he presents to us the divine life through the *lógos*. But this *lógos* is solely *light* (*phōs*). It is a light of "enlightenment." It appears to bear no kinship or relativity to the *hošek* of God in the Exodus event. John presents the *lógos* as the *life* and *light* of the person: "The *light* shines in the *darkness* and the *darkness* did not overcome it" (John 1:5, italics added). The *logos* is presented as the true light that *enlightens* every person. As if this one-sided distortion of the revelation of God were not enough, John proceeds to equate love of *darkness* and *evil*:

> This is the judgment, that the *light* has come into the world, and people loved *darkness* rather than *light* because their deeds were *evil*. For all who do *evil* hate the *light* and do not come to the *light*, so that their deeds may be exposed. But those who do what is true come to the *light*, that it may be clearly seen that their deeds have been done in God. (John 3:19-21, italics added)

Those who see in these verses the unequivocal rightness of light and wrongness of darkness are blind to the fact that light too lends itself to evil. Light blinds just as much as darkness. Light disguises evil. The evil that people do today occurs in the light, with the sanction of light. It is a mockery of the doctrine of evil to suggest that Satan loves darkness better as a cover than light. Satan is comfortable wearing both covers. For both belong to divine revelation. And the usurper does not seek to usurp one and not the other. Satan seeks to usurp both darkness and light. Satan seeks to usurp God. Satan cannot usurp God by seeking to usurp only part of what belongs to God, or being-itself, for darkness and light both belong to the being of God.

The Pauline corpus spells out in ethical terms what the Gospel of John proclaims in theological terms. Paul's allegiance to the Greek idealistic perception of human being and praxis in terms of light, may have been strengthened by his Damascus road experience narrated in Acts 26:13-18. On the way to Damascus, Paul saw a light (*phōs*) from heaven and a voice addressing him in the Hebrew language. This was for Paul both a conversion and revelatory experience. It bears the same character as the Exodus event or the transfiguration event in which a voice, presumably God's, is heard. In his allegiance to light, Paul writes that "the *night* is far gone, the *day* is at hand. Let us then lay aside the works of *darkness* and put on the armor of *light*" (Rom 13:12, italics added).

An undialectical use of Greek idealistic language in which darkness is negated can have disastrous consequences especially when it is used to lend support to spurious racist claims. Paul's goal and intention, for example in 2 Cor 6:14–7:1, is to draw a clear contrast between sinful existence and christological existence (sinlessness). He uses the best linguistic metaphor from Greek idealistic language to accomplish this task. But the price he pays for using a language foreign to Jesus is what can be construed as the "de-ontologization" of darkness. That which has being is denied being so that it may serve as the "scapegoat," the "foil," in contrast to that which has being. Light therefore is used to denote sinlessness and being in Christ. Darkness becomes sinfulness and that which is anti-Christ.

The undialectical identification of darkness as good and light as evil, or vice versa, leads all theological discourse to the impossible possibility: on the one hand, the Protestant requirement that all *dark* creatures must become "*enlightened*" in order to be saved, and on the other, the liberationist requirement that all *light* creatures must become "*darkened*" in order to be saved. The theological solution to this dilemma is to allow both *darkness* and *light* to be what they are as they both point to and participate in the being of God. The equality of darkness and light in the being of God (aseity) must be reflected in the image of the human beings who were created both dark and light to reflect God's image. God then is for me (*pro me*) only as God affirms others, for God is indeed God of all. Theological presuppositions which seek to limit God either in aseity or promeity, i.e., God solely as light or God solely as darkness, render the vastness of God a mockery.

Given the positivity of the Old Testament *ḥošek* and '*eš*, notwithstanding Paul's deliberate use of the Greek light–dark contrast for dogmatic and soteriological reasons, 2 Cor 6:14–7:1 points to Yahweh only as it affirms the *ḥošek* and '*eš* associated with Yahweh. In this regard, the passage speaks not against the being of *darkness* but the relation of *sin*. God is for being and against sin:

> Do not be mismatched with unbelievers. For what partnership is there between righteousness and lawlessness? Or what fellowship is

156

there between light and darkness? What agreement does Christ have with Beliar? Or what does a believer share with an unbeliever? What agreement has the temple of God with idols? For we are the temple of the living God; as God said: "I will live in them and walk among them, and I will be their God, and they shall be my people. Therefore come out from them, and be separate from them, says the Lord, and touch nothing unclean; and then I will welcome you, and I will be your father, and you will be my sons and daughters, says the Lord Almighty." Since we have these promises, beloved, let us cleanse ourselves from every defilement of body and of spirit, making holiness perfect in the fear of God. (2 Cor 6:14–7:1)

Overcoming De-ontologization

The theological circle must purge "de-ontologization," the process whereby that which has being is denied being, and afforded being only by becoming that which it cannot become. It cannot become other than what it was created to be. The history of Protestant theological deontologization of darkness in the name of theological clarity, abstract thought, harmatiological precision, or soteriological discussion, has come to an end. For the dark beings of this world will no longer believe there is no darkness in God, since a host of Old Testament witnesses speak to the contrary. The theological agenda is not to replace light in the being of God, but to allow darkness its equal place.

On Friday, May 24, 1991, the history of this denial was at least partially overcome. The nation of Israel finally recognized and admitted the dark Ethiopic Jews, after centuries of denial. This was a momentous theological occurrence. Yet many Protestant theologians were content to downplay its significance—understandably so, for this recognition was a stab in the heart of the theological agenda that has barred darkness from being, from participation in the people of God and in the being of God (being-itself). Speaking of this theological occurrence, New York's Mayor David Dinkins remarked: "Israel is the first country in the world to welcome Black Africans not just as free men and women—not just as automatic citizens—but as brethren."[32]

The Re-ontologization of Darkness

Re-ontologization, the systematic restoration of darkness and being dark to the being of God, is critical. It is a process that must be self-critical. It must be a dialectical process which does not de-ontologize light or ontologize sin. It is a restorative process, inasmuch as it

157

seeks to restore what according to the Old Testament sources belongs intrinsically not only to the being of God but to being itself. Paul Tillich and James Cone helped to shake the foundations. The walls have come tumbling down indeed. Israel itself has helped finish the demolition process. Now is the time to rebuild and restore that which rightfully points to God and participates in being itself: darkness.

CHAPTER 12

Interdependence as a Normative Value in Pastoral Counseling with African Americans

Carolyn L. McCrary

In West Africa, the Yoruba people have a proverb which says: "Omo omode ko to pepe, t' abalagba ko wo keregbe." It means: "The small hand of the child cannot reach the high shelf. The large hand of the adult cannot enter the narrow neck of the gourd." Ogunbowale interprets this proverb to mean that "adults and children need each other. None can exist without the other, and each must respect the other. . . ."[1] In essence, this is the type of interdependence in human relationships that concerns me in this paper—a Womanist kind of interdependence. "I am because we are, and since we are, therefore I am,"[2] speaks poignantly and ontologically of our interrelatedness. The African proverb just cited graphically reminds us of the vulnerability, the concreteness, and the often precarious nature of our dependency, and of our blatant need for one another, young and old, large and small, female and male.

In western culture, dependency is viewed as a pathological state, i.e. hysterical behavior, substance abusers, partners in abuse/co-dependents, etc. Independence and the illusion of self-sufficiency is held in highest regard.[3] In this paper I present some of the main theological and psychological tenets which undergird the African American value of interdependence. As such, I introduce neither a new concept nor a new norm, but I present an essential quality of African American culture that should be appreciated, relished, and utilized—particularly in the discipline of pastoral counseling.

My understanding of interdependence as a normative value in pastoral counseling is heavily influenced by the theology of community in the writings of the late Howard Thurman and the Bantu philosophy of African traditional religion. I also utilize the object

159

relations theory of W. R. D. Fairbairn to articulate some of the psychological intricacies of the processes of internalization. To articulate how I conceptualize and use the normative value of interdependence in pastoral counseling, I will discuss selected tenets from Howard Thurman's theology of community, using Bantu philosophy for elucidating a significant aspect of Thurman's thoughts and selected concepts from W. R. D. Fairbairn's psychology of object relations. To demonstrate, I will follow this discussion with a specific case. Then, I will conclude with implications of my model that are applicable in the ministry of pastoral counseling with African Americans.

Howard Thurman's Theology of Community

There are three major reasons why Howard Thurman's theology of community was chosen to provide the theological basis of the nature of interdependence. First, Thurman has struggled to articulate the complexities of community and the tendency toward "whole-making."[4] In Thurman's struggle to help us understand community, with special attention to the plight of African Americans, he has masterfully held in tension the needs and possibilities of the individual as persons with the needs and possibilities of the group as a whole—the community. Social transformation is also a goal of Thurman's work. He emphasizes, however, the transformation of the individual as a necessary priority for any meaningful and lasting transformation or liberation of a people, and particularly of African Americans.[5]

Second, the development of a proper identity is in Thurman's view crucial for each person.[6] Although this cannot be accomplished developmentally without the nurture of primary and secondary family units, or positive input from the larger society as a whole, Thurman adds insistently that it is the religious experience of each individual, her/his personal encounter with God, and the mystical union of creature and creator, that gives ultimate meaning, direction, and identity to each person.[7] Two ramifications of the "personal religious experience" are important for pastoral counseling: (a) the conscious awareness of the pastoral counselor's own ultimate gift of love, identity, interdependency, and the need to share those appropriately with others; and (b) considering the state of crisis, suffering, and anxiety with which the counselee usually comes to counseling, the counselor, through the quality of the pastoral relationship that is offered, can enhance the counselee's movement toward an ultimate interpretation of such a meaningful occurrence in her or his life.

Third, a crucial dimension of Thurman's concept of community is reconciliation, which has reference to the rejoining of self to God, of self to others, and of self to self.[8] This attention to the fragmentation that can and does exist in the lives of persons is particularly important for the present discussion involving the fractured egos and the sense of alienation experienced by African Americans. It is also important for us to note here that though African Americans do suffer psychologically as well as in other ways, because of the oppression of racism and sexism in the United States, such oppression is not the only catalyst for psychological fragmentations and feelings of alienation in the African American personality; nor would the removal of such oppression be the only "balm" that would "heal the sin-sick soul."[9] And, although being reconciled and loving of one's enemies—White persons included—is not in the primary concern of most liberation theologies that are grounded in the African American experience, Thurman does advocate passionately that loving one's enemies is a necessity for each person, not for the sake of the enemy, but for the sake of the self:

> Yet you must find a way to love your enemy, if you want to be whole; not if you want to redeem your enemy, but because you want to be whole. A part of you is caught in the deed which [the enemy] has done and you must get you out of it to restore wholeness to yourself.[10]

There are four tenets of Howard Thurman's theology of community: unity, actualization of potential, love, and reconciliation. The first two, unity and actualization of potential, will be highlighted here.

Unity: The Belief That the Contradictions in Life Are Neither Final nor Ultimate

A good sense of what Thurman means by community can be found in the following statement about the religious person in the midst of the contradictions of experience:

> Ultimately, all the dualisms of his experience as a creature must exhaust themselves in a corroborating unity fundamental to life and not merely dependent upon that which transcends life by whatever name he seeks to patronize it.[11]

This "corroborating unity" is the basic tenet of Thurman's concept of community (and therefore of his theology), and he says about it "the literal fact of the underlying unity of life seems to be established beyond doubt."[12] Thurman takes great pains in *The Search for Common Ground* to point out the tendency toward community or the penchant toward harmonious unity in all life by looking at the creation myths of various cultures, the life sciences, the philosophy behind utopias, and the social psychology of change in America.

As for the forces of evil, destruction, and division, Thurman acknowledges them, but only as against life, not supported by life and as "not aligned with the ultimate intent of life."[13] Ultimate for Thurman is a milieu of oneness where each person, by the grace of God, is permitted to develop and fulfill her or his meaning and purpose/potential in life. For Thurman, "the contradictions of life are not final or ultimate," especially in light of the indomitable human/divine spirit.[14]

Interestingly enough, Thurman's concept of unity bears much resemblance to the Bantu-Rwandaise philosophy of being. Thurman's emphasis upon unity as the all-embracing essence of creation grounds us meaningfully in our African tradition at the point of attempting to define the very nature of relationships. The African scholar, Alexis Kagame, in his work *La Philosophie Bantu-Rwandaise de L'être*,[15] highlights for us the concept of *Ntu*, which is the common denominator, the common ground (so to speak) of the four categories of Bantu-Rwandaise philosophy.

The Four Categories of Being and Their Qualifications in Bantu-Rwandaise Philosophy

The four categories of being in Bantu-Rwandaise philosophy are: (1) *Muntu* = human being (plural: *Bantu*); (2) *Kintu* = thing (plural: *Bintu*); (3) *Hantu* = place and time; and (4) *Kuntu* = modality. According to Janheinz Jahn:

> All being, all essence, in whatever form it is conceived, can be subsumed under one of these categories. Nothing can be conceived outside them. . . . Everything there is must necessarily belong to one of these four categories and must be conceived of not as substance but as force. [The human] is a force, all things are force. . . . *Ntu* is the universal force as such, which, however, never occurs apart from its manifestation: *Muntu, Kintu, Hantu*, and *Kuntu*. *Ntu* is Being itself, the cosmic universal force, which only modern rationalizing thought can abstract from its manifestations. *Ntu* is that force in which Being and beings coalesce. . . .[16]

Two aspects of *Ntu* are important for us in this discussion: (1) that it is the unifying force which bespeaks the connecting essence of all that is; and (2) that at the fundamental core, there is an interconnectedness and an interdependence of being of everyone and everything, trees, rocks, rivers, air, water, animals, birds, insects, time, place, and form. One cannot, therefore, relegate someone or something outside one's realm of care and concern. For since we are all inextricably joined to everyone else and everything else—at the point of *Ntu*—then whatever we do to another being, is done at the fundamental level of our own being. Thus, Bantu philosophy is different from most Western philosophies at this foundational level. In Western philosophy, not everyone and everything is valued in terms of being significantly related and inextricably intertwined with one's being as a human being. René Descartes postulates "Cogito, ergo sum," or "Je pense, donc je suis": "I think, therefore I am."[17] Thinking, in this view, becomes the essential criterion of worthwhile being. This mind-set is a direct antecedent to the behavior of discriminating between plundering, and raping people and nature, both of which are considered outside of or not belonging to one's realm of being, and, therefore, outside of the scope of one's ultimate and intimate care and concern.

Another dimension of *Ntu* important for us today is that when we speak of the category of *Muntu*, "être qui a l'intelligence,"[18] we are not just talking about the living breathing human being, but about the dead as well. "For the concepts *Muntu* and human beings are not coterminous, since *Muntu* includes the living and the dead, orishas, and loas." *Muntu* includes the ancestors, especially those who have recently died, the "living dead." The *bazima* are the living and the *bazimu* are the dead.[19] Kagame reminds us that in his language life and existence are not identical. The dead are not alive, but they do exist.[20] And it is by way of the Magara system—the Life Force which can strengthen or weaken the other—that the living and the dead are able to influence and help each other.[21]

The Magara system is, therefore, an important concept for pastoral counselors, in that it helps us to assume the posture of traditional African elders by being fully aware of, as well as users of, the power of familial and communal influences, living and dead, conscious and unconscious. Moreover, the Magara system can give us a way to articulate our insights in other than object relations terminology. It provides us with a method to help reconcile and bless persons wrecked by alienation and isolation.

By and large the Bantu-Rwandaise system of *Ntu* supports my strong belief in the interrelatedness and interdependence of human being and nature. Thurman believes that in life and death humans are always involved in the cycle of life intertwined with nature, and to perceive differently is but "one of the deceptive aspects of mind" in human beings.[22]

Actualization of Potential: The Move Toward Real "Whole-making"

The second tenet of Howard Thurman's theology that supports our value of interdependence is the actualization of potential, which is integral to his understanding of the principle of unity. The presence of unity is made manifest in its ability to allow each life form to actualize its potential. "Actualization of potential," expressive of its fundamental unity, involves several dimensions. We shall highlight only two: (1) "a proper sense of self" and (2) "a communal family."

Thurman's discussion of the actualization of potential is grounded in his belief that the human being is a "creature grounded in creature-liness." This notion ties every person to every other person, creature, life process, entity, and creation as well as to itself as a mind and a body. For Thurman, it is fruitless to talk of wholeness, or the "whole-making tendency" of the mind, without serious inclusion of the physical body. It is with proper recognition of the body (its potentials and limitations) that one develops an adequate sense of self.[23] Thurman sees the sense of self that is rooted in the experience of the person's body as his or her own, as rooting one into the "urgency" of all living things to actualize their potential as a body. It is upon this philosophical-corporeal base that Thurman places his crucial building blocks for the actualization of potential: a person's need to be loved, to be understood, to be cared for, to have a proper sense of self.[24]

A Proper Sense of Self

In determining the precise nature of Thurman's concept of the "sense of self," Luther Smith's work, *Howard Thurman: The Mystic as Prophet*, is helpful. Smith identifies three dimensions: the self-fact, the self-image, and self-love.[25] Concerning the self-fact and self-image, Smith explains two important affirmations. "First, since a person's 'fact,' one's inherent worth, is of ultimate value, it is important that one's self image conforms to one's self fact." Thurman is persistent in his passionate cry that we are all God's children, regardless of race, creed, color, gender, economic, social, or physical standing. Each one of us is of God and God is in each one of us. For Thurman, this is the center of religion and the starting point for theology. In an article entitled "What Can We Believe In?" Thurman's first response is "not only can I believe in myself, but I 'must' believe in myself."[26]

A Loving and Communal Family

The task comes in the recognition of our divine value. Smith tells us that "though one's fact is inherent, the nurture of this fact toward a healthy self-image is a social function."[27] The family is usually the primary context for this occurrence. In the first place, one's personal stability depends on [one's] relationships with others. For in order to answer the question, "Who am I?" the individual must go on to ask, "To whom, to what do I belong?" This primary sense of belonging, of counting, of participating in situations, of sharing with the group, is the basis of all personal stability. And from it is derived the true sense of self.[28] It is important to note the priority that Thurman places on relationships, particularly familial ones. This primary group has the opportunity to interact with the developing child so as to influence and reflect the child's own unique makeup, which Thurman calls *persona.*[29]

Thurman is also quite adept in his description of the consequences of personal development when there is, in the family, no pivotal point around which positive self-awareness emerges. According to Thurman, the rejected child becomes the rejecting child, enraged, withdrawn, and alienated, mainly because the child is assaulted by an insensitive environment before she or he has the necessary tools with which to cope.[30]

Accordingly, the two major tenets of Howard Thurman's theology grounded us and creation ontologically as one—as a whole. Yet Thurman also narrows the focus and speaks to us of the necessary "building blocks" that each of us needs in order to become whole: self-fact, self-image, self-love, proper nurturing, and parental guidance, all shaped around and related to the personal religious experience.

Let us now turn to W. R. D. Fairbairn, who, by way of his object relations theory of the personality, gives us a language and method for discussing the psychological process of internalization that comes as a result of acceptance, love, nurture, rejection, and deprivation.

W. R. D. Fairbairn and An Object Relations Theory of the Personality

The concept of "object relations" has its psychological origin in the work of Sigmund Freud, who used it in respect to the internalization of a person's external world, particularly significant others such as parents, during the earliest years of life. Freud, however, did not develop a system which detailed the specific processes of internalization, or an expanded theory of object relations.[31] W. R. D. Fairbairn, along with other writers of the British school of object relations such as Melanie Klein, D. W. Winnicott, and Edith Jacobsen, focused more on the pre-oedipal period of development (prior to age 4–5), the symbiotic relationship of mother and child, and the internalization of significant persons technically referred to as "objects."

Two particular dimensions of Fairbairn's object relations theory concern us here. They are: (1) his rejection of the drive/structure model of personality development as he opts for a relational/structure model;[32] and (2) the choice of dependency as the essential quality by which relations are distinguished. Fairbairn views all relationships to rest in some basic way upon a state of dependency and, therefore, does not reduce dependency to a negative status to be shunned after a brief interlude in early childhood. All of us remain dependent upon the continued interrelating of others all our lives, although it is the nature of dependency constantly to change. Dependency is no longer a bad word for mature relationships. In fact, mature dependency is the goal of development in Fairbairn's theory.

Such a posture has relevance for African Americans and other counselees in that the denotation and connotation of the "dependent person" have been broadened and enhanced toward the ideology that being intimately and consciously related in a needful way to someone all one's life is a natural thing to be grasped and not denied—the crucial factors being the changes in the nature, and/or the degree, of the dependency, and the timing of those changes. This attitude and the concomitant values of reciprocity and sharing fit better, in a foundational way, into the African American worldview and its value system which reflects interdependence as a positive way of living. The attainment of a state of existence called independence is put in its proper perspective as an arrival at a transitional stage of development that reflects quasi-independence at most. For Fairbairn, the three stages of development are (1) infantile dependency, (2) the transitional stage of quasi-independence, and (3) mature dependency.

Fairbairn sees himself as not only in conflict with certain traditional psychoanalytic formulations, but as offering a theoretical interpretation of personhood that is not biologically based on instincts, but rather relationally based on the quality of the dependence between persons. In his article "Synopsis of an Object Relations Theory of the Personality," Fairbairn challenges another pillar of classical psychoanalytic theory by stating that "an Ego is present at birth"[33] and, additionally, that it is inherently dynamic and whole.

Fairbairn sees the psychic core of the human being as innate,

166

dynamic, and whole. The central ego, as psychic structure and psychic energy with libidinal aim, is focused from the beginning on relating to the object for the sake of relationship. This object relations theory of the personality counters the classical Freudian instinct theory of the person in a striking way. Fairbairn believes that the fundamental goal of recognition, preservation and restoration of psychic wholeness is the goal of all mental health and, therefore, of psychotherapy.[34]

For Fairbairn, psychopathology involves the internalization and the consequent splitting of the object—which actually means the object representation and the accompanying affect. The preambivalent, or mostly "unsatisfying object" is internalized (unconsciously) by the infant/young child as a way to control or coerce it. The "unsatisfying object" is then split by the central ego into the "good object" and the "bad object." The "bad object" is further split into the "rejecting object" and the "exciting object." While the "good object" remains cathected to the central ego and partially conscious as the "ideal object," the "rejecting object" and the "exciting object" are repressed by the corresponding dimensions of the now split ego. The libidinal ego represses the exciting object and the anti-libidinal ego represses the rejecting and exciting objects. Consequently, the picture of the endopsychic structure is of a split object and a divided ego. Herein lies the problem for the client and a task for the pastoral counselor. There must be a reconciliation of these dimensions of the psyche for health and wholeness to occur.

In light of the above idea about internalization of object relations and the consequent endopsychic structuring, I offer the following definition of interdependence:

> Interdependence refers to that state of communal existence wherein each person is appropriately recognized for her/his uniqueness and ultimate worth, encouraged in her/his need to be significantly related to others, enabled in the fulfillment of her/his potential of worth and purpose, and supported in her/his responsibility for the survival, the physical well being, and positive mental, psychological, economic, and spiritual development of the group as a whole.

Let us now look briefly at a case that we will then analyze from our community object relations perspective of interdependence.

Case Study

Susan is a twenty-nine-year-old light-skinned African American woman who is single and a full-time undergraduate student. Susan came to counseling expressing feelings of loneliness, depression, isolation, and thoughts about suicide. She says, "Nothing seems to go right, so why am I here? . . . I'm not like a lot of people, like everybody else. . . . I feel different. . . . I have no friends." She is the daughter of a prominent professional couple who separated when she was ten years old. Susan felt torn by the separation and has subsequently spent time living with each parent. Susan has two brothers and two sisters, and though she doesn't feel particularly close to any of them, she does share some things with her younger sister. Susan always attended church regularly, as did the rest of the family, and they all worked with various groups and activities sponsored by the church. Now Susan says that these kind of activities "just keep me busy at running away from myself. . . . I don't even know if I'm on speaking terms with God anymore, especially since God isn't answering any of my questions." She characterizes her relationship with her mother as "better all the time . . . she thought me crazy, odd and different." She says that her mother is overly protective of her, especially since her earlier bout with depression. Susan says that though her mother had it hard, having grown up with only one parent, she (her mother) still doesn't really seem to understand her.

Of her relationship with her father, she says, "He used to be closer to me . . . now it seems that he doesn't have the time, especially since his promotion several years ago." Susan says that her father's work always came first in his life. However, she remembers her early childhood years as being rather happy as she tagged along with her father, even at work sometimes. She also speaks warmly and affectionately about her relationship with her paternal great-grandmother, who she says was her "buddy," who thought she was special. Susan felt pressured in her immediate family as a result of being the oldest girl, as if "I had to be special and do certain things. . . ." She feels as if she had disappointed her family in some regard, but even more herself. Susan longs to be involved in a significant relationship, preferably marriage, and to have a child.

Susan reflects that she never really had friends growing up. Most of her socializing was with the family. She laments the fact that they always attended integrated schools where African American people were always in the minority. She feels that her association with men has been limited as well. She sees herself as having been restricted in her association with men, and when she did start relating to men she found herself being used, abused, or misused by them. The one significant relationship that she does talk about ended abruptly when she thought that she was pregnant. "He broke off the relationship because he didn't want to consider any kind of commitment." Susan sees sexual intimacy as a "chore . . . a way of punishing myself."

Susan's recurring theme is her lack of significant positive relationships, male or female. She sees herself as the problem. She wants to know if and/or how she can change so that her life will be less lonely and more meaningful. Her most recent and painfully faced question is: "How do I cope if nothing's going to change?"

Clinically, Susan is depressed, isolated, and is experiencing an emerging anger relative to her disappointment with non-gratifying internal and external object relationships. Her depression is reflected in her low self-esteem, her sense of hopelessness about her life, and her repressed affect which until recently served to cloak her anger at not being significantly related. Susan is frustrated that her "good girl" role has not resulted in rewarding and gratifying relationships, particularly with her mother. She has, until recently, successfully repressed this anger for fear that she might destroy what little power and control she feels with her internalized bad—particularly rejecting— objects.

The turmoil between Susan's parents and their subsequent divorce created deep feelings of instability in Susan and negatively affected her oedipal development. In later childhood, Susan experienced with her father overprotection and arbitrary censorship of extra-familial, especially male, relationships. The relatively closed system in which Susan grew up inhibited free and open-ended experiencing and thereby reinforced the retreat to the internalized, split, and repressed world of bad object relationships. The one sanctioned exception to the closed system in Susan's life was the family church whose values and traditions transmitted by the "mothers and elders" served to counteract some of the negativity in her life and represented a place of refuge for contact with real object relationships.

Community and Mature Dependence: Differentiation Toward Interdependence

In Fairbairn's view, differentiation is a process of individuating as a person in the context of a nurturing and facilitating environment. The intense anxiety manifested in the oscillation and the vacillation between symbiosis and separation[35] testifies to the conflicting urges involved in the struggle to move from identification to individuality. For Thurman and Fairbairn, in the movement toward both community and mature dependence, the "give and take" dynamics involved in interpersonal relating is key. In this light, I discuss (1) the recognition of the nature of self, (2) surrendering of self, (3) response, and (4) the mourning process: surrendering of object representations.

Consider the following encounter with Susan which occurred in the early phases of our counseling relationship:

> *Susan*: I can remember even as a little girl saying "I want a job and a husband and a little chocolate-colored baby boy, with jet black curly hair . . . so I could raise him right . . . not to be trifling, lazy . . . and know how to treat a woman right. . . . I've always wanted to have a baby . . . to be a mother . . . but that's just par for the course, too. My dreams never seem to come true.
>
> *Counselor*: You wanted and still want to take care of someone and love someone special.
>
> *Susan*: Yeah. But it seems that all I've ever done is taken care of people . . . even my daddy and brothers and sisters . . . but it's never been my turn . . . they all seem to think I don't need like they do. . . .
>
> *Counselor*: Now that has you pretty upset.
>
> *Susan*: Shoot yeah! I do and do for everybody and don't get nothing back. But I just don't seem to be able even to know what to do for me. I don't know how to do for me. In fact, I'm scared to do for me. It might not turn out right . . . me doing for me, might turn out like me . . . not right.
>
> *Counselor*: Yes Susan, you do sound like you're scared to stretch out there.
>
> *Susan*: I just wonder what I'm going to do about myself . . . if I'm going to be able to do anything . . . or is it just too late for me. . . . (She cries. I hand her a tissue and I touch her hand.)

Recognition of the Nature of Self

From Thurman's perspective one would say that Susan is having problems with her sense of self in terms of the "nature of the self." Discovering the true nature of the self has to do with the proper cultivation of the relationship between the self-fact and the self-image; the cultivation of the "inner life." To put it bluntly, the inner life of Susan was in shambles and in need of a personal encounter with God. An encounter with self not predicated on an encounter and recognition of one's unique gift of transcendence, results in meaningless and powerless thought and behavior.[36] Susan apparently had tried to deal with feelings of alienation in various ways but without relief. Though she was having definite problems with her self-image, she seemed to have had an inkling that there was more to herself than what she was interpreting in her own behavior, as well as in the behavior and attitudes of other people toward her.

170

Susan had plenty of questions about herself, especially about her worth, her meaning to others, and her purpose for living. Her busy schedule, and her work in trying to help other people, did not fill the void or give her ultimate meaning. Susan's anger at God was an indication that her questions about the "nature of self" were of ultimate concern.

Surrender: Openness/Response to the Divine

According to Thurman, a primary response to transcendent encounter in a personal religious experience involves "a central surrender of the self to God." This surrender, which he likens in essence to commitment, and in difficulty to a child's achievement of selfhood, is "rugged, tempestuous, and ruthless." In Thurman's view, self-conscious surrender can be accomplished in two different ways. The first "may be a self-conscious yielding of the very center of one's being to God—the yielding of that of which the ego itself is but the shell, the facade, the protection, really."[37] This is a change that one is not capable of effecting on one's own, but which is an inner revolution of the innermost self effected by God.

The other way by which the surrender is accomplished is in terms of particular situations or events. Even over a long period of time, the person may make little surrenders, apparently insignificant surrenders, morally indecisive surrenders, but always holding back the ultimate, the final surrender. Nevertheless, deep within oneself one knows that it is impossible to hold out indefinitely against the ultimate demand. Whether a one-time self-conscious decision, or a long, arduous, and protracted surrender of the central nerve of one's innermost being, the ramifications of surrender to God are profound and extensive.[38]

Of particular importance to Susan are the ramifications of wholeness, power, and freedom. Susan was feeling the continual alienation in her being as if it were an impending doom. This she felt powerless to halt, let alone to change. Susan's sense of loneliness, isolation, and lack of love are exemplified in her intense desire for a baby, "ever since she was a little girl;" someone she could love deeply and profoundly and who would love her back, she thought, with the same intensity. Her sense of alienation and helplessness was further compounded by the ramifications of racism and discrimination that impacted the family value system regarding color and beauty. She felt that her own color was "holding her back" and/or "keeping people from experiencing the real me." She said, "A lot of times, I could just tell that all that the Black guys would see would be my long straight hair and my light skin. They never wanted me for *me*." Susan seems to have thought that a "chocolate colored boy baby with jet black hair" would give her a sense of belonging and, all in all, make her a whole person.

Susan's sense of alienation and internal fragmentation, which were negatively affecting her motivation and leaving her feeling powerless, was reflected in what she called her "love-hate relationship" with herself. Obviously, Susan was having a running battle with her mother over her selfhood. Susan seemed to be fighting desperately to affirm her self-fact, that indeed she was full of worth and value, but her mother's image of her as "crazy and odd," which was slowly eating away at Susan's own estimation of herself, was gaining ground. Having to fight so hard thus far in her life for every bit of affirmation that she received, and often overestimating herself in such achievement, made surrender, in the Thurmanian sense of the process, a very arduous task.

Response

Were surrender to occur for Susan, Thurman advocates that she could find motivation in "an integrated basis for action . . . a core of purpose . . . for her life and for living." Adjacent to this new-found purpose is "the releasing in the individual of new and great powers." Thurman's discussion of the origin and potency of these powers brings to mind the plight and possibilities of Susan:

> From where comes these powers? They are inherent in the individual, at least in part. Before surrender, the individual spends enormous energies in scattered efforts, activities, and functions of various kinds. He is unable to bring to bear the resources of his life upon any single end. But when he surrenders and has now a new center which takes the form of a central demand, then his powers are pooled, are focused, and may be directed to achieve impossible ends.[39]

When one surrenders the central nerve of one's innermost being to God and as commitment is made, "a different kind of value is placed on physical existence" and even death of the body is no ultimate threat. Relative to the issue of surrender, Susan's question also has to do with loyalty to God, or to parents. "A soul-shaking conflict of loyalty" may be experienced by the person, in response to which a decision must be made. . . ."[40]

Susan expresses the turmoil: "These feelings of trying to stretch out there on my own stuff seems to be getting me in big trouble." In a letter written and read to me by Susan, after about a year in counseling, she expresses the fear, anxiety, and trepidation of trying to realize and be her God-given self:

> This newly awakened independence is okay, but it seems like I'm just as alone now as I was before. Through all of these sessions I've become more aware to pinpoint, to feel, rationalize, really learn more about me, what to accept, what to throw out, what to redo. I feel like I've only covered a cornerstone and I still have a milestone to go. But I feel like however I go, I'm damned if I do, damned if I don't.
>
> The gist of what you said is I'm all right as me and I don't have to give, or as I would say, create situations like I used to. And possibly I can't radiate fully because I don't know my own secret. If that's true then why am I still in the situation that I'm in and alone. And I said I didn't want to discuss this issue anymore. I feel like I'm trapped in a world that isn't mine.
>
> I've had these really crazy mini-dreams which always show me falling apart. Why haven't I written them down? To be frank, I just wanted to forget them. . . .
>
> The scary part is not wanting to wind up the way folks said that I would, and the way I had conditioned myself, but not knowing how to change.

Thurman would say that Susan is in the process of losing her life, so that she can find it in surrender to God, which is a religious experience where "there is no loss of being but rather an irradiation of the self that makes it alive with 'Godness' in various ways." Of those ways mentioned by Thurman, a sense of wholeness and a feeling of integration would be beneficial for Susan.

The Mourning Process

Fairbairn would say that Susan was in the midst of a process of mourning. Fairbairn, following in the psychoanalytic tradition, emphasizes the need of persons to expel and to mourn past self and object images in order for the process of differentiation to occur. In addition to achieving greater object constancy (a kind of homeostatic balance in the face of frustrating internal and/or external objects), mourning aids in the integration of the rejecting object, the exciting object, and the ideal object.[41] Here I believe that Fairbairn's description of the mourning process—the struggle to be free of inner conflict and bad internalized objects—is related to the religious concept of salvation. He puts it this way:

> On the one hand, it [salvation] presents itself as a need to be saved from inner conflicts, corresponding to the religious need for the

to be saved from the power of internalized bad objects, corresponding to the religious need for the casting out of the devil.[42]

Whereas Thurman spoke of surrendering the "nerve center of consent," Fairbairn has in mind the surrendering of unconscious self and object images that influence attitude and behavior. An important fact that Thurman, Fairbairn, and Susan would have us to note is the intense difficulty in the surrendering, releasing, and mourning of intimate relationships that profoundly affect one's worldview, one's attitude, and one's behavior. The resistance to such a process has been duly noted in Susan's letter. The opportunity for both counselor and counselee to deal with these repressed images and their corresponding impulses and memories will present itself (in transference, dreams, behavior, and in other ways) time and time again, despite the conscious and unconscious efforts on the part of the counselee to flee them or the counselor's "pressing" the counselee to confront and "release" them. This time of surrendering and mourning is also a time when more mature ways of coping are developed in the personality. Primary and infantile mechanisms such as projection, splitting, and identification, are gradually replaced by repression, sublimation, and displacement. These secondary and more mature ways of coping with internal and external relationships reflect more openness and versatility and less hostile identification with past significant others. The surrendering and mourning of the oppressive and divisive internalized relationships permits more integrated behaviors and defense mechanisms.

One of the issues in my therapy with Susan was to allow her to release some of her hostile feelings about her mother, and also to begin to take a look at how a large part of her behavior was in retaliation and reaction to her mother's treatment of her. Susan needed to examine what choices in life were really hers and what choices were made from the pressures of internal and external relationships. We focused on a psychological separation of Susan and her mother. In addition to the therapeutic relationship, Susan now has one female friend and a church mother as participants in her support system during her process of mourning. The result is that she no longer has to fear isolation and abandonment if and when she chooses to separate from her mother. Susan may never completely heal from the hurt caused by her relationship with her mother. But there were some indications that repressions were being lifted and some externalizations of internal images. Susan was still able to see realistically the persecutory, judgmental, and verbally abusive behavior of her mother (the rejecting object), while yet feeling a bond and need for her mother reflected in her desire to be accepted by and acceptable to her mother (the exciting object). She even began to see some things that she actually admired about her mother, such as the "wheeling and dealing that she did in order to raise five children almost by herself . . . and how she could always find very good bargains to keep us in style and looking nice" (the ideal object).

Conclusion

We have seen by way of theological and psychological theories and case material that dependency, with its attendant ramifications, is not necessarily a bad or detrimental state of being. On the contrary, in terms of relationships, dependency is crucially necessary at appropriate times and in appropriate degrees. Independence is at best a transitory state. It is, rather, interdependency that reflects appropriate timing and responses of ever recurring dependency needs, along with reciprocity, mutuality, giving, receiving, reliance, and responsibility, as well as the simultaneous experience of finitude and limitlessness.

With interdependence as a normative value in pastoral counseling, one is able to meet persons, especially African American clients, at the points of their needs and strengths, while valuing both as part of the process of creation, and especially of the human condition. The pastoral counselor, while affirming the ultimate worth and value of persons, recognizes the deep-seated internal pain of fragmentation, splitting, and alienation, and is able to "stand at the foot of the cross" patiently waiting and working with persons as they externalize, express, expel, and re-internalize or gather together dimensions of themselves that heal toward wholeness.

CHAPTER 13

Black Methodist Protestants, 1877–1939: Protest and Change Among African Americans Within Predecessor Organizations of The United Methodist Church

James M. Shopshire

Introduction

I was appointed as pastor of the Bethlehem Methodist Church in 1964 while in seminary and as a probationary member of the Georgia Conference of The Methodist Church. During my two-year appointment at Bethlehem, I became aware of its history as one of the Black congregations of the Methodist Protestant Church. Having already developed a strong interest in the history and sociology of Black religious experiences, I was curious about a Black Methodist congregation in the Deep South that appeared to be related to the historic Methodist Protestant Church and decided to do some exploratory study.

While in seminary I wrote a brief paper about the Bethlehem church and the group of Black congregations in Georgia that formed a racially separate movement within the White Methodist Protestant Church. Dr. Charles Copher, my professor and a member of the Bethlehem congregation, read the paper and observed that I had identified an important area for additional study and encouraged me to do more. Now, nearly thirty years later, I am pleased to honor Dr. Copher by offering this brief socio-historical assessment of Black people in the Georgia Annual Conference of the Methodist Protestant Church (Colored)—the times, the social context, the nature of the protest, and the organizations—using my knowledge of the Bethlehem congregation that I served as my primary example.

The Bethlehem Congregation and Black Methodist Protestant Beginnings

The early story of the Bethlehem Methodist Protestant Church is sketchy at best. Organized sometime prior to 1877, the little group of people who became the Bethlehem congregation was allowed to worship in "a small, frame, unpainted church owned by White people" in the area called "Lick Skillet, Georgia." Later, the area became Adamsville. The congregation formally became Bethlehem in 1877 when the Whites sold the building to Black people whose descendants have continued in membership to the present day.[1]

The relationship of the Bethlehem congregation to the Methodist Protestant Church is more difficult to trace in detail. In the historical sketch of the Bethlehem United Methodist Church written for the 111th church anniversary (1987), the relationship of the Black and White conferences of the Methodist Protestant Church is described in the observation that the "Colored" Annual Conference of Georgia was organized by the authority of the 47th Georgia Annual Conference of the Methodist Protestant Church [White] during its November 2–6, 1877 session in Poplar Springs (Clayton County, Georgia).[2]

Only a year earlier, the 46th Annual Conference of the Methodist Protestant Church of Georgia had formed the Sandy Creek Mission for Blacks, which included "Bethlehem, Sand Creek, and surrounding country."[3] Again, one finds indication that the Bethlehem congregation and others were already organized before they were designated "Colored Missions" of the White Methodist Protestant Church of Georgia. The following statement lends additional support to the claim:

> Rev. James Robinson, who was received as a delegate from the Colored mission at this conference, was appointed to the Sandy Creek Mission as Superintendent, and Rev. Silas Montgomery was appointed as his assistant. (Rev. George Barge was appointed to the Campbellton Circuit, which included Zion, Rocky Head, and Poplar Spring).[4]

Hence, the Black churches or charges apparently were already formed and functioning. The White Methodist Protestant Annual Conference of Georgia simply helped to constitute the missions and circuits into an organization that became the Georgia Annual Conference of the Methodist Protestant Church (Colored).

The extant *Minutes* of the Georgia Annual Conference of the Methodist Protestant Church (Colored) are currently the primary sources of information on trends and developments at Bethlehem throughout its 62 years as a Black Methodist Protestant congregation. Reconstructing the story is complicated by the fact that the statistical changes reported in the Annual Conference *Minutes* seem inconsistent at various points. For example, the *Minutes of the Eighth Session of the Georgia Annual Conference, Methodist Protestant Church (Colored),* convened at Warner's Chapel, Atlanta, November 4th, 1885, reported that Bethlehem had 2 ministers, 2 preachers, 2 churches, 200 members, church property valued at $320, 1 Sabbath school, 4 teachers, 40 scholars, 150 volumes in the library, and paid a salary of $21.[5] The following year, the *Minutes of the Ninth Session of the Georgia Annual Conference, Methodist Protestant Church (Colored),* convened at Zion Church, Campbellton, November 17, 1886, reported that the Bethlehem Circuit had 2 ministers, 2 preachers, 2 churches, 102 members, church property valued at $500, 2 Sunday schools, 5 teachers, 57 scholars, 116 volumes in the library, and paid a salary of $71.35.[6]

The difference in membership between 1885 and 1886 draws immediate attention. The question is why the reported membership became halved over the course of a year, down from 200 to 102. Except for the possibility of a typographical error or the intentional manipulation of the numbers, some decisive occurrence took place to drastically decrease the membership. Thirty years later, in the year leading up to World War I, the *Minutes of the Thirty-eighth Annual Session of the Georgia Annual Conference of the Methodist Protestant Church Colored, of Georgia* held in Bethlehem Church, Adamsville, November 16–17, 1916, show that Bethlehem had 1 minister, 1 preacher, 1 church, 50 members, church property valued at $13.00 (probably a typographical error), 1 Sunday school, 6 officers-teachers, 72 scholars, no mention of library or number of volumes, and paid a salary of $41.00.[7]

Several observations concerning Bethlehem are appropriate at this point. First, Bethlehem apparently was a "station" church during 1916. That is to say, only one congregation was reported to be on the charge. The membership of 50 was up from the 31 reported in 1913,[8] another year during which Bethlehem was a station church. Although the membership count was down in comparison with other years after the turn of the century, it can be accounted for, in part, because of the station church status as compared to the years in which there were two or more churches (congregations) on the charge or circuit.

Second, through 62 years, Bethlehem was indeed a protesting congregation. The central matters of protest were concerned with church autonomy and polity. At Bethlehem, and other Methodist Protestant conferences, bishops and presiding elders were not considered necessary. Elected presidents of the annual conference, "stationing committees," and duly certified lay delegates were believed to provide ample structure and leadership for the churches and annual conference. Reference to actions of committees and ministers elected to serve as president of the annual conference abound in the *Minutes of the Georgia Conference (Colored) of the Methodist Protestant Church.*

Third, over the years of its Methodist Protestant affiliation, Bethlehem appears to have experienced slow growth in membership with fluctuations up and down. Although Bethlehem was consistently among the largest of the Black Methodist Protestant congregations in Georgia, the number of members attached to its name and its general status among the congregations varied with the changes associated with composition as a one-church charge to two or more congregations as a circuit.

Even as a more complete story of Bethlehem begins to emerge, it must be acknowledged that careful research is needed to fill the blank spaces. Records of the intervening years for Bethlehem are partial and scattered in the memories and homes of members, some of whom can recall the final years of the Black Methodist Protestant (Colored) Annual Conference. The same is true for Rocky Head, Poplar Springs, and other congregations that were absorbed into the Georgia Conference of the Methodist Church in 1939 and continue as part of the North Georgia Conference of The United Methodist Church.

The Methodist Protestant Church (Colored) in Georgia

The mergers that concluded the history of the Methodist Protestant Church caused the Bethlehem Methodist Protestant Church to become Bethlehem Methodist Church in 1939, and the Bethlehem United Methodist Church after 1968. The Bethlehem congregation, and others in the Georgia movement, had their beginning in the decade of 1870s (or earlier) after the end of what has been termed "Radical Reconstruction" by some historians. The evidence indicates that, from the beginning, the Black congregations of Methodist Protestantism were organized by Black people for Black people, but the "Colored" Methodist Protestant Annual Conference organization was authorized by, and with the assistance of, White people in the Georgia Conference of the Methodist Protestant denomination. Placed in perspective, this was not a unique development, as the other White Methodist bodies and other denominations were "solving their race problem" by forming similar segregated structures.

Despite racial segregation and subordination, some Black people chose to remain in the predominantly White structures of American Methodism. Yet, the tendency was to resist outside organizational control of the type which probably would have been imposed had they truly been part of the Methodist Episcopal Church, the Methodist Episcopal Church, South, or one of the African American Mission/Annual Conferences authorized by the General Conference of the Methodist Episcopal Church in 1864 and 1868.[9] From 1877, when the independent Black Methodist Protestant Conference was organized with the Henry Mission, the Campbellton Circuit, and the Sandy Creek Mission, the matter of autonomy was addressed for Black people who wanted to be Methodist Protestants. At the same time, the matter of maintaining racial segregation was addressed for Whites.

Although relatively small throughout its history over six decades, the African American branch of the Methodist Protestant Church in Georgia was a viable annual conference organization. The Statistical Report of the *Minutes of the Sixth Annual Conference of the Methodist Protestant Church (Colored) for the Georgia District, 1883*, lists the following circuits or congregations:[10]

Circuit/Congregation	Ministers	Preachers	Members	Churches
Rocky Head Circuit	3	1	286	1
Polar Springs Circuit	2	2	3	2
Laual Mission*	–	–	–	–
Palmetto Circuit	1	1	42	1
Sandy Creek Mission	1	1	67	1
Wilkerson Mission	–	2	16	1
Burks Chapel*	–	–	–	–
Barge's Chapel	1	6	26	1
Bethlehem Circuit	3	1	101	2
Mableton Mission*	–	–	–	–
Carroll Circuit	1	3	8	3
Coweta Mission	–	1	31	1
Friendly Hill Mission	1	0	43	2
Henry Mission*	–	–	–	–
Fairburn	–	–	30	–
	13	18	734**	15

* = No statistics reported
** = Actual total is 723. The report shows a total of 734.

In 1885, the statistical report in the *Minutes of the Eighth Session of the Georgia Annual Conference, Methodist Protestant Church (Colored)* gave similar figures to 1883, but with slight increases in some categories and significant increases or grievous errors in others. The increase to 17 churches appears to show slight growth in congregations. The same is true of the 743 members and 29 preachers reported. The jump to 98 ministers may indicate a typographical error:[11]

Circuit/Congregation	Ministers	Preachers	Members	Churches
Bethlehem	2	2	200	2
Wilkerson Mission	2	1	57	2
Palmetto Circuit*	80	1	–	2
Coweta Mission No. 1	2	5	31	1
Poplar Springs	1	4	83	1
White Oak Circuit	1	1	14	2
Jesup Mission	1	3	7	2
Concord Circuit	1	2	79	2
Rocky Head Station	4	1	191	1
Fairburn Circuit	–	1	11	0
Atlanta Mission	2	7	4	2
Coweta Mission No. 2	1	1	45	1
St. Paul Chapel	1	–	23	1
	98	29	745	17

* = Eighty ministers is very likely a typographical error, as is the total of 98. However, it is reported here exactly as it appears in the *Minutes*.

The *Minutes of the Tenth Session of the Georgia Annual Conference of the Methodist Protestant Church (Colored)*, convened in Smith's Chapel, at Ivey's Station, Wilkinson County, October 19, 1887, provides a listing of the location and dates of the first ten annual conference sessions, as shown on the following page.[12]

Virtually no written reports were made with reference to the social, cultural, political, and economic condition of African Americans, located in a segregated Southern state dominated by Whites, in the printed *Minutes* and records of the Methodist Protestant Georgia Annual Conference (Colored). In "post-Reconstruction" Georgia, it was probably the better part of wisdom not to publish statements representing their real attitudes toward racial segregation and subordination in the church and society. Even after the turn of the century and into the 1930s, the pattern persisted of simply reporting on devotions, Scripture titles and hymns, or resolutions pertaining to operations and finance. For example, consider this typical report in the *Minutes of the*

Annual Sessions			
Place	Date	President	Secretary
1. Rockhead*	Oct. 31, 1878	G. N. Barge	J. T. Robison**
2. Bethlehem	Dec. 13, 1879	G. N. Barge	J. T. Robison**
3. Rockhead*	Dec. 9, 1880	G. N. Barge	S. D. Wilson
4. Friendly Hill	Nov. 10, 1881	G. N. Barge	J. W. Whittaker
5. Poplar Springs	Nov. 9, 1882	G. N. Barge	I. C. Robison
6. Atlanta	Nov. 7, 1883	J. T. Robison**	W. E. Spain
7. Macedonia	Nov. 4, 1884	J. T. Robison**	W. E. Spain
8. Atlanta	Nov. 4, 1885	J. T. Robison**	W. E. Spain
9. Campbellton	Nov. 17, 1886	J. T. Robison**	W. E. Spain
10. Smith's Chapel	Oct. 19, 1887	E. Henry	W. E. Spain

* = Several of the Minutes have *Rocky Head* instead of *Rockhead*.
** = The spelling differs in several places; J. T. Robinson is the correct name above.

Fifty-first Session of the Annual Conference of the Methodist Protestant Church (Colored) of Georgia convened at Rocky Head M. P. Church, Ben Hill, November 20–24, 1929:

Friday Night. 7:20 o'clock, Bro. E. L. Green led devotions. Lined Hymns 307 and 312. Bros. J. W. Wheat and J. C. Mangram led in prayer. Revs. C. Mangram and E. L. Hickson ascended the rostrum. Rev. C. Mangram lined Hymn 307. Rev. E. L. Hickson arose and selected the text—Daniel 1st chapter and 8th verse. With much power he demonstrated the work intrusted to him.

Rev. C. Mangram closed, lining hymn 312. The President led in prayer. The stewards came and collected $2.05.

We stood adjourned.[13]

In the same annual conference of 1929, a rather tough resolution was passed regarding the right to hold office or serve as a conference delegate if claims were not paid. The text of the resolution as it was adopted is presented below as reported on p. 10 of the *Minutes*:

Be it resolved, That, seeing the need of more finances in our Church and Conference, if any official belonging to the local church fail [*sic*] to pay his respective claims to the Quarterly or the Sub-District Conference, said member will not be eligible as a delegate to the District Conference, not to the Annual Conference; and also subject to removal from any office.

consolidated by all the delegates of the Fifty-first Annual Conference.[14]

A few general observations need to be made concerning the Methodist Protestant Church (Colored) in Georgia. First, the number of ordained elders who were eligible for conference membership tended to outnumber the missions and circuits that were available for them to serve. It is readily acknowledged that additional study needs to be made of the way ministers were assigned to serve. However, a review of the *Minutes* suggests an indistinct pattern where, in some years, a number of circuits and missions were not assigned to a minister who was a member of the conference and, therefore, had to depend on the services of local preachers or other substitutes. In other years, it appears that the stronger churches or circuits received not only what appeared to be the strongest ordained pastoral leadership, but also the benefit of assistant ministers. It is not clear whether those assistant pastors were ordained members of the Annual Conference or lay preachers. The category of "unstationed ministers" was defined by the practices of the annual conference.

Second, there were typical Methodist concerns and practices that were carefully attended in the Georgia Conference (Colored) of the Methodist Protestant Church. For example, temperance was emphasized in virtually every annual conference session. In the *Minutes of the Thirty-eighth Session of the Georgia Annual Conference of the Methodist Protestant Church Colored, of Georgia* held in Bethlehem Church, Adamsville, November 16–17, 1916, a short report was made that gives insight into the social consciousness of Black Methodist Protestants in Georgia. The following was given under the heading "temperance":

> We, your Committee, beg to report: Seeing how intemperance is dragging our people down, ruining homes and reducing churches, we beg our people to look high and help save our race. Respectfully submitted, Rev. R. B. Butler, Rev. W. H. D. Gilbert, Rev. S. Mayo, James T. Thurmon, W. F. Davis.[15]

In the year 1925, the *Minutes of the Forty-Seventh Session* received the report below from the Committee on Temperance:

> Mr. President and Conference: We, your Committee on Temperance, beg to make this our report:
> We recommend that all ministers, preachers, and members refrain from strong drinks, alcoholic or any habits that point downward. Let them act as becomes the saints of God. Be sober, kind, loving and virtuous, true at home and abroad, that their Christian

loving and virtuous, true at home and abroad, that their Christian influence may win souls and bring them to Christ, and the church will be an edifice and God will bless our labor.

Respectfully submitted, Rev. W. H. White, Rev. J. W. Robinson, T. M. Varner, G. N. Barge, C. W. Williams.[16]

The Temperance Committee was a standing committee of the Annual Conference as set forth in The Rules of Order. The "Rules" for the Ninth Session of the Georgia Methodist Protestant Conference (Colored) were in part stated as follows:

4. All Committees shall be appointed by the President, except when otherwise directed in the Book of Discipline or by special vote of the Conference.

5. Unfinished business—one minister and two laymen.

6. Finance—three ministers and two laymen.

7. Itineracy and Orders—three ministers.

8. Boundaries—seven laymen.

9. Publication of *Minutes*—the Secretary.

10. Temperance—three ministers and two laymen.

11. Official Character—three ministers and two laymen.

12. Statistics—one minister and one layman.[17]

This committee structure was largely maintained throughout the history of the Black Methodist Protestant Conference. Slight variations were made over the years, mainly in terminology, but not function.

Statistics were important enough to merit a Standing Committee in the Annual Conference. The penchant for record keeping was not lost in the "Colored" Protestant Conference of Georgia. A note in the *Minutes of the Sixth Annual Conference*, encouraged the following: "Brethren, please bring in your papers and statistical reports next term more plainly written than they were before; I may be able to make a more correct minute than this is, Yours sincerely, William E. Spain secretary of conference."[18] Despite what appear to be glaring typographical errors and inconsistencies in the *Minutes*, the location of statistical records and data may afford a near complete set of information for the sixty-two years of the Black Methodist Protestant Conference in Georgia.

Education was another continuing concern of the Black Methodist Protestant Conference in Georgia. An education committee was not maintained among the standing committees over the years. Financial concerns with education came often, to which direct responses were made. Support to a theological school is mentioned in several of the conference *Minutes*. The school is not named. A "Literature Committee" is included among the standing committees in the mature years of the Black Methodist Protestant (Colored) Conference. The primary function seems to have been to promote the use of Sunday school and other literature from the Methodist Protestant Publishing Board.

It seems fitting to characterize the cultural agenda as a "split agenda" in the Black Methodist Protestant Conference in Georgia. Such a statement takes into consideration the variety of observable practices and emphases that constituted the way of life for the conference. Temperance was emphasized, as was the case with most Methodist bodies. The same was true for the importance given to maintaining records and statistics, as well as supporting Christian educational endeavors. Each of the three emphases just mentioned had their roots in Methodism and, therefore, represented the deep attachment of African American people in and around Atlanta to values of the Methodist cultural agenda.

There was another agenda in the practices and procedures of Black Methodist Protestants, more subtle, and yet, no less real. That agenda was concerned with survival and accomplishment in times that can only be characterized as hostile for African American people. There were several allusions to things that do detriment to a people, alcoholic beverages and other "habits that point downward." Other matters come to light only when the fuller situation in life is considered. The weight of White racism on Black people was not reflected in the *Minutes* and written records of the Conference. The palpable silence of the conference on what was a critical life and death matter for Black people cried out for recognition.

How, then, was the cultural agenda of Black folk expressed? I maintain that it was expressed in the patterns of worship and praise, in association and development which echoed the work of the antebellum "Invisible Institution" and the "Underground Railroad." Although deradicalized in the Wilmorian sense,[19] the Black Methodist Protestants of Georgia took the opportunity for autonomy and moved on to develop their own organization around some of their vital interests.

Although the content of the worship services and sermons are not available on the written record, the importance of the Bible, preaching, the worship services, conference gatherings and official responsibilities, and to a degree, the caring for the life of the people, is evident in the *Minutes* of each of the conference sessions.

Thus, the split cultural agenda was carried in the full range of experiences of the people, in the Black-ness and the Methodist-ness of the African American people in the Methodist Protestant movement of Georgia.[20]

The Societal Context of Atlanta, the South, and the Nation

The African American quest for autonomy in religion and church organization was not an isolated phenomenon in Atlanta, the South, or the United States of the 1870s. Many intertwining developments characterized the period. Most Black people in the South were scarcely twelve years past the bondage of slavery. Being no strangers to work, African American people had in that short span of time, with their energy and ingenuity, already begun to fuel positive social and economic development. However, many powerful social forces were at work in Atlanta, the South, and the nation during the 1870s when the Black Methodist Protestants were organizing. Some of the forces at work helped, and some hindered progress toward equity and justice for all in the American society. Virtually all of the forces that can be identified were related to pernicious and pervasive racism and efforts to segregate people along the lines of socially constructed understanding of race.

Economy and the Societal Context

There were economic upheavals. The 1870s were depression years. Crippling railroad strikes took place, including the typical interaction between unions and labor, but with the overlay of racism. White hostility toward Black people ballooned out of fear that large numbers of African Americans would enter the work force of the railroad industry.[21] Black people were held in the unskilled ranks and were subject to the most vicious forms of differential treatment in the transportation, manufacturing, food processing, construction, and service industries.[22] The Freedman's Bureau, established by Congress in 1865 gave important assistance to Black freedpersons and poverty-stricken Whites during its seven year existence. Not only did it contribute significantly to the survival of former African American slaves, but it opened the door slightly for compensatory assistance to Black self-reliance in community and economic development.

Politics: Atlanta, the Regional South, and the Nation

In politics, "Reconstruction" failed for African Americans. The supposed gains toward equity were quickly negated and reversed. The election of Rutherford B. Hayes as president of the United States and subsequent withdrawal of federal troops from the South, the eventual relaxation of other restraints on the South, such as supervision of elections, ended all prospect of freedom, justice, and peace in a reconstruction of the federal union.[23] Disenfranchisement of Black people, the institutionalization of Jim Crow, a surge in lynching and brutal riots and attacks on Black people and other atrocities became the order of the day.

Education in American Society

The impact of the economy and polity had expected impact on other institutions such as education. The first Atlanta public school system was fully operational by 1873.[24] This had little meaning for Black citizens as elementary or higher education was not available to most African Americans. Atlanta University was chartered as a center of higher education for Black students in 1867. It was already clear that alternative institutions for the education of Black people had to be developed.

The Freedman's Aid Society of the Methodist Episcopal Church began to establish schools and colleges immediately after the Civil War and within 18 months of its start on November 1, 1866, had directly assisted in establishing 59 schools in the South.[25] Among the colleges established or moved to Atlanta were Morehouse (1867), and Clark University (1869; later Clark College, and now Clark Atlanta University). Twenty-two of the historically Black colleges were organized during the decade of the 1870s; all of them were located in the South.[26]

Religion and the Churches: Institutions of the Society

Religious institutions and other voluntary associations afford significant cultural data about a society. They variously influenced and were influenced by the larger social reality. Most of the American Protestant churches danced around the race issue and compromised by organizing separate structures, often to accommodate the demands of the Southern churches.

A number of "Colored" church denominations emerged during the Reconstruction era. The Cumberland Presbyterian (Colored) body was organized in 1869, at Murfreesboro, Tennessee with its first synod in 1871, and first general assembly in 1874. Similar organizations were formed for the Regular Baptists (Colored) and the Congregational Methodist (Colored) groups. The "Colored Methodist Episcopal Church" was organized in Jackson, Tennessee, in 1870.[27] These churches, along with movements such as the Black Convention Movement, continued to attract African Americans from all over to grapple with questions of how to respond to the significant religio-political agenda of the times. The impetus to get organized was occasioned by the need to survive; to throw off exploitation; to foster associations and organizations that Black people would direct and control; and the development of Black interests and resources in a depressed and racist economic climate.

The General Conference of the Methodist Episcopal Church again extended its compromise with racial segregationists by voting to authorize mission conferences (1864) and later annual conferences (1868) for African Americans. No fewer that 11 mission conferences were formed in the middle to the late 1860s including the Georgia Mission Conference, October 10, 1867.[28] Five mission conferences were formed during the decade of the 1870s.[29] The formation of mission conferences in the Methodist Episcopal Church and in the Methodist Protestant Church is evidence of a continuing trend toward forming independent and racially segregated Black structures in Methodist bodies.

In fact, the Southern White Methodist Protestants were not appreciably different from the Methodist Episcopal Church, South, with reference to race. Before the Civil War the White Methodist Protestants approved eloquent statements about the evils of slavery, but there is precious little in the extant records about genuine action to oppose slave-holding among ordained ministers or the lay members of local churches.[30] Likewise, in the post-war period, when separation characterized the law and etiquette of race relations, one could hear the pronouncements but see little by way of direct and uncompromising action in opposition to patterns of racial segregation after "emancipation" of the slaves and "reconstruction" of the Union.

Perhaps the same resistance would have been present had the White Methodist Protestant Church in Georgia defied the law and conventional etiquette of race relations during that period and included Black clergy, lay persons, and congregations in the larger Methodist Protestant movement in Georgia.[31] An interpretive reading of the history of the period suggests that the "Colored" people would have had precious little control over, or participation in, the White conference organization had they been included.

Among other possibilities, then, the Black Methodist Protestant conferences functioned to provide African Americans, who did not choose to join one of the other African Methodist protest and independence movements, with organizational structures that they controlled. They, too, were the precursors of the Central Jurisdiction which came with the 1939 merger of the Methodist Protestant and two Episcopal bodies which resulted in The Methodist Church.

Racial separation, the Jim Crow laws, and the tendency of White people to discount the value of Black organizations and Black people were, no doubt, strong contributing factors in the social movement of Black people to organize their own congregations and still participate in the larger Methodist Protestant movement concerning the issues of lay representation and the episcopacy. Whites in Georgia generally sanctioned the efforts of Blacks to start their own organizations, that is, as long as those organizations were separate and deemed not to threaten the cultural ethos and prevailing social arrangement among the socially defined races of Black and White people.

The self-identification of a little band of Black congregations in Georgia with the Methodist Protestant Church in the states of the Deep South raises interesting questions. Had African Americans, so soon after the end of slavery and in the throes of "reconstruction," renewed the dream of viable participation in the churches without respect to the social distortions of race? What were the similarities in the protest of Black people and that of White people? Although the protest agenda of White Methodist Protestants was relatively clear, was there a significant hidden agenda of Black people in taking on the organizational identity of Methodist Protestants? Did the Black clergy leaders manipulate the Methodist Protestant agenda for political gain? Why was there virtually no explicit protest by Black Methodist Protestants against the "mission conference" status given to them by the General and Annual Conferences of the Methodist Protestant Church?

The presence and work of the Methodist Protestant Church in the Deep South was itself an interesting aspect of Methodist religious history. The issue of race coexisted all along with the central issues of Methodist Protestantism. The opposition to slavery consumed considerable energy in the pre-Civil War Methodist Protestant General Conferences, yet, a spirit of compromise was always strong for the sake of the unity of the Methodist Protestant organization. One need only scan the *Proceedings of the General Conference of the Methodist Protestant Church, 1858*, to get a flavor of the tension occasioned by the issue of race.[32]

Although the predominantly White Methodist Protestant conferences were viable entities in the southeastern and southcentral regions of the United States, the strongest areas of the movement were in the mid-Atlantic region and the Midwest. The conferences of those two regions held the strongest position against slavery, and after the Civil War, opposed segregation. They also compromised, time and again, with the Southern contingent, in order to preserve harmony and unity in the church.

Concluding Summary

Set within all of the cultural, social, political, and economic currents of the times, the Black Methodist Protestant Church (Colored) of Georgia came into being. While it functioned in some very important ways to enhance the lives of it members, it also dysfunctioned in some regards by using critical resources in practices and operations which were more deadly than life-sustaining. The Methodist Protestant Church (Colored) of Georgia was not a unique institution within Methodism or among the denominational churches. It was almost predictable given the need of Black people for autonomy and the persistent desire of the majority of White people for a racially segregated church and living context.

CHAPTER 14

The Transmission of Faith
to Young African American Children

Janice E. Hale

We've come this far by faith,
Leaning on the Lord;
Trusting in his Holy Word,
He's never failed us yet.
Oh, can't turn around
We've come this far by faith.

—African American gospel song
by Albert G. Goodson

Any study of faith in young Black children must flow from an analysis of the development of faith in African American culture. In order to understand faith in African American culture, we must explore and analyze the roots of African American culture in general, and we must consider the religious experience of African Americans by beginning with the African heritage. In this essay, I will trace the core of values that characterize African American culture. These values, which are inextricably bound to the Black religious tradition, had their genesis in the African heritage, but were shaped by the common experience of American slavery. I will identify the ways in which this perspective of faith has been transmitted to Black children generation after generation through the oral tradition, and show how it is active in the cosmology of contemporary African Americans.

Jack Daniel and Geneva Smitherman[1] make the point that a traditional African worldview colors the culture of African Americans. Even though they acknowledge differences in the many tribes, languages, customs, physiognomies, spirits, and deities that exist throughout the African continent, these are only surface variations on the deep structure themes that characterize traditional African culture.

Leonard Barrett[2] makes the point that there is documentation that West Africa in the fifteenth century, before the entrance of the Europeans, had already passed through several centuries of cultural development and had reached a stage comparable to the most developed countries of Europe of that period. This development was evident in all areas of human expression, but was most important in the religious system of Africa.

Barrett maintains that the African traditional religion was the motivating force of all African peoples and it continued to be expressed by Africans in bondage. "The slave master was able to claim the body of the slave, but the worldview of the African was nurtured in his soul, and his soul was impregnable."[3] This was expressed in the spiritual, "Jordan river, chilly and cold, chills the body not the soul." Indeed, as C. Eric Lincoln states, "it was mainly their dynamic and pragmatic religion which helped the slaves survive in their new environment."[4]

Barrett describes the African worldview as being dynamic:

> The universe is a vast system consisting of God, the supreme power who created it, spirits and powers who rule over every aspect of this creation, and, at the center [humans]. All things below [humans], all lower biological life was created for [humans], and the inanimate things serve [humans] also.[5]

The whole system is alive, as presented by Barrett, because it is energized by a spiritual force that emanates from the Supreme Being. Human being depends upon maintaining a harmonious relationship between humanity, God, and nature.

However, Africans do not conceive of the world as a place in which to contemplate life; they see it as an arena for activity. Barrett makes the point that the African's aim is to live strongly. Prayers are for long life, health, and prosperity; the strengthening of family, clan, and tribe because each person lives through them. The ancestors are the guardians of posterity, and human beings are heavily dependent upon them for all aspects of life.

Barrett judges that the pragmatism in the African worldview finds its greatest expression in African folklore and proverbs. The main theme of the folktales is the will to survive in adverse conditions. Here we find the ever-recurring theme of the weak against the strong, and here the stress is on cunning, craftiness, and speed. These folktales gained new significance in the slavery of the New World because they contained the collective wisdom of the African people.[6] Barrett points out that the worldview of Africa is above all life affirming:

194

In them we find instructions for the preservation of life, leading a moral life, living cautiously, loving God, and holding respect for the aged, as well as the wisdom of gratitude and the beauty of temperance.[7]

The slaves brought with them to the New World the wisdom of their forbears. The African culture they brought laid the foundation for the African American culture that was transmitted to their descendants. Barrett affirms that "this worldview found expression in the spirituals, music, dance, and the general life-style of later generations who came to be known as African Americans."[8]

Lawrence Levine[9] points out that retention of traditional African beliefs and practices was facilitated by the delay that occurred in the conversion of the African slaves to Christianity. There was considerable debate for over two hundred years among Whites as to whether to give their religion to their bondsmen. They were afraid that freedom would result from baptism and that time for labor would be lost, given the fact that labor was prohibited on Sunday in the Christian tradition. They also feared that the slaves would develop notions of religious equality.

This vacillation on the part of the slaveholders, in Levine's view, required the slaves to accommodate their African religious beliefs and practices to the demands of the harsh economic and social system they found themselves in. Accommodation was necessary because of the suppression of their freedom to worship in traditional ways, an example of which was the prohibition against using the drum. When conversion did come, it was not at the expense of the slave's prevalent folk beliefs.

In fact, Levine makes the point that there were numerous points of intersection between the beliefs of the African and those of people from other European countries who held beliefs that the slaves could adopt or adapt without doing essential violence to their own worldview. "The African practices and beliefs which had the best chance of survival in the New World were those that had European analogues, as so many of the folk beliefs did."[10]

The concept of faith is particularly germane to this discussion because there is an inextricable relationship between magic, medicine, religion, and faith. Faith is particularly strong when a people feel a lack of control over their existence. Levine points out that the absence of power helped to perpetuate the slaves' sacred universe and to intensify their search for supernatural aid and solutions. As Bronislaw Malinowski put the point:

We find magic wherever the elements of chance and accident, and the emotional play between hope and fear have a wide and extensive range. We do not find magic wherever the pursuit is certain, reliable and well under the control of rational methods and technological processes. Further, we find magic where the element of danger is conspicuous.[11]

In Levine's view, the slave's magical folk beliefs were a central and necessary part of existence. They stood beside his Christian myths and supplemented and fortified them. Both were sources of strength and release. They served to preserve their sanity. Christianity assured them that the present condition eventually would change and that retribution would come in this world and in the next. It also reinforced their feelings of dignity and self-worth. Their folk beliefs provided hope and a sense of group identification, but also provided the slaves sources of power and knowledge that were alternative to those existing in the master class.

These beliefs that were closely associated with magic and faith in the religious realm were also expressed in medical practices as well. Levine points out that

while slaves acknowledged the medical care extended to them by their masters—"Our white folks was good as dey knowed to be when us got sick," Callie Elder testified—there is evidence that in doctoring, as in preaching, slaves frequently distrusted the whites and preferred their own doctors and remedies.[12]

In his book *Black Self-Determination: A Cultural History of the Faith of the Fathers*, V. P. Franklin[13] argues that the shared experience of slavery served as the foundation for the "cultural value system" that was handed down from the Africans to their American-born offspring, the African Americans. His book is a cultural history of the experiences that formulated the African American cultural value system in the United States. Franklin utilizes

the testimony and narratives of enslaved and free African Americans from the end of the eighteenth century to the beginning of the twentieth, as well as African American folk songs, beliefs and religious practices, in an attempt to provide a viable explanation of the meaning and significance of self-determination, freedom, resistance and education in the lives and experiences of the masses of African Americans in this society.[14]

There is implicit agreement among scholars[15] that analysis of constructs such as faith as they are expressed in African American culture can only be properly understood when their genesis is studied in the context of slavery. Central in the religious expressions of the slaves were the spirituals. C. Eric Lincoln (1974) wrote:

> Blacks feel more deeply than do others, and it is that broader, deeper spirituality which has enabled black people to endure. The spirituals are songs, prayers, praises and sermons. They have been mistakenly derided by those who cannot distinguish between the experience of slavery and the creative genius of a people in spite of slavery.[16]

John Wesley Work, writing in 1915, summarized the essence of the spiritual in the culture of the slave poetically: in the minds of Negroes their

> music has held and still holds, positions of variable importance. In the darkness of bondage, it was [their] light; in the morn of [their] freedom, it was [their] darkness, but as the day advances, and [they are] being gradually lifted up into a higher life, it is becoming not only [their] proud heritage, but a support and powerful inspiration. The songs of the slave were [their] sweet consolation and his messages to Heaven, bearing sorrow, pain, joy, prayer, and adoration. Undisturbed and unafraid, [they] could always unburden [their] hearts in these simple songs, pregnant with faith, hope and love.[17]

Franklin observes that African Americans created their own version of Christianity. The southern plantation encompassed two worlds, one the master's and one the slave's. "The gospel of the oppressor taught obedience and submission, and it was rejected by the enslaved. The gospel of the oppressed spoke of freedom, the ultimate justice of God, and His support for His chosen people."[18] Levine notes that not only did slaves believe that they were the chosen people of God, but there is evidence that many felt that their owners would be denied salvation. He cites the story told of a slave's reaction to the news that he would be rewarded by being buried in the same vault with his master: "Well massa, one way I am satisfied, and one way I am not. I like to have good coffin when I die (but) I fraid, massa, when the debbil come take you body, he make mistake, and get mine."[19]

Features of the Slave Religion

There are certain themes identified by Levine as characterizing the religion of the slaves that inform our study of faith in the contemporary African American community.

(1) The God of whom the slaves sang was neither remote not abstract, but as intimate, personal, and immediate as the gods of Africa had been: "O when I talk, I talk with God"; "Mass Jesus is my bosum

friend"; "I'm goin' to walk with (talk with, live with, see) King Jesus by myself, by myself "; these were refrains that echoed through the spirituals.[20]

(2) Descriptions of the Crucifixion communicate a sense of the actual presence of the singers: "Dey pierced Him in the side . . . Dey nail Him to the cross . . . Dey rivet His feet . . . Dey hanged Him high . . . Dey stretched Him wide. . . ." "Oh sometimes it causes me to tremble, tremble, tremble, Were you there when they crucified my Lord."[21]

(3) The slave's Bible was constructed primarily from the books of Moses in the Old Testament and of Revelation in the New. All that lay between, even the life of Jesus, they rarely cared to read or hear. The lives of Daniel, David, Joshua, Jonah, Moses, and Noah struck the imagination of the slaves because they experienced deliverance in this world. Over and over their songs dwelt upon the spectacle of the Red Sea opening to allow the Hebrew slaves past before inundating the mighty armies of Pharaoh. They lingered delightedly upon the image of little David humbling great Goliath with a stone—a pre-technological victory which postbellum Negroes were to expand upon in their songs of John Henry. They retold in endless variations the stories of the blind and humbled Samson bringing down the mansions of his conquerors; of the ridiculed Noah patiently building the ark which would deliver him from the doom of a mocking world; of the timid Jonah attaining freedom from his confinement through faith.[22] The parallels between these Old Testament figures and their plight as slaves was clear. Levine notes that in "O my Lord delivered Daniel," the slaves observed and responded logically, "O why not deliver me, too?"

> He delivered Daniel from de lion's den,
> Jonah from de belly ob de whale,
> And de Hebrew children from de fiery furnace,
> And why not every man?[23]

(4) Although Jesus was omnipresent in the spirituals, it was not the Jesus of the New Testament of whom the slaves sang. He was Jesus transformed into an Old Testament warrior—"Mass Jesus" who engaged in personal combat with the devil; "King Jesus" seated on a milk-white horse with sword and shield in hand—"Ride on, King Jesus," "Ride on conquering King," "The God I serve is a man of war."[24]

This Old Testament and New Testament Jesus was eventually merged with Black Theology in the 1960s. James Cone, in *Black Theology and Black Power*,[25] declared that "Jesus is God [Godself] coming into the very depths of human existence for the sole purpose of striking off the chains of slavery, thereby freeing [humankind] from ungodly principalities and powers that hinder [their] relationship with God." Jesus' definition of his ministry in Luke 4:18 is important here:

> If God is omnipotent and in control of human history, how can God's goodness be reconciled with human servitude? If God has the power to deliver black people from the evil of slavery as he delivered Moses from Pharaoh's army, Daniel from the lion's den, and the Hebrew children from the fiery furnace, why then are black slaves still subject to the rule of white masters?[26]

Cone argues that the slaves do not really question the justice and goodness of God. They affirm that God is righteous and will vindicate the poor and the weak. The singers of the spirituals are concerned about the faithfulness of the community in a world full of trouble. They do not wonder about whether God is just and right; they are concerned that the sadness and pain of the world will cause them to lose faith in the gospel of God.

The slaves faced the reality of the world, "ladened wid trouble, an' burden'd wid grief," but they believed that they could go to Jesus and get relief. They appealed to Jesus not so much to remove the trouble, (although they wanted it removed), but to keep them from "sinkin' down":

> Oh, Lord, Oh, My Lord!
> Oh, My Good Lord! Keep me from sinkin' down.
> Oh, Lord, Oh My Lord!
> Oh, My Good Lord! Keep me from sinkin' down.[27]

The songs of the slaves affirmed the knowledge that "trouble don't last always." They also sang, "Sometimes I feel like a motherless child, A long way from home"; but as Cone notes, they were confident that Jesus was with them and had not left them completely alone.[28]

A preoccupation in the spirituals seemed to be, according to Cone, the threat that the present realities of despair and loneliness would disrupt the community of faith. They feared the agony of being alone in a world of hardship and pain.

> I couldn't hear nobody pray,
> Oh, I couldn't hear nobody.
> Oh, way down yonder by myself,
> And I couldn't hear nobody pray.[29]

199

The spirituals lamented the loss of community and felt that this constituted the major burden. They felt that the suffering was not too much to bear if you had brothers and sisters to go down in the valley and pray with you.

Cone notes further that there were not direct attacks upon God in the spirituals. If the slaves truly believed that God was in control of history, why were they silent about God's neglect to end slavery? The answer is that not all slaves had an unquestioning faith in God. Cone and Levine identify open rebellion against God that is exemplified in secular music (the blues). Sterling Brown reports that blacks sang:

> I don't want to ride no golden chariot;
> I don't want no golden crown;
> I want to stay down here and be,
> Just as I am without one plea.

They also sang:

> Our father, who is in heaven,
> White man owe me eleven and pay me seven,
> Thy kingdom come, they will be done,
> And if I hadn't took that, I wouldn't had none.[30]

Cone analyzes that the "theological assumption of Black slave religion as expressed in the spirituals was that slavery contradicts God and that he will therefore liberate Black people".[31] The slaves were keenly aware of their oppression and lack of freedom. However, they felt that the same God who delivered the Israelites would deliver them. A central theme in Black slave religion and in the development of faith was of God's involvement in history and God's liberation of the oppressed in bondage. When the slaves sang:

> Sometimes I'm up, sometimes I'm down,
> Oh, yes, Lord!
> Sometimes I'm almost to the ground,
> Oh, yes, Lord!

they were exemplifying the fact that God was always with them and that "trouble would not have the last word."[32]

Cone contends that the slaves knew that God was in control and would liberate them. This was expressed when they sang:

> Do, Lord, remember me.
> Do, Lord, remember me.
> When I'm in trouble,
> Do, Lord, remember me.

When I'm low down,
Do, Lord, remember me.
Oh, when I'm low down,
Do, Lord, remember me.[33]

Transmission of Faith Through the Oral Tradition

We come now to the central issue of this paper, which is the transmission of faith to young children. I have chosen to approach this process from the perspective of the transmission of faith through the culture rather than from the perspective of development of faith in young children. It is almost so obvious that it is unnecessary to point out that there is virtually no empirical or conceptual literature to guide this inquiry. The process of faith development in Black children must await empirical investigations, but I hope the themes developed here might assist more comprehensive studies. In the previous section we reviewed the substance of the religion of African Americans that shaped the expression of faith. In this section, we will examine the mechanisms by which that faith was transmitted to each succeeding generation.

Ella Mitchell[34] has outlined the cultural vehicles that enabled the slaves and freedmen to transmit cultural values that included faith. She marveled as a child over the eloquent exegesis of her two grandmothers, who made magnificent comments on the Bible. She wondered how they could have gleaned such insights, being barely literate, not having had the benefit of a printed curriculum or trained church school teachers. She grew to understand that the oral tradition in Black culture had been the vehicle for absorption of religious insights. This point coincides with one made by Levine when he pointed out that even when literate, the slaves favored the songs and prayers from their oral tradition over those contained in hymn and prayer books:

> When Baptist Negroes attended the church of their masters, or when their mistress sang with them, they used hymn books, but their own meetings they often made up their own words and tunes. They said their songs had more religion than those in the books.[35]

Mitchell points out that the slaves found it necessary to make adaptations in their traditional ways of communicating because of the oppression of slavery. Drumming was suppressed, for example. However, the descendants of Africa had a wide variety of cultural vehicles for transmitting their culture.

Storytelling was an extremely lively and popular art form used in teaching. The story that was written by Alex Haley into his best-selling book *Roots* is an example of the way important historical information was transmitted intergenerationally through the oral tradition.[36] Audience participation was expected and the stories were enlivened by the mixing in of poetry and music, and even dance and drumming. These performances might serve any number of very practical functions, "such as a dispute to be settled, a bargain to be driven, a child to be corrected, or a friend to be advised of the error of his/her ways. To say nothing of work made easier by singing, and fields thus converted into classrooms with 'live entertainment.' "[37]

Proverbs were a poetic art form with poetic beauty. They peppered spontaneous discussions and served as pearls of wisdom for the survival of the extended family/tribal unit. Mitchell stresses that there was no way of escaping this ingenious educational system because the children were surrounded by the lessons of their ancestors, dead and living in such a natural way that they did not recognize it as a lesson! Traditional African religious gatherings were forbidden, and the authorized worship that was supervised by the slaveholders was so unsatisfying that the slaves went underground to worship authentically. Likewise, they developed instructional and socializing techniques for their children that were difficult to squelch. Mitchell points out that parents were required to work from "can to cain't" (sunup to sundown) so the task of transmitting the culture fell to the elderly grandparents who cared for and taught the small children too young to work: "until they were large enough to work, there was plenty of time to listen to tales and take advantage of the peak learning years."[38] When the children went to the fields, their education into the culture continued with the singing of spirituals and work songs and the telling of stories, proverbs, and folktales.

There was no effort on the part of the slaveholders to control the activity in the cabins after sundown. This was a period of time that the slave could use for reading the Bible or, when that was impossible because of illiteracy, telling stories and transmitting meaning and comfort. Mitchell points to the numerous slave narratives that "attest to the fact that slave children were exceptionally well trained in devious ways of coping with masters, and in Bible wisdom, prayer, and trust."[39]

An important aspect of the slave child rearing system that is described by Mitchell was closely shared living or enforced intimacy. This was very analogous to the intimacy of the small African village. She points out that the belief system of African Americans was more "caught than taught." Thus, slave children got their cues for coping by watching their parents and other significant adults at very close range. They were together in cotton and corn fields, in small cabins and in the highly restricted life of the slave quarter. Persons were so close that, blood relations or no, one had to treat all as persons and indeed as kin. Training for coping with tragic mistreatment was thus handed down most effectively with no formal instruction, but lots of casual oral communication.[40]

Self-esteem is another value that is closely related to faith and that was taught and learned in the intimacy of the slavery experience. Mitchell points out that "the lesson was learned so well that despite the ravages of dehumanization, very few slaves ever gave up and fully accepted the servile image thrust upon them."[41] Even though there was precious little time for any adult save the elderly to spend with them, love was lavished on babies and children. As John W. Blassingame notes:

> Since slave parents were primarily responsible for training their children, they could cushion the shock of bondage for them, help them understand their situation, teach them values different from those their masters tried to instill in them, and give them a referent for self-esteem other than their master.[42]

Mitchell correctly stresses that the message of self-respect and psychic survival could not be communicated openly. However, her "caught-not-taught" process was especially useful. Casual conversation and example could quietly nourish healthy self awareness in the hearts of even the youngest children."[43]

Another important contextual variable in the life of the slave that Mitchell highlights is the power of messages between children, parents, and other adults because of the urgency of the situation. Children learned early that they were surrounded by danger and potential death. "The gravity of their plight was obvious, and slave parents dared not try to protect their offspring from hard reality. The best evidence of this fact is the sophistication among small children in dealing with situations where survival was at stake."[44] The stereotype of slave children as happy-go-lucky is entirely false.

A happier aspect of slave child rearing that Mitchell describes was the more typical formal religious instruction. Whether the slaves could read or not, Bible teaching was the closest thing they could get to formal training. Such training was regarded not only as spiritual food, but also as a means of uplift and improvement of their condition. Franklin has identified the drive toward education as a key cultural value in the minds of African Americans as illustrated in the following folk song:

> When I done been 'deemed en done been tried,
> I'll sit down side de lamb.
> Can't you read? Can't you read?
> When I done been ter heaven den,
> I can read my title clean.
> I's goin' ter git my lesson,
> I's goin' ter read,
> I's goin' ter read my title clean.[45]

In a similar fashion, W. E. B. DuBois argued at the turn of the century that:

> We believe in work. We ourselves are workers, but work is not necessarily education. Education is the development of power and ideal. We want our children trained as intelligent human beings should be and will fight against any proposal to educate black boys and girls simply as servants and underlings, or simply for the use of other people. They have the right to know, to think, to aspire.[46]

The unifying thread in the vehicles of socialization that Mitchell describes is the oral tradition brought to the New World from Africa. Stories such as the Br'er Rabbit stories were told to socialize Black children in how to outfox a system that was oppressing them. The Br'er Rabbit stories were told to prepare Black children to survive the hardships of life in America. The oral tradition continued to transmit Black culture even after emancipation. The enforced intimacy of slavery did not change dramatically under sharecropping or even urban living for the freedmen. There was a new emphasis on formal living for the freedmen. There was a new emphasis on formal education: reading, writing, and arithmetic. However, as Mitchell points out,

> this latter did not take the place of the oral tradition in the deeper matters of how to cope in oppression and the development of an adequate belief system. In fact, formal education itself was often fused or blended with oral traditional forms of instruction in many creative ways.[47]

The Proverb Tradition in Socializing African American Children

While there is no attempt to argue that proverbs are exclusively found in African and African American culture, they are in keeping with a very strong African tradition. Jack Daniel[48] points out that many

204

African scholars have observed that the proverb is perhaps the richest and most plentiful literary device found in Africa. Proverbs have served to preserve religious principles and transmit folk wisdom across generations. As Daniel states:

> There is practically no such thing as a traditional African child who has not been raised on a steady diet of what "they say." And throughout Black America, there are many Blacks who use these old saying to help raise their children by giving oral summations of life's many lessons.[49]

The suggestion is made here that important folk wisdom about faith is transmitted to Black children through proverbs that helps them make sense out of the universe and achieve a sense of serenity as they must cope with events that they cannot control.

Daniel and Smitherman have identified five significant areas for the analysis of proverbs:

1. Proverbs are an index of cultural continuity and integration.
2. Proverbs are significant in the socialization process—how do Black parents utilize proverbs to guide the thought and action of their children in a hostile environment, in contradistinction to other child-rearing practices?
3. Proverbs are central to mental development and abstract thinking and reasoning—training in proverbs can supplement formal education, particularly in the area of critical thinking.
4. Proverbs are significant rhetorical devices in arguments, debates, verbal dueling, and other interaction contracts where persuasion and manipulation of the rhetorical situations are paramount.
5. Proverbs are indices of cultural assimilation.[50]

Following are examples of proverbs compiled by Daniel[51] that transmit wisdom that are pertinent to faith. These are gleaned from hundreds of proverbs that address a wide range of subjects. They are given in the categories assigned by Daniel:

Human Control and Responsibility

The more you stir mess, the more it stinks; If you fall, don't wallow; If we send no ships out, no ships will come in; If you don't climb the mountain, you can't view the plain; If you can't take it, you can't make it; If you can't stand the heat, get out of the kitchen; Take life as you find it, but don't leave it the same; Games can't be won unless they are played; When things get tough, remember that it's the rubbing that brings out the shine; Where there's a will there's a way; Stumbling blocks may be carved into stepping stones; and, Necessity is the mother of invention.

Natural Relationships

What is done in the dark will come to light; The darkest hour is just before the dawn; A place for everything, and everything in its place; Where there is smoke, there is fire; What goes around, comes around; What goes up must come down; Cream rises to the top; A little light in a dark place can serve a large purpose; Every dog will have [its] day.

The Inevitability of the Good with the Bad

You must take the bitter with the sweet; Life is not a bed of roses; Every good thing has to come to an end; You can't be the salt of the earth without smarting some; Easy come, easy go; You can't eat your cake and have it too; You have to crawl before you walk; Things that are hard to bear are sweet to remember; Into each life some rain must fall; and, Games can't be won unless they are played.

Faith Taught by the Hero/Heroine in Black Children's Folktales and Literature

An important source of faith to Black children is found in folktales and children's literature that socializes Black children to achieve power in the midst of a powerless community. The Br'er Rabbit story stars an animal trickster with clear parallels between his and the fox's status and that of the slave and the slaveholder. There are also numerous folktales that star the slave as trickster.

Additionally, there is a body of literature that features heroes from the fictional John Henry to Harriet Tubman, who led over 300 Blacks from slavery to freedom, to Joe Louis who stood up to society and refused to accept the "place" reserved for African Americans. A vast amount of literature geared to Black children falls into the contributionism category. This literature tells the stories of real life Black heroes and heroines such as Jackie Robinson, Marian Anderson, and Booker T. Washington, who emerged from humble beginnings, suffered racial indignities, but managed to triumph and become achievers.

These stories transmit the message to Black children that there is a great deal of quicksand and many land mines on the road to becoming a Black achiever in America. However, they also transmit the message that it is possible to overcome these obstacles. These stories help Black children de-personalize oppression when they encounter it and enable them to place their personal difficulties into the context of the overall Black liberation struggle.

It was my contention that it is the proverbs, the folktales and more recently, the heroes and heroines that are taught during the Black History celebrations that keep Black children grounded in the African American tradition of faith. A key to the African American notion of faith is its importance in facilitating survival. Nowhere in African American literature is the notion of survival through faith transmitted more effectively than in the classic poem by Langston Hughes:

> Well son, I'll tell you:
> Life for me ain't been no crystal stair.
> It's had tacks in it,
> And splinters,
> And boards torn up,
> And places with no carpet on the floor—
> Bare.
> But all the time
> I'se been a-climbin' on,
> And reachin' landin's
> And turnin' corners,
> And sometimes goin' in the dark
> Where there ain't been no light.
> So, boy, don't turn back.
> Don't you set down on the steps.
> 'Cause you finds it kinder hard.
> Don't you fall now—
> For I'se still goin', honey.
> I'se still climbin',
> And life for me ain't been no crystal stair.[52]

CHARLES B. COPHER

Curriculum Vitae

Education

1947	Ph.D., Boston University Graduate School, Boston, MA
1941	B.D., Oberlin Graduate School of Theology, Oberlin, OH
1939	B.D., Gammon Theological Seminary, Atlanta, GA
1938	A.B., Clark College, Atlanta, GA

Professional Career

1978—	Professor Emeritus and Lecturer in Ancient Black Biblical Studies, Interdenominational Theological Center
1972–1978	Vice President for Academic Affairs, Interdenominational Theological Center
1968–1984	Member, The Judicial Council, The United Methodist Church
1948–1978	Professor of Old Testament Studies and Dean of Instruction, Interdenominational Theological Center
1942–1948	Pastor, Fourth Methodist (now Union) United Methodist Church, Boston, MA
1941–1942	Pastor, Eleventh Street (now Asbury) United Methodist Church, Columbus, OH
1939–1941	Pastor, Rust Methodist Church, Oberlin, OH

Selected Bibliography

Dissertation

"Isaiah's Philosophy of History" (Ph.D. dissertation, Boston University Graduate School, 1947).

Books, Articles, and Essays

Black Biblical Studies: An Anthology of Charles B. Copher (Chicago: Black Light Fellowship, 1993).
"The Black Presence in the Old Testament," in *Stony The Road We Trod*, ed. Cain Hope Felder (Minneapolis: Fortress Press, 1991), 146–64.

"The Bible and the African Experience: The Biblical Period," *The Journal of the Interdenominational Theological Center* 16 (1988), 32–50.

"Biblical Characters, Events, Places and Images Remembered and Celebrated in Black Church Worship," *The Journal of the Interdenominational Theological Center* 14 (1986), 75–86.

"Three Thousand Years of Biblical Interpretation with Reference to Black Peoples," *The Journal of the Interdenominational Theological Center* 13 (1986), 225–46.

"Egypt and Ethiopia in the Old Testament," *The Journal of African Civilization* 6 (1984), 163–78.

"Blacks and Jews in Historical Interaction: The Biblical/African Experience," *The Journal of the Interdenominational Theological Center* 3 (1975), 9–16.

"The Black Man in the Biblical World," *The Journal of the Interdenominational Theological Center* 1 (1974), 7–16.

"Perspectives and Questions: The Black Religious Experience and Biblical Studies," *Theological Education* 6 (1970), 181–88.

"Abishag," *Encyclopedia Britannica*, 1964 Edition.

"Brotherhood of Man, Fatherhood of God," *Together* (February, 1962), 45–77.

"The Biblical Position of Race: Presumed Positions; Revelations of Investigations; The Way Out and the Destination" (three lectures), Columbus, Ohio: *Ohio Methodist Interracial Conference Report* (April 2, 3, 4, 1959), 68ff.

"The Bible and the Christian Faith," *Child Guidance In Christian Living* 17 (1958), 1.

"The Theological Basis for Human (Race) Relations," *Report of Interracial Leadership Conference*, Wesley Memorial Church, Atlanta, GA (January 28–29, 1957), 21–25.

"All Men Are Brothers," *Christian Advocate* 131 (1956), 10–11.

"My Sabbatical Year," *The Foundation* 46 (1956), 13ff.

"The Figure of the Shepherd," *The Foundation* 44 (1954), 32.

"My Six Weeks in Israel," *The Foundation* 44 (1954), 7.

"Books in the Field of Old Testament for the Christian Minister," *The Foundation* 41 (1951), 12–14.

"Isaiah's Faith and Ours," *The Foundation* 41 (1951), 4–5.

"Boston and the Negro," *The Central Christian Advocate* (March 18, 1948), 184(8)–185(9).

"Ministers of Christ in an Age of Crisis," *The Foundation* 38 (1948), 4–7.

"Why I Should Know and What I Should Know About Tuberculosis," *The Foundation* 29 (1939), 13–17.

"Every Christian a Missionary," *The Foundation* 27 (1937), 7–8.

"The Christian Missionary: A Needed Pioneer in Our Modern World," *The Foundation* 25 (1935), 17–18.

Book Reviews

The Everlasting Covenant: Content and Value of the Old Testament, by H. R. Weaver, *The Church School* 19 (1965), 33.

The Latter Prophets, by T. Henshaw, *The Journal of Bible and Religion* 28 (1959), 346.

Discovering Buried Worlds, by A. Parrot, *The Foundation* 47(1957), 22.

The Messianic Idea in Israel: From Its Beginning to the Completion of the Mishnah, by J. Klausner, *The Journal of Bible and Religion* 25 (1957), 63.

The Old Testament Since the Reformation, by E. G. Kraeling, *The Pastor* 19 (1956), 41.

The Book of Daniel, ed. J. A. Bewer, *The Journal of Bible and Religion* 24 (1956), 68.

The Messianic Idea in Israel: From Its Beginning to the Completion of the Mishnah, by J. Klausner, *The Foundation* 45 (1955), 18.

The Book of Ezekiel, ed. J. A. Bewer, Vol. 1, Chapters 21–24; Vol. 11, Chapters 25–48, *The Journal of Bible and Religion* 23 (1955), 143.

The Development of Negro Religion, by R. Johnston, *The Foundation* 45 (1955), 23.

Mercy and Sacrifice: A Study of the Book of Hosea, by N. Snaith, *The Pastor* 17 (1954), 45.

A Theology of Salvation, by U. E. Simon, *The Foundation* 44 (1954), 12.

Mandate to Humanity, by E. M. Poteat, *The Foundation* 43 (1953), 14.

The Word in Season, by H. Wagner, *The Foundation* 41 (1951), 14.

Through Christ Our Lord, by G. Harkness, *The Foundation* 40 (1950), 7.

Your Life Counts, by H. Rubert, *The Foundation* 40 (1950), 7.

The Dignity of Man, by L. H. Hough, *The Foundation* 40 (1950), 7.

The Craft of Sermon Illustration, by W. E. Sangster, *The Foundation* 40 (1950), 7.

A Treasury of Sermon Illustrations, by C. L. Wallis, *The Foundation* 40 (1950), 7.

As a Mighty Stream, by J. Morgenstern, *The Foundation* 40 (1950), 7.

The Psalms, by E. A. Leslie, *The Foundation* 40 (1950), 7.

The Religious Pilgrimage of Israel, by I. G. Matthews, *The Journal of Religious Thought* 5 (1948), 98–99.

ABBREVIATIONS

AA	*American Anthropologist*
AB	Anchor Bible
ACNT	Augsburg Commentary on the New Testament
ANET	J. B. Pritchard, ed., *Ancient Near Eastern Texts Relating to the Old Testament* (Princeton: Princeton University Press, 1969)
BAGD	W. Bauer, W. F. Arndt, F. W. Gingrich, and F. W. Danker, *Greek-English Lexicon of the New Testament and Other Early Christian Literature* (Chicago: University of Chicago Press, 1979)
BDB	F. Brown, S. R. Driver, and C. A. Briggs, *Hebrew and English Lexicon of the Old Testament* (Oxford: Clarendon Press, 1952)
BJMP	*British Journal of Medical Psychology*
BTB	*Biblical Theology Bulletin*
CBC	Cambridge Bible Commentary
CBQ	*Catholic Biblical Quarterly*
ExpT	*Expository Times*
FRLANT	Forschungen zur Religion und Literatur des Alten und Neuen Testaments
GNS	Good News Studies
HDR	Harvard Dissertations in Religion
HSM	Harvard Semitic Monographs
IB	*Interpreter's Bible*
IBC	Interpretation: A Bible Commentary for Teaching and Preaching
ICC	International Critical Commentary
IEJ	*Israel Exploration Journal*
IJP	*International Journal of Psychoanalysis*
JAH	*Journal of American History*
JBL	*Journal of Biblical Literature*
JBS	*Journal of Black Studies*
JITC	*The Journal of the Interdenominational Theological Center*
JPE	*Journal of Political Economy*
JRH	*Journal of Religion and Health*
JSH	*Journal of Southern History*
JSOTSS	Journal for the Study of the Old Testament–Supplement Series
KJV	King James Version
NCBC	New Century Bible Commentary
NF	Neue Folge

NIGTC	The New International Greek Testament Commentary
NKJV	New King James Version
NovT	*Novum Testamentum*
NRSV	New Revised Standard Version
NTS	*New Testament Studies*
OBO	Orbis biblicus et orientalis
OTL	Old Testament Library
QJS	*Quarterly Journal of Speech*
RelEd	*Religious Education*
RSV	Revised Standard Version
SBLDS	SBL Dissertation Series
SBLSBS	SBL Sources for Biblical Studies
TDNT	G. Kittel and G. Friedrich, eds., *Theological Dictionary of the New Testament* (Grand Rapids: William B. Eerdmans, 1964–76)
TDOT	G. J. Botterweck and H. Ringgren, eds., *Theological Dictionary of the Old Testament* (Grand Rapids: William B. Eerdmans, 1973—)
VT	*Vetus Testamentum*
WBC	Word Biblical Commentary

NOTES

Notes to Preface

1. Gayraud Wilmore, *Black and Presbyterian* (Philadelphia: The Geneva Press, 1983), 93–100.

Notes to Chapter 1

1. BDB, 497.
2. Cf. Ps 65:3; the KJV reads "purge away"; the NRSV reads "you forgive our transgressions"; and the NKJV reads "you will provide atonement."
3. The KJV reads "thou shalt purge them away."
4. For another passage in which the KJV has "reconcile," see Ezek 45:20, "so shall ye reconcile the house."

Notes to Chapter 2

1. Earlier versions of this article were presented in the Rhetorical Criticism Section of the Society of Biblical Literature at its Annual Meeting in Chicago in November, 1988, and for the Atlanta Old Testament Consortium in April, 1993.
2. Count C. F. Volney, *The Ruins of Empires* (New York: Peter Eckler, 1890), 150–51.
3. S. Freud, *Moses and Monotheism* (New York: Vantage Books, 1939), 16–65.
4. J. G. Jackson, *Man, God, Civilization* (Secaucus, NJ: Citadel, 1972), 232–33.
5. For example Noth has argued, "It might even be that such a story arose as an aetiology of the name. Ancient Israel did not know that Moses is in reality an Egyptian name, that it is a shortened form of Egyptian names like Athmosis, Thutmosis, etc." (Martin Noth, *Exodus*, OTL [Philadelphia: Westminster Press, 1962], 26.) Similarly George W. Coates, in *Moses: Heroic Man, Man of God*, JSOTSS (Sheffield: Sheffield Academic Press, 1988), 42, argues that "[The pericope] provides the occasion to introduce the Egyptian name of the child. . . . This observation does not support a conclusion that, as a matter of historical fact, Moses was really an Egyptian." So also Umberto Cassuto, *A Commentary on the Book of Exodus* (Jerusalem: Magnes, 1987), 21; Brevard Childs, *The Book of Exodus: A Critical, Theological Commentary*, OTL (Philadelphia: Westminster Press, 1974), 19; Childs, "The Birth of Moses," *JBL* 84 (1965), 114; Gordon F. Davies, *Israel in Egypt:*

Reading Exodus 1–2, JSOTSS (Sheffield: Sheffield Academic Press, 1992), 114; John I. Durham, *Exodus*, WBC (Waco, TX: Word Books, 1987), 17; and J. Philip Hyatt, *Exodus*, NCBC (Grand Rapids: William B. Eerdmans, 1971), 65. While Bloom disagrees with Noth on the claim that the ancient writer did not know the Egyptian meaning, he does not speculate on the nationality of Moses (cf. Harold Bloom and David Rosenberg, *The Book of J* [New York: Grove Weidenfeld, 1990], 243).

6. George V. Pixley, *On Exodus: A Liberation Perspective* (Maryknoll, NY: Orbis Books, 1987), 7.

7. For a discussion of the function of this unit in the development of the traditions in Exodus 1–6 see George W. Coats, "A Structural Transition in Exodus," *VT* 2 (1972), 129–42.

8. For a discussion of the construction *ûmošeh hayah rôʿeh*, "and Moses was a shepherd," where we have a subject + the perfect of *hyh* + the participle as complement, see H. Donner, "Psalm 122," in *Text and Context: Old Testament and Semitic Studies for G. C. Fensham*, ed. W. Classen, JSOTSS 48 (Sheffield: Sheffield Academic Press, 1984), 81–91.

9. Childs, *Exodus*, 68–69; Durham, 29; Noth, 41.

10. One could argue that, since Moses was not in Egypt, he was not one of the oppressed ones. The point being made here, however, is that the use of the possessive pronoun, *your*, as opposed to *our*, serves to separate him from membership in the group.

11. Interestingly Coats (*Moses*, 63) argues that this set of question-response is "one in a series of reassurances addressed to Moses in the light of his objections to the commission." He does not, however, raise the question of why there is a "series" in a genre which usually only contains one such formulation. Rather his attention is drawn to arguing for a word-play on the formulaic use of *'hyh* (63–65).

12. For a discussion of the syntax of these verses see Durham, 38–9.

13. As he states, "The heroic tale of individual victory with the result of marriage into the clan's leading family thus characterizes this stage of the Moses tradition" (Coats, *Moses*, 51). On the other hand J. G. Williams refers to this narrative as an example of the *betrothal type scene* and explains the use of the appellation, "Egyptian" as the narrator's attempt to remind the audience of "Moses's Egyptian [*sic*] acculturation" (cf. James G. Williams, *Women Recounted: Narrative Thinking and the God of Israel*, Bible and Literature Series [Sheffield: Almond Press, 1982], 43–46).

14. This relationship between Exod 3:1a and 2:16–22a is discussed by P. Weimer, *Die Berufung des Mose: Literaturwissenschaftliche Analyze von Exodus 2,23–5,5*, OBO 32 (Göttingen: Vandenhoeck & Ruprecht, 1980), 213–15.

15. Cf. my discussion of the positive view of Africans both in these centuries and the respective pentateuchal sources in "Beyond Identification: The Use of Africans in Old Testament Poetry and Narratives," in *Stony the Road We Trod: African American Biblical Interpretation*, ed. Cain Hope Felder (Minneapolis: Fortress Press, 1990), 165–84.

See also my discussion of this anti-African bias in the P narratives in

"They're Nothing But Incestuous Bastards: The Polemical Use of Sex and Sexuality in Hebrew Canon Narrative," in *Reading From This Place: Social Location and Biblical Interpretation*, ed. Fernando F. Segovia and Mary Ann Tolbert (Minneapolis: Fortress Press, 1994).

16. Gen 10 and 17.

17. Cf. Lev 18:2-5.

18. J. Cheryl Exum, "Let Every Daughter Live," *Semeia* 28 (1983), 67, begins this narrative block in 1:22 so as to keep symmetry of structure with three units beginning with Pharaohnic instructions (18, 15, and 22).

19. Given this stress on a Levitical connection, it is surprising that others have not suggested that the source here is P. Perhaps this is the place to note that I am using both synchronic and diachronic methods in this interpretation. This is the case, since I do not see them as mutually exclusive, rather as mutually enhancing. Thus, what is to follow is a literary critical reading of the Exod 2:1-10 narrative, with an eye toward how this reading can be fit into the ideology of the P school as serving its political interests.

20. Cf. my discussion of this narrative technique in *David in Love and War: The Pursuit of Power in 2 Samuel 10–12*, JSOTSS 75 (Sheffield: Sheffield Academic Press, 1990), 100–101 and 117–18. Similarly, Davies (93) notes that "verse 2c–d, which interrupts the birth description and begins the complication. . . ."

21. As will be shown below, the fact that the Egyptian princess uses bad Hebrew grammar in naming him points to the unusual nature of the name.

22. Cf. *ANET*, 119.

23. Hugo Gressman, *Mose und seine Zeit*, FRLANT, NF 1 (Göttingen: Vandenhoeck & Ruprecht, 1923), 346.

24. Cf. Freud, *Moses and Monotheism*, 3–15. Coats (*Moses*, 47) also argues that this is not the intention of the narrative, although he does not note that the intention of the narratives is to do the exact opposite.

25. The omission of this element to the text was identified and "corrected" by the rabbinic tradition. As A. Kensky ("Moses and Jesus: The Birth of the Savior," *Judaism* 42 [1993], 43–44) notes: "The Midrash connects the birth of Moses with the decrees of Pharaoh, or, rather, it connects the decrees of the coming birth of the Hebrew savior. Of this prediction there are several versions. According to the Jerusalem *Targum* (on Exod 1:15), Pharaoh had a dream in which he dreamt that all of Egypt was on one scale and a young goat was on the other. The latter outweighed the former. This dream was interpreted to Pharaoh to mean that an Israelite child would be born who would destroy all of Egypt. Josephus relates that the announcement to Pharaoh of the birth of this child is made by one of the sacred scribes (*Antiquities* II, 1.205); in *Exodus Rabbah* (I, 22), Pharaoh is informed of the impending birth of a redeemer by his astrologers. In response to this announcement, Pharaoh issues a decree to the entire nation, or, alternatively, only to the Israelites, to cast their male-children into the river (*B. Sotah* 12a, *Exodus Rabbah* I, 18; cf. Exod 1:22)."

26. Cf. Norman K. Gottwald's discussion of ʿapiru and its relationship to the term Hebrew in *The Tribes of Yahweh: A Sociology of the Religion of Liberated Israel, 1250–1050 BCE* (Maryknoll, NY: Orbis Books, 1979), esp. 390–409 and 419–25. Given his arguments this unit may be P's attempt at fusing Hebrew and Israelite.

27. As Renita J. Weems ("The Hebrew Women Are Not Like the Egyptian Women: The Ideology of Race, Gender and Sexual Reproduction in Exodus 1," *Semeia* [1992], 28) states, "At the heart of his and the Egyptians' dread of the people of Israel is their fundamental assumption that Egyptians and Hebrew were different." I would differ with this analysis to the extent that it appears that the narrator wants the reader to perceive this to be the case, i.e. that there is a fundamental difference, and reinforces this through the speeches of the Egyptian characters in the narratives in Exod 1–2.

28. So Exum (75), who states, "Men are strikingly absent. . . . It is a woman's story in so far as their action determines its direction. But while narrative attention focuses on the activity of women, their attention centers on Moses. . . . An inherent narrative irony presents itself; without Moses there would be no story, but without the initiative of these women, there would be no Moses!" Similarly Weems (25–33) concentrates on the other women in the narrative.

In contrast to this, there are also heavily androcentric interpretations of this narrative complex, such as that of Davies. On the one hand he argues, "And how will Moses' origins here affect his future as an adult? He is nursed by his *mother*, named by the *princess*; he is adopted by the second but not abandoned by the first. His future is mysterious because he is still passive" (96; emphasis mine). On the other hand, after acknowledging these women he speaks of "This intense narrative concentration on the boy" (98).

29. This interpretation is in contrast to that of Davies who writes, " . . . we can justly ask if the Creation story is the taproot of Moses' birth story. . . . It is not. . . . the narrative is unlikely to cast Moses' mother in any role previously played by God, as though her son were her own handiwork. Children come from God's bounty, and even a hint otherwise would be no introduction to the Exodus where God alone is victorious" (105). One has to wonder whether such a statement speaks to the problem of what is theologically conceivable by the exegete, as opposed to narrative intention.

30. See also Exum, 76; Kensky, 43; James L. Kugel, "The Adverbial Use of *kî tôb*, *JBL* 99 (1980), 433–35; and J. Gerald Janzen, "Kugel's Adverbial *kî tôb*: An Assessment," *JBL* 102 (1983), 99–106.

31. Cf. Cassuto, 17–18.

32. Again, rabbinic tradition attempts to explain away this feat of the woman. As Kensky (48) notes, "The Jerusalem *Targum*, several of the later Midrashic works, and the commentary of Rashi, explain that Moses was born prematurely, after six months, and that his mother was thus able to hide him until the time that the Egyptians expected her to give birth.

However, a tradition found in the Babylonia Talmud (*Sotah* 12a) gives a different explanation, namely that Yokheved was able to hide Moses for three months because she was already pregnant for three months at the time of her remarriage with Amram. The Egyptians suspected that she would give birth nine months after her remarriage, and so Yokheved was able to avoid the watchful eyes of the Egyptians for three months."

Again these readings do not take into account the argument here. They do not, in other words, speak to how she was able to hide him in the time he would make the most noise. The androcentric nature of these readings miss part of the special nature of this woman.

33. Interestingly the omission of the father from the narrative was "corrected" by Josephus in a most heavy handed androcentric manner such that it points to how much this biblical narrative stresses the role of the woman (cf. *Antiquities* II, 1.220).

34. In this regard I am following Jon D. Levenson and Baruch Halpern, who assert Nabal is to be seen as a chieftain; see "The Political Import of David's Marriages," *JBL* 99 (1980), 507–18. See also Alice Bach's treatment of the Abigail marriage in *The Pleasure of Her Text: Feminist Readings of Biblical and Historical Texts* (Philadelphia: Trinity Press International, 1990), 25–44.

35. This birth sequencing is also a problem in Num 26:59, which lists Miriam as being younger than Moses and Aaron. A proposed resolution to this problem is found in Rabbinic sources, which speculate to there having been a divorce and remarriage between Amram and Yokebed, which led to a situation of children from both marriages, with the ones in Exod 2:3 being from the remarriage period (cf. Kensky, 44, for citations).

36. It should be noted that since Exod 1:8 there has been a sarcastic portrayal of the Pharaoh which is intended to undermine ancient Israelite reverence for Egyptian wisdom. On the one hand the king is "one who did not know Joseph." Thus, he is portrayed as a leader who is ignorant of his own nation's history. On the other hand, he wants to deal shrewdly with the situation, *habah nith akkemah* (Exod 1:10), but his plans are both irrational and unsuccessful. Thus, the actions of the king call into question the very idea of Egyptian wisdom.

37. This omission seems to be missed by many commentators; cf. E. Neufeld, "The Redemption of Moses," *Judaism*, 42 (1993), 50.

38. For an alternative reading of the daughter of Pharaoh's character portrayal, see Danna Nolan Fewell and David M. Gunn, *Gender, Power and Promise: The Subject of the Bible's First Story* (Nashville: Abingdon Press, 1993), 93; and Terrence Fretheim, *Exodus*, IBC (Louisville: John Knox Press, 1991), 38.

Notes to Chapter 3

1. William Julius Wilson, *The Declining Significance of Race: Blacks and Changing American Institutions*, 2nd ed. (Chicago: University of Chicago Press, 1980).

2. Ibid.

3. Contrast this to the portrait of mid-twentieth century in Nicholas Lemann, *The Promised Land: The Great Black Migration and How It Changed America* (New York: Alfred A. Knopf, 1991), 37.

4. Theodore Walker, Jr., *Empower the People: Social Ethics for the African-American Church* (Maryknoll, NY: Orbis Books, 1991), 36–48.

5. Ibid.

6. Robert M. Franklin, *Liberating Visions: Human Fulfillment and Social Justice in African American Thought* (Minneapolis: Fortress Press, 1990), 43–73. Dwight N. Hopkins, *Shoes That Fit My Feet: Sources for a Constructive Black Theology* (Maryknoll, NY: Orbis Books, 1993), 131–69.

7. George A. Lindbeck, *The Nature of Doctrine: Religion and Theology in a Postliberal Age* (Louisville: Westminster/John Knox Press, 1984), 118; Stephen B. Reid, *Experience and Tradition: A Primer in Black Biblical Hermeneutics* (Nashville: Abingdon Press, 1990), 18–24.

8. Vincent L. Wimbush, "The Bible and African Americans: An Outline of an Interpretive History," in *Stony the Road We Trod: African American Biblical Interpretation*, ed. Cain Hope Felder (Minneapolis: Fortress Press, 1991), 81–97.

9. I. A. Richards, *Practical Criticism: A Study in Literary Judgment* (New York: Harcourt, 1929), 174–76.

10. Ibid.

11. Ibid.

12. Philip R. Davies, "The Social World of the Apocalyptic Writings," in *The World of Ancient Israel: Sociological, Anthropological and Political Perspectives*, ed. R. E. Clements (Cambridge: Cambridge University Press, 1989), 251–71.

13. Gerhard E. Lenski, *Power and Privilege: A Theory of Social Stratification* (Chapel Hill: University of North Carolina Press, 1966), 304f.

14. Ibid.

15. R. Linton, "Nativistic Movements," *AA* 45 (1943), 230–40; A. F. Wallace, "Revitalization Movements," *AA* 58 (1956), 264–81.

16. Thomas W. Overholt, *Prophecy in Cross-Cultural Perspective*, SBLSBS 17 (Atlanta: Scholars Press, 1986), 16–19.

17. Thomas W. Overholt, *Channels of Prophecy. The Social Dynamics of Prophetic Activity* (Minneapolis: Fortress Press, 1989), 27–68.

18. Albert Memmi, *The Colonizer and the Colonized* (Boston: Beacon Press, 1965).

19. Victor Tcherikover, *Hellenistic Civilization and the Jews*, trans. S. Appelbaum (New York: Atheneum, 1970).

20. John G. Gammie, "Spatial and Ethical Dualism in Jewish Wisdom and Apocalyptic Literature," *JBL* 93 (1974), 356ff.

21. John A. Dearman, *Studies in Religion and Culture in the Old Testament* (Peabody, MA: Hendrickson, 1993), 261–63.

22. W. Lee Humphreys, "A Lifestyle for Diaspora: A Study of the Tales of Esther and Daniel," *JBL* 92 (1973), 211–23.

23. H. P. Müller, "Märchen, Legende, und Endwartung," VT 26 (1976), 338–50.

24. Andre Lacocque, *The Book of Daniel* (Atlanta: John Knox Press, 1979). See also L. M. Wills, *The Jew in the Court of a Foreign King: Ancient Jewish Court Legends*, HDR 26 (Minneapolis: Fortress Press, 1990).

25. Danna Nolan Fewell, *Circle of Sovereignty: A Story of Stories in Daniel 1–6*, JSOTSS 72 (Sheffield: Almond Press, 1988), 66.

26. Ibid.

27. Ibid.

28. Lenski, 201.

29. Ibid., 284.

30. Randall C. Bailey, "Beyond Identification: The Use of Africans in Old Testament Poetry and Narratives," in Felder, ed., *Stony the Road We Trod*, 165–84.

31. See 1 Maccabees.

32. John J. Collins, *The Apocalyptic Vision of the Book of Daniel*, HSM (Missoula, MT: Scholars Press, 1977).

33. W. E. B. DuBois, *Souls of Black Folks* (Greenwich: Fawcett, 1961), 16f.

34. August Meier, Elliot M. Bodwick, and Francis L. Broderick, eds., *Black Protest Thought in the Twentieth Century* (New York: Macmillan, 1985), 53.

35. Ibid., 55.

36. Ibid., 68.

37. Ibid., 71.

38. Ibid., 48.

39. Ibid.

40. Ibid., 49–50.

41. Ibid., 49.

42. Franklin, 44f.

43. Ibid., 54–59, 69.

44. DuBois, 129.

45. Wills, 194.

46. Cornel West, *Prophesy Deliverance! An Afro-American Revolutionary Christianity* (Philadelphia: Westminster Press, 1982), 69–91.

47. Ibid., 78–80.

48. Ibid., 80–85.

49. Robert B. Coote, *Amos Among the Prophets: Composition and Theology* (Philadelphia: Fortress Press, 1981), 32; and John A. Dearman, *Religion & Culture in Ancient Israel*, 185–98.

50. West, *Prophesy Deliverance!*, 85–91.

51. Ibid., 72–78.

52. Wilson, *The Declining Significance of Race*.

Notes to Chapter 4

1. See Cain Hope Felder, *Troubling Biblical Waters: Race, Class and Family* (Maryknoll, NY: Orbis Books, 1989); Cain Hope Felder, ed., *Stony*

the Road We Trod: African American Biblical Interpretation (Minneapolis: Fortress Press, 1991); Alfred G. Dunston, *The Black Man in the Old Testament and its World* (Philadelphia: Dorrance, 1974); and Cheikh Anta Diop, *The African Origin of Civilization: Myth or Reality?* (Westport and New York: Lawrence Hill, 1974 [1955]).

2. Charles B. Copher, "Three Thousands Years of Biblical Interpretation with Reference to Black Peoples," *JITC* 13/2 (Spring, 1986), 231.

3. For the use of the language in John, see Raymond E. Brown, *The Community of the Beloved Disciple* (New York: Paulist Press, 1979), 13–91.

4. Nils A. Dahl, "Nations in the New Testament," in *New Testament Christianity and Africa: Essays in Honour of Henry Sawyer,* ed. Mark E. Glasswell and Edward W. Fashole-Luke (London: SPCK, 1974), 57.

5. Martin Dibelius, *Gospel Criticism and Christology* (London: Ivor Nicholson & Watson, 1935), 47.

6. Martin Dibelius, *From Tradition to Gospel,* trans. Bertram Lee Woolf, 2nd rev. ed. (Cambridge and London: James Clarke & Co. Ltd, 1971), 1–35; Rudolf Bultmann, *The History of the Synoptic Tradition,* trans. John Marsh (Oxford: Basil Blackwell, 1963), 1–7; and Martin Kahler, *The So-called Historical Jesus and the Historic Biblical Christ,* trans. and ed. Carl E. Braaten (Philadelphia: Fortress Press, 1964), 42–122.

The cultic orientation of John is obvious: "But these things are written so that you may come to believe that Jesus is the Messiah, the son of God, and that through believing you may have life in his name" (John 20:31, NRSV).

7. E.g., Howard C. Kee, *Jesus in History: An Approach to the Study of the Gospels* (New York: Harcourt, 1971), 29–103; and John S. Kloppenborg, *The Formation of Q: Trajectories in Ancient Wisdom Collections* (Studies in Antiquity and Ancient Christianity; Philadelphia: Fortress Press, 1987).

8. See especially, Helmut Koester, *Ancient Christian Gospels: Their History and Development* (Philadelphia: Trinity Press International, 1990), 43–47.

9. Charles H. Talbert, *What Is a Gospel? The Genre of the Canonical Gospels* (Library of Early Christianity; Philadelphia: Fortress Press, 1977); and David E. Aune, *The New Testament in Its Literary Environment* (Philadelphia: Westminster Press, 1987), 11–157.

10. For a contemporary acknowledgment of this, see Helmut Koester, "Jesus the Victim," *JBL* 111/1 (1992), especially 8–10.

11. See Morna D. Hooker, *A Commentary on the Gospel of St. Mark* (Black's New Testament Commentaries; London: A & C Black, 1991), 372; Hugh Anderson, *The Gospel of Mark,* NCBC (London: Marshall, Morton & Scott, 1976), 340; and C. S. Mann, *Mark: A New Introduction with Introduction and Commentary,* AB (Garden City, NY: Doubleday, 1986), 645.

12. E.g., Weddig Ficke, *The Court-Martial of Jesus,* trans. Salvator Atanasio (New York: Grove Weidenfeld, 1987), 17–18, 95–108.

13. Ibid., 18–21. Also for this assessment, see J. C. O'Neill, *The Theology of Acts in Its Historical Setting,* 2nd ed. rev. (London: SPCK, 1970), 59–99; and Koester, "Jesus the Victim," 10.

14. E.g., Ficke, 100–102; Theodore S. Weeden, Sr., "The Cross as Power in Weakness: Mark 15:20*b*–41," in *The Passion in Mark: Studies in Mark 14–16*, ed. Werner H. Kelber (Philadelphia: Fortress Press, 1976), 115–34.

15. E.g., Eduard Schweizer, *The Good News According to Mark*, trans. Donald H. Madvig (Atlanta: John Knox Press, 1970). Scholars like Dennis Sweetland (*Our Journey with Jesus: Discipleship According to Mark*, GNS 22 [Wilmington: Michael Glazier, 1987]) and Vernon K. Robbins (*Jesus the Teacher: A Socio-Rhetorical Interpretation of Mark with a New Introduction* [Minneapolis: Fortress Press, 1992]) believe that Mark especially focuses on the theme.

16. Brian K. Blount, "A Socio-Rhetorical Analysis of Simon of Cyrene," *Semeia* 63 (1993), 171–98.

17. Frans Ventur, *Man From Cyrene* (Philadelphia: Muhlenburg Press, 1962), 222–23.

18. Cf. Burton L. Mack and Vernon K. Robbins, *Patterns of Persuasion in the Gospels* (Somona, CA: Polebridge, 1989).

19. Thus Frank J. Matera, *The Kingship of Jesus: The Composition and Theology of Mark 15*, SBLDS 66 (Chico, CA: Scholars Press, 1985), 45.

20. Ibid., 40

21. See Kenneth E. Bailey, "The Fall of Jerusalem and Mark's Account of the Cross," *ExpT* 102/4 (January, 1991), 104; also Anderson, *The Gospel of Mark*, 340.

22. Blount, "A Socio-Rhetorical Analysis of Simon of Cyrene." Here my intent is not to deny what Blount and others offer regarding the pastoral nature of the Gospels. Rather it is to ask if the Gospels can help us with historio-ethnographic issue for the world of Jesus as well.

23. See Robert F. Funk (with Mahlon H. Smith), *Mark-Red Letter Edition* (Somona, California: Polebridge, 1991), 53–56.

24. See Kieth Nickle, *The Synoptic Gospels: Conflict and Consensus* (Atlanta: John Knox Press, 1980), 40–41; and Vincent Taylor, *The Formation of the Gospel Tradition* (London: MacMillan & Co., 1935), 44–62.

25. Thus Donald Juel, *The Gospel of Mark*, ACNT (Minneapolis: Augsburg Press, 1990), 218; and Vincent Taylor, *The Gospel According to St. Mark* (London: MacMillan & Co., 1959), 587.

26. Taylor, *The Gospel According to St. Mark*, 587.

27. Dibelius, *From Tradition to Gospel*, 182–83.

28. The ensuing dialogue with Peter in 14:29ff makes it quite clear that the disciples will fall away and they all do in 14:50.

29. See John H. Reumann, "Psalm 22 and the Cross: Lament and Thanksgiving for Jesus Christ," *Interpretation* 28/1 (January, 1974), 39–43.

30. See Dibelius, *From Tradition to Gospel*, 184, and Bultmann, *History of the Synoptic Tradition*, 280, who respectively think that the stress on scripture fulfillment in the context of the Passion have to do with "shame and disgrace" caused by Jesus' death and the church's need "to solve the problem of a crucified Messiah."

31. See BAGD.

32. For Matthew's preference for this verb, see my "Studies in Luke's

Editorial Methods and Their Situations" (Ph.D. diss., Harvard University, 1975), 19–25.

33. Thus Luke 9:47, 14:4, 20:20; and Acts 9:27, 16:19, 18:17. See also G. Delling, *"epilambánō," TDNT,* 4:9.

34. Here I take the position, based on Mark 15:21, that Simon is an example not of a disciple but of a conscript, a victim of the Roman power to command in occupied territories. For the political situation of first century Palestine, see Richard Horsley and John S. Hanson, *Bandits, Prophets and Messiahs: Popular Movements in the Time of Jesus* (Minneapolis: Winston, 1985); and Richard Horsley, *Jesus and the Spiral of Violence: Popular Jewish Resistance in Roman Palestine* (San Francisco: Harper & Row, 1987).

35. This view is promoted in Eurocentric lexical and exegetical commentary materials on the Simon passage.

36. E.g., Schweizer, 343.

37. See N. Avigad, "A Depository of Inscribed Ossuaries in the Kidron Valley," *IEJ* 12/1 (1962), 1–12 who gives details regarding the finds as well as of the site.

38. Thus C. S. C. Williams, *The Acts of the Apostles* (New York: Harper and Bros., 1957), 154; Gerhard A. Krodel, *Acts,* ACNT (Minneapolis: Augsburg Press, 1986), 226–28; and Felder, *Troubling Biblical Waters,* 47–48, n. 52.

39. Whether Basilides and his followers produced the document cannot be determined from the treatise itself. If they did not, this means that Simon (rather than Jesus) was thought to have been crucified by more than one group in Egypt. For the Nag Hammadi collection and the story of its discovery, see James M. Robinson, ed., *The Nag Hammadi Library,* rev. ed. (San Francisco: Harper & Row, 1988); for the Simon tradition, see "The Second Treatise of the Great Seth," VII.2.56, in Robinson, 362–71.

40. Thus George R. Beasley-Murray, *John,* WBC (Waco, TX: Word Books, 1987), 144–45; Rudolf Bultmann, *The Gospel of John: A Commentary,* trans G. R. Beasley-Murray (Philadelphia: Westminster Press, 1971), 680, n. 3; and Hooker, 372.

41. See the critical apparatus in Nestle-Aland, *Novum Testamentum Graece,* 26th edition (Stuttgart: Deutsche Bibelstiftung, 1979).

42. See Aziz S. Atiya, *A History of Eastern Christianity* (London: Methuen and Co., Ltd., 1986), 13–48; and Atiya, *The Copts and Christian Civilization* (Salt Lake City: University of Utah Press, 1979).

43. See Bruce J. Malina, "Reading Theory Perspective: Reading Luke-Acts 1–23," in *The Social World of Luke-Acts: Models for Interpretation,* ed. Jerome H. Neyrey (Peabody, MA: Hendrickson Publishers, 1991); and Malina and Neyrey, "First-Century Personality: Dyadic, Not Individual," ibid., 72.

44. Malina and Neyrey, "First-Century Personality," 72.

45. Ibid., 73.

46. Ibid., 86.

47. Ibid.

48. For insights on ethnic demographics in the ancient world with special attention to the African presence issue, see Stanlake Samkange, *African Saga: A Brief Introduction to African History* (Nashville and New York: Abingdon Press, 1971), 98–108; Frank M. Snowden, Jr., *Blacks in Antiquity: Ethiopians in the Greco-Roman Experience* (Cambridge: Harvard University Press, 1970), 1–155; and Snowden, *Before Color Prejudice: The Ancient View of Blacks* (Cambridge: Harvard University Press, 1983), 3–17.

Regarding the Cyrenian population, Josephus, quoting the geographer Strabo, notes the following (*Antiquities* XIV.115): "There were four classes in the city of Cyrene. The first consisted of the citizens, the second of the farmers, the third of peasant resident aliens (*metics*), and the fourth of Jews." Victor Tcherikover views Josephus's second group (farmers) as peasants and assumes they "were native Libyans reduced to serfdom by the Greek population of the towns"; see *Hellenistic Civilization and the Jews*, trans. S. Applebaum (New York: Atheneum, 1970), 331.

49. For Greco-Roman attitudes towards Blacks and Black African occupations in Greco-Roman lands, see Snowden, *Blacks in Antiquity*, 186–88.

50. Countee Cullen, "Simon the Cyrenian Speaks," in *On These I Stand: An Anthology of the Best Poems of Countee Cullen* (New York and Evanston: Harper and Bros., 1947 [1929]), 8.

Notes to Chapter 5

1. See especially, Bruce J. Malina, *The New Testament World: Insights from Cultural Anthropology* (Louisville: John Knox Press, 1981); Malina, *Christian Origins and Cultural Anthropology: Practical Models for Biblical Interpretation* (Atlanta: John Knox Press, 1986); Malina and Jerome H. Neyrey, *Calling Jesus Names: The Social Value of Labels in Matthew* (Sonoma, CA: Polebridge Press, 1988); and Malina, "First Century Personality: Dyadic, Not Individual," in *The Social World of Luke-Acts: Models for Interpretation*, ed. Jerome H. Neyrey (Peabody, MA: Hendrickson Publishers, 1991), 67–97.

2. The designations "Mediterranean" and "Mediterranean society" are used here in accordance with their meaning in Malina's social and sociological analyses of the NT. As such, the terms refer to the agrarian cultures of the eastern Mediterranean basin that are linked through trade, economics, politics, and warfare. The terms are not restricted to the societies traditionally referred to as Graeco-Roman but are inclusive of North Africa and, especially, Egypt.

3. Malina, *New Testament World*, 51–70; see also Malina and Neyrey, *Social World*, 67–97, for a subsequent expansion of the theme.

4. Malina, *New Testament World*, 53; cf. Malina and Neyrey, *Social World*, 72–74, 83–84.

5. The second, or Three Zone Model, is attributed to Bernard de Geradon, "L' homme a l'image de Dieu," *Nouvelle Revue Theologique* 80 (1958), 683–95. According to Malina (and de Geradon), "The way the

human being is perceived as fitting into his rightful place in his environments, physical and social, and acting in a way that is typically human, is by means of his inmost reactions (eyes—heart) as expressed in language (mouth—ears) and/or outwardly realized in activity (hands—feet). These three zones comprise the non-introspective makeup of man and are used to describe human behavior throughout the Bible, from Genesis to Revelation" (Malina, *New Testament World*, 60–61).

6. Ibid., 57. The term *dyadism* derives from the Greek word meaning "pair" or "a twosome."

7. Ibid., 55. Cf. Malina and Neyrey, *Social World*, 74–75, 86–90, for a discussion of group embeddedness in relation to family and clan, place of origin, group of origin, inherited craft-trade and parties-groups.

8. Ibid. Cf. also Malina and Neyrey, *Social World*, 73.

9. The quotation is from Clifford Geertz, "From the Native's Point of View," in *Meaning and Anthropology*, ed. Keith H. Basso and Henry A. Selby (Albuquerque: University of New Mexico Press, 1977), 221–37, cited in Malina, *New Testament World*, 55.

10. See also Malina's further remarks: "The dyadic personality is thus a person whose total self-awareness emphatically depends upon such group embeddedness" (*New Testament World*, 55); and "It is the group that is unique, individualistic, not the representative of the group" (ibid., 56). Cf. also Malina and Neyrey, *Social World*, 73.

11. Ibid., 54; cf. Malina and Neyrey, *Social World*, 67–68, 72.

12. To my knowledge, the term *dyadism* is not a psychological or psychoanalytic term. Malina's employment of this term appears to derive from its social and cultural anthropology. See, for example, the introductory discussion to the articles in Jack M. Potter, May N. Diaz, and George M. Foster, eds., *Peasant Society: A Reader* (Boston: Little, Brown & Co., 1967), cited by Malina, *New Testament World*, 156, n. 1, and the discussion of "model personality" in Malina and Neyrey, *Social World*, 68–69.

13. Cf. Malina and Neyrey, *Social World*, 73, citing Murray Bowen, *Family Therapy in Clinical Practice* (New York: Jason Aronson, 1978), 468, 492–96.

14. Malina, *New Testament World*, 68.

15. Ibid., 68–69. Malina's subsequent analysis employs yet a further testing model. In *Social World*, the distinctive characteristics of persons in strong group cultures (e.g., dyadism, social thinking, honor and shame, morality and deviance, values and virtues) form the parameters of the investigation; cf. Malina and Neyrey, *Social World*, 83–94. For a description of strong group cultures, see Malina's modification of Mary Douglas's grid and group model in Malina, *Christian Origins*, 1986), 13–27.

16. To comply with the model, all translations of NT text are taken from the RSV unless otherwise stated. As such, the use of chauvinist and exclusionist language in the translation is solely the responsibility of the translators.

17. A selective sample of Acts convinced me that this was unnecessary

since it largely duplicated the findings already achieved in analyzing Luke's Gospel.

18. The database is derived from a computer version of the 26th edition of Nestle-Aland using a software search function. To repeat the sample, one should take into consideration (and heed!) the discussion of standard Greek-English-German concordances in Kurt Aland and Barbara Aland, *The Text of the New Testament*, trans. Erroll F. Rhodes (Grand Rapids: William B. Eerdmans, 1989).

19. BAGD, *"éntimos,"* 268.

20. Cf. Anders Nygren, *Eros and Agape* (Chicago: University of Chicago Press, 1982); E. Stauffer, *"agapáō, agápē, agapētós," TDNT*, 1:35–38, 44–54.

21. W. Dittenberger, *Orientis graeci inscriptionis selectae* (Leipzig: Hirzel, 1903–05), 96; the text appears also in J. M. Creed, *The Gospel According to St. Luke* (New York: St. Martin's Press, 1969), 101, n. 5.

22. The subject of *apésteilen* (he sent) is the centurion.

23. *Exousía* (authority), implicit in 7:3, is explicitly stated in 7:8*a*, implied in 7:8*b*, and ascribed to Jesus in 7:7*b*. Cf. Foerster's observation concerning legal authority; authority "is illusory unless backed by real power. . . . Thus, it is not always possible to separate between authority and power, between *exousía* and *dýnamis*. . . ." (W. Foerster, *"éxestin, exousía," TDNT* 2:563).

24. The contrast of *worthy-unworthy* occurs in 7:4, 6, 7, signaled by the noun *axios* and its verb *exiosa* and the related adjective *hikanós*. *Áxios* in the elder's address to Jesus could be translated "appropriate" (e.g., "It is appropriate for you to do this for him"), but ruled out by 7:6, 7.

25. Cited by Joseph Fitzmyer, *The Gospel According to Luke I-IX*, AB (Garden City, NY: Doubleday, 1981), 652. For the alternative, see I. H. Marshall, *The Gospel of Luke*, NIGTC (Grand Rapids: William B. Eerdmans, 1983), 281.

26. Malina, *New Testament World*, 55.

27. Apparently the authority referred to here is Herod Antipas, as Roman forces were not in Galilee prior to 44 CE. Cf. A. N. Sherwin-White, *Roman Society and Roman Law in the New Testament* (Oxford: Oxford University Press, 1963), 123ff.

28. Soldiers and slaves are meant here, but also, the elders. On the elders see below.

29. Elders, without the definite article (cf. 7:3), refers to local leaders of the synagogue, or, to other local civil leaders. Cf. Gunther Bornkamm, *"presbýteros," TDNT* 6:660.

30. The term friends (*philoí*) in 7:6 covers a wide semantic field embracing a variety of social relations. Among these are familial relations, intimates outside the family, members of philosophical schools, persons associated with the wealthy, associates of political leaders and those associated with the Hellenistic royal court. Typically, the term expresses equality, but, as its use in the Hellenistic court attests, the equality may be real or simply ascribed. In our test, the term signifies those related to the

centurion on the order of a "member of a circle of friends around a leader" (Gustav Stahlin, *"philéō, kataphiléō,"* *TDNT* 9:146–48, 154–55, 159–64). The relevant semantic field of "friends" in 7:6, therefore, is the political, legal court, or patron-client relationship and not "close personal friends." The centurion *sent* the friends to Jesus just as he sent the elders! Note also the use of the first person in the exchange between the "friends" and Jesus. *Client*, thus, is more expressive of the meaning in 7:6 and the equality traditionally associated with the term is probably ascribed and not real.

31. Since Jesus is subject to the civil authority of the centurion (as authorized by the king), he is clearly a social inferior, but, as a healer, and miracle-worker, he is also religiously superior. What is significant in the story, as Jesus' pronouncement makes clear, is that the centurion *ascribes* authority/power to Jesus equivalent to that which he claims for himself. The depth structure of the exchange makes this clear: the centurion has authority over others (soldiers, slaves, elders, friends), Jesus has authority over others (demons, illness). Honor and reciprocity are also at stake in the exchange. As the centurion commands and is obeyed, he requests and expects Jesus to command and be obeyed. Cf. Malina and Neyrey, *Social World*, 25–65.

32. Cf. Malina and Neyrey, *Social World*, 49.

33. Rudolf Bultmann, *History of the Synoptic Tradition*, trans. John Marsh (New York: Harper & Row, 1963), 38–39.

34. Cf. for example, Plummer's remark concerning the centurion that is repeated again and again in the commentaries: "He has become in some degree attracted to Judaism (v. 5), and was an illustration of the great truth which Luke delights to exhibit, that Gentile and Jew alike share in the blessings of the kingdom." Alfred Plummer, *A Critical and Exegetical Commentary on the Gospel According to St. Luke*, ICC (New York: Charles Scribner's Sons, 1896), 194.

35. Cf. Eduard Schweizer, *The Good News According to Luke* (Atlanta: John Knox Press, 1984), 131; Schweizer notes that the inclusion of Gentiles in Luke is linked to the shaming of Israel.

36. Dyadic personalities, according to Malina, "do not seem to go through the stages of ego formation typical of Western individualistic persons" (Malina and Neyrey, *Social World*, 74). The model, however, does not sufficiently clarify the process of individuation and ego formation that, in fact, does take place. Note, for example, that Malina recognizes that "Some passages seem to predict that allegiance to Jesus will mean loss of biological family (12:51-53, 14:25-26, 18:29), but the gaining of a new, fictive family (8:19-21)" (ibid., 86) and he questions, "what new dyadic identity is signalled when the presumption of Israel as a chosen race, set apart, is debated in Acts 10–11" (ibid). In these instances, however, Malina argues that the principle is the same: "individuals are known in terms of parents, family and kin—biological or fictive" (ibid). That may be true, but the question remains. What are the distinctive factors (religious, cultural, social) that alter the symbolic world of groups to the degree that alternative

interpretations of history, legacy and an individual's relation to the group emerges?

37. In either case, however, the alternate ego structure does *not* mean that the ego is deficient. It simply means that the ego in the dyadic personality functions differently than the ego in Western individualistic culture.

38. Cf. Malina, *New Testament World*, 99.

39. Other relevant texts in Luke that need investigation in light of the process of individuation in first century society are: Luke 6:23, 26, 32-33, 38; 7:33; 10:1-16, 38-42; 11:29-32; 14:14, 24, 28; 12:11-12; 16:13; 17:24; 18:9-14, 32; 21:12-19. Cf. note 36 above on the fictive family.

40. Cf. Vernon Robbins, "The Social Location of the Implied Author of Luke-Acts," in Malina and Neyrey, *Social World*, especially 315–18. Of particular interest for our text, however, is not simply the acceptance of the socially marginal, etc., but the inclusion within this group and the positive evaluation of certain members of the gentile military establishment which effected and maintained Rome's imperial claims on the Mediterranean world. See John's (?) advice to the soldiers: "Soldiers also asked him, 'And we, what shall we do'? And he said to them, 'Rob no one by violence or by false accusation, and be content with your wages' " (Luke 3:14, RSV).

Notes to Chapter 6

1. For discussion of the community behind the Fourth Gospel, see David Rensberger, *Johannine Faith and Liberating Community* (Philadelphia: Westminster Press, 1988), 15–36. There I built upon a consensus about the Johannine community that has developed from the work of J. Louis Martyn, *History and Theology in the Fourth Gospel*, rev. ed. (Nashville: Abingdon Press, 1979); "Glimpses into the History of the Johannine Community," *The Gospel of John in Christian History* (New York: Paulist, 1978), 90–121; Raymond E. Brown *The Gospel According to John*, 2 vols., AB (Garden City, NY: Doubleday, 1966–1970); Brown, *The Community of the Beloved Disciple* (New York: Paulist, 1979); Wayne A. Meeks, "The Man from Heaven in Johannine Sectarianism," *JBL* 91 (1972), 44–72; and others. See also, for example, D. Moody Smith, Jr., "Johannine Christianity," in *Johannine Christianity: Essays on Its Setting, Sources, and Theology* (Columbia: University of South Carolina, 1984), 1–36 (originally in *NTS* 21 [1975], 222–48); and Jerome H. Neyrey, *An Ideology of Revolt: John's Christology in Social-Science Perspective* (Philadelphia: Fortress Press, 1988).

2. See especially Meeks, "Man from Heaven."

3. Rensberger, 107–34.

4. Frederick Herzog, *Liberation Theology: Liberation in the Light of the Fourth Gospel* (New York: Seabury, 1972); José Porfirio Miranda, *Being and the Messiah: The Message of St. John* (Maryknoll, NY: Orbis Books, 1977).

5. Richard J. Karris, *Jesus and the Marginalized in John's Gospel*,

Zacchaeus Studies: New Testament (Collegeville, MN: Liturgical Press [Michael Glazier], 1990).

6. Ibid., 35–38. Among the commentaries, see for example G. R. Beasley-Murray, *John*, WBC (Waco, TX: Word Books, 1987), 119–20; and Brown, *John*, 1:325.

7. Karris, 40–41.

8. Contrast 7:31 with 7:25-30, and note that the people of Jerusalem, unlike the crowd, know about the "the Jews'" desire to kill Jesus (7:1, 19–20, 25). Cf. Beasley-Murray, 110.

9. Karris, 38–39.

10. See the groundbreaking work of J. Louis Martyn in *History and Theology*; also Rensberger, 41–49; Karris, 46–50; and Paul D. Duke, *Irony in the Fourth Gospel* (Atlanta: John Knox Press, 1985), 117–26.

11. Karris, 48–49.

12. Martyn, *History*, 71; Karris, 52. This is denied by Brown, *John*, 1:209, and Barnabas Lindars, *The Gospel of John*, NCBC (Grand Rapids: William B. Eerdmans, 1972), 217.

13. Karris, 62–65; Wayne A. Meeks, "Galilee and Judea in the Fourth Gospel," *JBL* 85 (1966), 159–69; Jouette M. Bassler, "The Galileans: A Neglected Factor in Johannine Community Research," *CBQ* 43 (1981), 243–57.

14. Meeks, "Galilee and Judea," 164–165; Brown, *John*, 1:187; Beasley-Murray, 73.

15. Karris, 63–64; Sean Freyne, *Galilee from Alexander the Great to Hadrian 323 B.C.E. to 135 C.E.: A Study of Second Temple Judaism*, University of Notre Dame Center for the Study of Judaism and Christianity in Antiquity, 5 (Wilmington, DE: Michael Glazier, 1980), 309–29.

16. Karris, 67–70.

17. See for example W. A. Meeks, *The Prophet-King: Moses Traditions and the Johannine Christology*, NovTSup 14 (Leiden: Brill, 1967), 314–19; O. Cullmann, *Der johanneische Kreis: Zum Ursprung des Johannesevangeliums* (Tübingen: J. C. B. Mohr, 1975), 49–52; and J. D. Purvis, "The Fourth Gospel and the Samaritans," *NovT* 17 (1975), 161–98, with references to earlier literature; and Brown, *Community*, 35–40.

18. Karris, 73–95; Brown, *Community*, 183–98; S. M. Schneiders, "Women in the Fourth Gospel and the Role of Women in the Contemporary Church," *BTB* 12 (1982), 35–45; Elisabeth Schüssler Fiorenza, *In Memory of Her: A Feminist Theological Reconstruction of Christian Origins* (New York: Crossroad, 1983), 326–33; and most recently Gail R. O'Day, "John," in *The Women's Bible Commentary*, ed. Carol A. Newsom and Sharon H. Ringe (Louisville: Westminster/John Knox Press, 1992), 293–304.

19. Brown, *John*, 1:454.

20. See Rensberger, 88–89.

21. Ibid., 92–95; earlier in Rensberger, "The Politics of John: The Trial of Jesus in the Fourth Gospel," *JBL* 103 (1984), 401–6. See also Duke, 126–37.

22. See for example Rudolf Bultmann, *The Gospel of John* (Philadelphia: Westminster Press, 1971), 669; Duke, 89.

23. Rensberger, *Johannine Faith*, 98–100; "Politics of John," 410–11.

24. Cf. Rensberger, *Johannine Faith*, 116–118.

25. C. K. Barrett, *The Gospel According to St. John*, 2nd ed. (Philadelphia: Westminster Press, 1978), 426.

26. U. C. von Wahlde has attempted to show that the use of "the Jews" to designate authorities belongs to a different stage of John's redaction than the use of "the Pharisees" in *The Earliest Version of John's Gospel: Recovering the Gospel of Signs* (Wilmington, DE: Michael Glazier, 1989), 31–36. I do not find his argument convincing.

27. See for example Brown, *John*, 1:lxx-lxxiii; Beasley-Murray, lxxxix. Sometimes, of course, "the Jews" is a more neutral religious designation (e.g., John 2:6, 13). It is occasionally suggested that *Ioudaioi* should sometimes be translated "Judeans" rather than "Jews" in John, but the value of this suggestion is limited. Even in chapter 11, where the suggestion is most commonly made, the *Ioudaioi* are hostile to Jesus and separate from him and his followers, and though some of them believe in him, others betray him to the Pharisees (11:8, 45-46).

28. Rensberger, *Johannine Faith*, 25–26, 42–43, 48–49; Martyn, *History*, 84–85; R. Schnackenburg, *Gospel According to St. John*, 3 vols. (New York: Crossroad, 1982), 1:165–67.

29. Brown, *John*, 1:130, 313, 325, 484; Bultmann, 133, n. 4; Schnackenburg, 1:365; 2:474, n. 28.

30. Emil Schürer, *The History of the Jewish People in the Age of Jesus Christ (175 B.C.–A.D. 135)*, rev. and ed. by Geza Vermes, Fergus Millar, and Matthew Black, 3 vols. (Edinburgh: T & T Clark, 1973–1987), 2:435, 3:92–100. For a good non-technical discussion, see Shaye J. D. Cohen, *From the Maccabees to the Mishnah* (Philadelphia: Westminster Press, 1987), 108–11. For terminology in use in the Jewish community of Antioch, see W. A. Meeks and R. L. Wilken, *Jews and Christians in Antioch in the First Four Centuries of the Common Era*, SBLSBS 13 (Missoula, MT: Scholars Press, 1978), 7–8.

31. Martyn, *History*, 86–89.

32. Among the commentaries, see for example Bultmann, 311; Lindars, 592; Schnackenburg, 3:296–97; Brown, *John*, 1:330, 2:959–60; see also Brown, *Community*, 72, n. 128.

33. Rensberger, *Johannine Faith*, 37–41, 48–49, 55–61, 67–70. For similar treatments of Nicodemus, see Meeks, "Man from Heaven," 55; Duke, 110; Alfred Loisy, *Le quatrième Evangile* (Paris: Picard, 1903), 305, 895–96; and Martinus de Jonge, "Nicodemus and Jesus: Some Observations on Misunderstanding and Understanding in the Fourth Gospel," in *Jesus: Stranger from Heaven and Son of God*, SBLSBS 11 (Missoula, MT: Scholars Press, 1977), 30–42.

34. D. D. Sylva, "Nicodemus and His Spices (John 19:39)," *NTS* 34 (1988), 148–51.

35. Karris, 97–101.

36. Cf. Rensberger, *Johannine Faith*, 115.

37. "Du reste, ces Juifs n'ont eu affaire qu'à son cadavre" (Loisy, 896).

38. Karris, 25–32.

39. The work of Obery M. Hendricks, Jr., bears on my subject matter at a number of points; see his "An Ideology of Domination: A Socio-Rhetorical Study of *Ioudáios* in the Fourth Gospel" (paper read at the Society of Biblical Literature Annual Meeting, San Francisco, November 23, 1992). Unfortunately, the manuscript for the present essay had already been completed before Hendricks's work came into my hands. His contention that the designations "Galilean" and "Jew/Judean" in John are ideological constructs referring respectively to the oppressed peasantry and to the aristocracy of wealthy priests demands careful consideration.

Notes to Chapter 7

1. Bruce Vawter and Leslie J. Hoppe, *A New Heart: A Commentary of the Book of Ezekiel*, International Theological Commentary (Grand Rapids: William B. Eerdmans, 1991), 3.

2. Joseph Blenkinsopp, *Ezekiel*, IBC (Louisville: John Knox Press, 1990), 8.

3. John W. Wevers, ed., *Ezekiel*, The Century Bible (London: Thomas Nelson & Sons, 1969), p. 1.

4. Keith W. Carley, *The Book of the Prophet Ezekiel*, CBC (Cambridge: Cambridge University Press, 1974), 248; Herbert G. May, "Introduction and Exegesis to Ezekiel," *IB* 6:269.

5. Ralph Klein, *Ezekiel: The Prophet and His Message* (Columbia: University of South Carolina Press, 1988), 6.

6. Carley, 247.

7. Vawter and Hoppe, 165. Vawter continues his discussion on an interesting note. The vision, he writes, "has attracted the interest of several patristic commentators, most of whom found here biblical warrant for the Christian belief in resurrection of the dead. . . ."

8. Ronald M. Hals, *Ezekiel*, FOTL 19 (Grand Rapids: William B. Eerdmans, 1989), 266.

9. Vawter and Hoppe, 166.

10. Carley, 269.

11. Ibid., 249.

12. Wevers, 277.

13. Carley, 247.

14. Aelred Cody, *Ezekiel, with an Excursus on Old Testament Priesthood* (Wilmington, DE: Michael Glazier, 1984), 175.

15. There is a little need to call attention to the use of this text to support the early Christian teaching of a bodily resurrection. There are other passages which indicate that in early Judaism, as it approaches the common era, there developed a belief in the bodily resurrection of the dead. There are several references including Dan 12:2-3, and Eccl 3:21.

Perhaps the most intriguing reference is found in 2 Kings 13:20-21. At least it is amusing (Vawter and Hoppe, 165).

16. See Num 19:16-18; 2 Kings 23:14, 16; and Ezek 39:15-16.

17. Vawter and Hoppe, 168.

18. Blenkinsopp, 172.

19. Hals, 266.

20. Blenkinsopp, 170; Vawter and Hoppe, 166.

21. Klein, 150.

Notes to Chapter 8

1. Toni Morrison, *Song of Solomon* (New York: Penguin, 1987). All subsequent citations used in this essay are drawn from this edition. All page citations are enclosed in parenthesis. The essay reflects a singular reading of Morrison's *Song of Solomon*; it does not consider the earlier or later novels written by Morrison.

2. In *Song of Solomon*, the past, present, and future all come together. Scholarship works that way as well. I owe a debt of gratitude to the venerable and vibrant Dr. Charles Copher, a former colleague at the Interdenominational Theological Center and a scholar for whom ebullience, eloquence and erudition have always been a way of life. Another debt is owed to Mark Jefferson, a bright and budding M.Div. student at Boston University School of Theology. Mark first suggested that I might explore Morrison's appropriation of the bible in her *Song of Solomon*. Later, as a research assistant, he helped me to crystallize most of the ideas which this essay develops.

3. These terms were drawn from one of Morrison's theoretical articles on the need to appreciate a text for its own inherent qualities. See Morrison, "Unspeakable Things Unspoken: The Afro-American Presence in American Literature," *Michigan Quarterly Review* 28 (1989), 10.

4. Examples of this perspective are: Jacqueline De Weever, "Toni Morrison's Use of Fairy Tale, Folk Tale and Myth in The *Song of Solomon*," *Southern Folklore Quarterly* 44 (1980), 131–44; A. Leslie Harris, "Myth as Structure in Toni Morrison's *Song of Solomon*," *Melus* 7 (1980), 69–70.

5. For a comprehensive list of the western allusions, see De Weever, 131–44.

6. The narrator says that Milkman "had a fine enough face. Taken apart, it looked all right. Even better than all right. But it lacked coherence, a coming together of the features into a total self. It looked very tentative. . . ." (69). Milkman's father, Macon Dead II, tells his son that he can never become a whole man if he does not know the whole truth about the strained relations between his parents. And Milkman himself on several occasions views his life as a stroll down a street with everyone going in the very direction he was coming from.

7. To take one example, the Icarus myth, Morrison makes the following observation: "If it [the flying motif in *Song of Solomon*] means Icarus to some readers, fine; I want to take credit for that. But my meaning is

specific; it is about black people who could fly. That was always part of the folklore of my life; flying was one of our gifts. I don't care how silly it may seem. It's everywhere—people used to talk about it, it's in the spirituals and gospels." See Thomas LeClair, "The Language Must Not Sweat," *New Republic* 21 (1981), 26–27. On the failure of western myths to explain *Song of Solomon*, see Trudier Harris, *Fiction and Folklore: The Novels of Toni Morrison* (Knoxville: University of Tennessee, 1991), 86. Morrison herself contends that the goal of her writing is to "centralize and animate information discredited by the West. . . ." See her "Memory, Creation, and Writing," *Thought* 59 (1984), 388. Elsewhere Morrison points out the insidiousness of judging African American literature "in terms of its referents to European criteria. . . ." See her "Unspeakable Things Unspoken," 10.

8. Morrison critiques the literary critics who aver that the addition of classical forms to African American art is a necessary refinement to Black art to give it a superior, complex texture. See her critique of Western art's hegemonic neutralization of African American culture in her "Unspeakable Things Unspoken," 10.

9. Harris (89) notes that Milkman's mistreatment of Hagar and his non-altruistic theft of Pilate's "inheritance" (a bag of bones) strains against the conventions of the classical hero myth.

10. Harris (95) suggests that Milkman is a Br'er Rabbit hero, not a classical one, because his character shows that "goodness alone is not the major prerequisite for heroism."

11. While De Weever's earlier work, "Toni Morrison's Use of Fairy Tale," gives prominence to the classical allusions in *Song of Solomon*, her later work, *Mythmaking and Metaphor in Black Women's Fiction* (New York: St. Martin, 1992), acknowledges Morrison's intertextuality and revision of classical myths in the novel (28–29). One revision De Weever notes (31) is that Milkman fails to "be reintegrated into his community and family."

12. After ruminating about her twist on the classical myths in *Song of Solomon*, Morrison notes: "I want to subvert his [the reader's] traditional comfort so that he may experience an unorthodox one: that of being in the company of his own solitary imagination." See "Memory, Creation, and Writing," *Thought* (1984), 387.

13. Examples are Susan Blake, "Folklore and Community in *Song of Solomon*," *Melus* 7 (1990), 77–82; Harris, 85–95; Cynthia A. Davis, "Self, Society and Myth," *Contemporary Literature* 23 (1982), 323–42; and Valerie Smith, *Self-Learning and Authority in Afro-American Literature* (Cambridge: Harvard University Press, 1987), 122–53.

14. Dolan Hubbard, "In Quest of Authority: Toni Morrison's *Song of Solomon* and the Rhetoric of the Black Preacher," *College Language Association Journal* 35 (1992), 288.

15. Susan Willis, "Eruptions of Funk: Historicizing Toni Morrison," in *Black Literature and Literary Theory*, ed. Henry Louis Gates, Jr. (New York: Methuen, 1984), 271.

16. Morrison, "Unspeakable Things Unspoken," 27.

17. On the impeding role of the flashbacks, see Smith, 135.

18. Several characters (Pilate, Macon Dead II, Guitar, and Freddie) tell travel stories, that is, stories depicting their journeys from one place to another.

19. To be sure, Milkman experiences a metamorphosis in the South, for there, free from the trappings of materialism and a "commodity culture," he learns that his status is not determined by his affluence. In Virginia, conspicuous consumption (a nice brim, a three piece beige suit, a gold Longines watch and Florsheim shoes) fails to win Milkman the respect of others. Indeed, in Virginia, where no one translates status in terms of commodities, for the first time, Milkman sees women walking without purses, with "nothing in their hands" (259). Yet Milkman's metamorphosis here does not merely indicate his growth as a hero, but symbolically it dramatizes the polarity between the tolerations and countenances of the North and the South, between two ways of life—one heavily influenced by individualism and materialistic pursuits and the other imbued with selflessness and simplicity.

20. On Guitar as Milkman's alter ego, see De Weever, *Mythmaking*, 29. Of course, later in the novel, Guitar, the once displaced orphan, takes on the same individualistic values possessing Milkman.

21. In the latter case, he even speaks of his past using a third person narration style, as if to distance himself from his own experiences.

22. See Anthony Berret, "Toni Morrison's Literary Jazz," *College Language Association Journal* 32 (1989), 267.

23. According to Alfred Lee Wright, the value of the blues for Morrison is that they "define the cultural rootedness of her characters." See Wright's "Identity, Family, and Folklore in African-American Literature" (Ph.D. diss., University of Toledo, 1992), 10.

24. Originating in the Mississippi Delta and other areas in the South in the latter nineteenth and early twentieth centuries, the blues were products of the slaves' folk traditions. As Betty Jean Phillips notes: "The sorrow songs of the spirituals, the moanful songs of work, the pathos of the field and the cry of sadness of the roustabout songs carried in them the element of the blues." Phillips, "African-American Folk Archetypes and Language in the African-American Oral Tradition and Their Influence on Selected Contemporary African-American Poets (Volumes I and II)" (Ph.D. diss., University of Minnesota, 1992), 168.

25. Milkman recalls vividly other occasions when Pilate sang the blues song, 300.

26. According to Wright (144), one of the extraordinary talents of both the blues pianist Art Tatum and the blues hornplayer Louis Armstrong was their improvisational style.

27. "Buckra" is an appellation for a white man. I owe this observation to Herbert Marbury, an M.Div. student at the Interdenominational Theological Center, Atlanta, GA.

28. Joseph Skerrett, "Recitation to the Griot: Storytelling and Learning in Toni Morrison's *Song of Solomon*," in *Conjuring: Black Women, Fiction*

and Literary Tradition, ed. Marjorie Pryse and Hortense J. Spillers (Bloomington: Indiana University, 1985), 201.

29. LeClair, 28.

30. This interpretation is given by Brenda Marshall in her "The Gospel According to Pilate," *American Literature* 57 (1985), 486–89.

31. Josie Campbell, "To Sing the Song, To Tell the Tale: A Study of Toni Morrison and Simone Schwarz-Bart," *Comparative Literature* 22 (1985), 399.

32. On the power play involved in affirming the uninscribed import of the name "Pilate," see Jan Stryz, "Inscribing an Origin in *Song of Solomon*," *Studies in American Fiction* 19 (1991), 31–40.

33. Note that throughout the novel, Milkman has always had a keen interest in flying (9, 31, 220, 302, 337).

Notes to Chapter 9

1. Antonio Gramsci, *Selections from the Prison Notebooks*, trans. and ed. Quinten Hoare and Geoffrey Norwell Smith (London: Lawrence & Wisehart, 1971), 5–23. See also Cornel West, *Prophesy Deliverance! An Afro-American Revolutionary Christianity* (Philadelphia: Westminster Press, 1982), 127.

2. Winthrop D. Jordan, *White Over Black: American Attitudes Toward the Negro, 1550–1812* (Baltimore: Penguin Books, 1969), 3–98.

3. H. Shelton Smith, *In His Image, But . . . : Racism in Southern Religion, 1780–1910* (Durham, NC: Duke University Press, 1972), 23–207.

4. E. S. Morgan, "Slavery and Freedom: The American Paradox," *Journal of American History* 59 (1972), 5–29.

5. Angela Y. Davis, *Women, Race and Class* (New York: Random House, 1981), 391–421.

6. J. William Harris, *Plain Folk and Gentry in a Slave Society* (Middletown, CT: Wesleyan University Press, 1985), 67.

7. Joseph R. Washington, Jr., *Anti-Blackness in English Religion, 1500–1800* (New York: The Edwin Mellen Press, 1984), 231–320.

8. Josiah Priest, *Slavery, As It Relates to the Negro, or African Race, Examined in the Light of Circumstances, History and the Holy Scriptures; with an Account of the Origin of the Black Man's Color, Causes of His State of Servantude and Traces of His Character as Well in Ancient and Modern Times* (Albany, NY: C. Van Benthuysen & Co., 1843).

9. Ibid., 393.

10. Davis, 3–29.

11. Oliver C. Cox, *Caste, Class and Race: A Study in Social Dynamics* (New York: Doubleday and Company, 1948), 353–91; Jordan, *White Over Black*, 321–25.

12. Frederick A. Ross, *Slavery Ordained by God* (Philadelphia: J. B. Lippincott & Co., 1857), 11–68.

13. William Sumner Jenkins, *Pro-Slavery Thought in the Old South* (Chapel Hill: University of North Carolina Press, 1935), 90–92.

14. L. R. Bradley, "The Curse of Canaan and the American Negro (Gen 9:25-27)," *Concordia Theological Monthly* (February, 1971), 100–5.

15. Frederick Perry Noble, *The Redemption of Africa* (Chicago: Flemming H. Revell, 1899).

16. Walter Rodney, *How Europe Underdeveloped Africa* (London: Bogle l'Ouverture, 1972), 7–30.

17. Lester B. Scherer, *Slavery and the Churches in Early America 1619–1819* (Grand Rapids: William B. Eerdmans, 1975), 29–81.

18. Davis, 165–96.

19. Washington, 231–320.

20. George Fitzhugh, *Cannibals All! or, Slaves Without Masters*, ed. C. Van Woodward (Cambridge: Belknap Press of Harvard University, 1960).

21. Washington, 1–35.

22. Ibid., 24.

23. Orlando Patterson, *Slavery and Social Death: A Comparative Study* (Cambridge: Harvard University Press, 1982), 1–14.

24. C. Eric Lincoln, *Race, Religion and the Continuing American Dilemma* (New York: Hill and Wang, 1984), 23–31.

25. Samuel Blanchard How, *Slaveholding Not Sinful. Slavery, The Punishment of Man's Sin, Its Remedy, The Gospel of Jesus Christ* (New Brunswick, NJ: J. Terhune's Press, 1856), 63–133.

26. Patterson, 81–121.

27. Ibid., 12–26; 38–84.

28. Adam Gurowski, *Slavery in History* (New York: A. B. Burdick. 1860), 165–71.

29. William A. Smith, *Lectures on the Philosophy and Practice of Slavery as Exhibited in the Institution of Domestic Slavery in the United States: With the Duties of Masters and Slaves* (Nashville: Stevenson & Evans, 1856).

30. Patterson, 17–34.

31. Alfred Conrad and John Meyer, "The Economics of Slavery in the Antebellum South," *Journal of Political Economy* 66/2 (1958), 95–130; Harold Woodman, "The Profitability of Slavery: A Historical Perennial," *Journal of Southern History* 29/3 (1963), 303–25.

32. Iveson L. Brookes, *A Defense of the South Against the Reproaches of the North: In Which Slavery Is Shown to Be An Institution of God Intended to Form the Basis of the Best Social State and the Only Safeguard to the Permanency of a Republican Government* (Hamburg, SC: The Republican Office, 1850), 45.

Notes to Chapter 10

1. Bert Lowenberg and Ruth Bogin, eds., *Black Women in Nineteenth Century American Life: Their Words, Their Thoughts, Their Feelings* (University Park, PA: The Pennsylvania State University Press, 1976), 220.

2. Ntozake Shange, *For Colored Girls Who Have Considered Suicide When the Rainbow Is Enuf* (New York: Macmillan, 1977), 43.

3. Jesus Christ is the focus of this paper; however it should be noted that the arguments being made are applicable to other topics and doctrines of Christian theology as well, e.g. God, Humanity, the Bible, religion, life, etc. In fact, the same arguments can be made of Christianity itself.

4. Sheila Collins, *A Different Heaven and Earth* (Valley Forge, PA: Judson Press, 1974), 51.

5. Elizabeth Dodson Gray, *Patriarchy as a Conceptual Trap* (Wellesley, MA: Roundtable Press, 1982), 17.

6. Jacquelyn Grant, *White Women's Christ and Black Women's Jesus: Feminist Christology and Womanist Response* (Atlanta: Scholars Press, 1989), passim.

7. The phrase is particularly familiar in Methodist structures, however here it refers to the claim of any church to being an "equal opportunity employer".

8. Joel Kovel, *White Racism: A Psychohistory* (New York: Columbia University Press, 1984), x, quoted in Grant, 199.

9. C. Eric Lincoln, *Race, Religion and the Continuing American Dilemma* (New York: Hill and Wang, 1984), 11–12, quoted in Grant.

10. Cf. Randall Bailey, "Beyond Identification: The Use of Africans in Old Testament Poetry and Narratives," in *Stony the Road We Trod: African American Biblical Interpretation*, ed. Cain Hope Felder (Minneapolis: Fortress Press, 1991), 180; and Cain Hope Felder, *Troubling Biblical Waters: Race, Class and Family* (Maryknoll, NY: Orbis Books, 1989), 42.

11. Joseph Johnson, "The Need for a Black Christian Theology," *JITC* 1 (1974), 25.

12. I have explored this theme in an article entitled "The Sin of Servanthood and the Deliverance of Discipleship," in *A Troubling in My Soul: Womanist Essays on Evil and Suffering*, ed. Emilie Townes (New York: Orbis Books, 1993). Suffice it to say here, the institution of domestic service and the relationship between Black and White women clearly demonstrate a problematic with the servanthood language and imagery.

13. Quoted by Mason Crum, *Gullah: Negro Life in the Carolina Sea Islands* (Durham, NC: Duke University Press, 1940), 204–5. Taken from Albert Raboteau, *Slave Religion* (New York: Oxford University Press, 1978), 163.

14. Thomas R. Frazier, ed., *Afro-American History: Primary Sources* (Atlanta: Harcourt, 1970), 93.

15. Interview with Matthew Johnson, pastor of United Institutional Baptist Church, Greensboro, NC, April 10, 1992.

16. Harold Carter, *The Prayer Tradition of Black People* (Valley Forge: Judson Press, 1976), 49.

17. Jarena Lee, *Religious Experiences and Journals of Mrs. Jarena Lee* (Philadelphia: Printed and published for the author, 1849), 15–16.

18. Robert Wright, "Interview with Fannie Lou Hamer," August 9, 1968, 26. The text is located in the Civil Rights Documentation Project, Moorland-Spingaarn Research Center, Howard University, Washington, D.C.

Notes to Chapter 11

1. Karl Barth, Church Dogmatics, III.1 (Edinburgh: T & T Clark, 1970), 104.
2. Ibid., 105.
3. Ibid.
4. Ibid., 106.
5. Ibid., 110.
6. Ibid., 123.
7. Ibid., 104.
8. Ibid., 106ff.
9. Ibid., 123.
10. Paul Tillich, Systematic Theology, 3 vols. (Chicago: University of Chicago Press, 1967), 1:238.
11. Ibid., 1:239.
12. Ibid.
13. Ibid., 1:250. Italics added.
14. Ibid., 1:250–51.
15. Ibid.
16. Ibid.
17. Ibid.
18. Ibid., 1:253.
19. Ibid.
20. Ibid.
21. James H. Cone, A Black Theology of Liberation (Philadelphia: J. B. Lippincott Co., 1970), 33–34.
22. Ibid., 35–36.
23. Ibid., 54–74.
24. James H. Cone, Black Theology & Black Power (New York: Seabury Press, 1969), 52.
25. Cone, A Black Theology of Liberation, 122.
26. Ibid., 132.
27. Ibid., 140–41.
28. Ibid.
29. Ibid.
30. Ibid., 178.
31. Ibid., 118.
32. Israel Outreach (July 1991), 3.

Notes to Chapter 12

1. P. O. Ogunbowale, The Essentials of the Yoruba Language (London: University of London Press, 1970), 139.
2. John S. Mbiti, African Religions and Philosophy (Garden City, NY.: Anchor Books, 1970), 141. This African principle is also seen in the work of womanist scholars; see, for example, Jacquelyn Grant, White Women's

Christ and Black Women's Jesus: Feminist Christology and Womanist Response (Atlanta: Scholars Press, 1989), and Alice Walker, *In Search of Our Mothers' Gardens* (San Diego: Harcourt, Brace, Jovanovich, 1983).

3. In his brief overview of the "Overly Dependent Person" and the "Overly Independent Person" in the *Dictionary of Pastoral Care and Counseling*, gen. ed. Rodney J. Hunter (Nashville: Abingdon Press, 1992), R. S. Sullender states that "compared to the 'dependent personality,' modern psychology has devoted relatively little attention to the problems of the excessively independent person. This is due in part to a strong cultural bias in America that defines independence and even excessive independence as desirable. Western culture admires the 'rugged individualist.'" Robert Bellah and other writers in *Habits of the Heart* (Berkeley: University of California Press, 1985) document this penchant in the United States culture toward "rugged individualism" and alleged independence. See also Pamela Couture, *Blessed Are the Poor? Women's Poverty, Family Policy, and Practical Theology* (Nashville: Abingdon Press, 1991).

4. Howard Thurman, *The Search for Common Ground: An Inquiry into the Basis of Man's Experience of Community* (New York: Harper & Row, 1971).

5. Howard Thurman, *Creative Encounter: An Interpretation of Religion and the Social Witness* (New York: Harper & Bros., 1954); *Jesus and the Disinherited* (Nashville: Abingdon-Cokesbury Press, 1949); and *The Luminous Darkness: A Personal Interpretation of the Anatomy of Segregation and the Ground of Hope* (New York: Harper and Row, 1965).

6. Howard Thurman, *Deep Is the Hunger* (New York: Harper and Bros., 1951), 63.

7. Howard Thurman, *Disciplines of the Spirit* (New York: Harper and Bros., 1963), 121–22; and Thurman, *The Search for Common Ground*, 78–79.

8. Thurman, *Disciplines of the Spirit*, 105. Cf. Carolyn McCrary, *Interdependence As a Norm for an Interdisciplinary Model of Pastoral Counseling* (Ph.D. diss., Interdenominational Theological Center, 1989), 86–94.

9. Edward P. Wimberly and Anne Streaty Wimberly, *Liberation and Human Wholeness: The Conversion Experiences of Black People in Slavery and Freedom* (Nashville: Abingdon Press, 1986).

10. Howard Thurman, *The Growing Edge* (New York: Harper and Bros., 1956).

11. Thurman, *The Search for Common Ground*, xiv.

12. Thurman, *Disciplines of the Spirit*, 104.

13. Luther Smith, *Howard Thurman: The Mystic as Prophet* (New York: University Press of America, 1981), 46.

14. Thurman, The *Search for Common Ground*, 6.

15. Alexis Kagame, *La Philosophie Bantu-Rwandaise de L'être* (Brussels, 1956), 71–120.

16. Janheinz Jahn, *Muntu: The New African Culture*, 4th edition (New York: Grove Press, 1958), 100–101.

17. Norman Geisler and Paul Feinberg, *Introduction to Philosophy: A*

Christian Perspective (Grand Rapids: Baker Book House, 1990), 92; cf. René Descartes, *Meditations on First Philosophy*, 2nd rev. ed. (Indianapolis: Bobbs-Merrill, 1960), Meditation 2.

18. Kagame, 209.

19. Jahn, 107–8.

20. Kagame, 128–36.

21. Jahn, 101–11.

22. Thurman, *The Search for Common Ground*, 83.

23. Ibid., 80.

24. Ibid., 8.

25. Smith, 50.

26. Cf. Howard Thurman, "What Can We Believe In?" *JRH* 12 (1973), 111–19.

27. Smith, 63

28. Thurman, *Deep Is the Hunger*, 63.

29. Ibid.

30. Thurman, *The Search for Common Ground*, 82.

31. In Sigmund Freud's last book, *An Outline of Psychoanalysis*, the title of the last unfinished chapter is "The Internal World," which can be interpreted as a reference to the processes of internalization and object relation theory. See also Sigmund Freud, *The Ego and the Id*, Standard Edition, Vol. 19 (London: Hogarth Press, 1961), 13–66; and *Group Psychology and the Analysis of the Ego*, ed. James Strachey (New York: W. W. Norton Co., 1959), esp. 41.

32. Jay R. Greenberg and Stephen Mitchell, *Object Relations in Psychoanalytic Theory* (Cambridge: Harvard University Press, 1983), 151–87.

33. W. R. D. Fairbairn, "Synopsis of an Object Relations Theory of the Personality," *IJP* 44 (1963), 224.

34. Henry Guntrip, *Psychoanalytic Theory and the Self* (New York: Basic Books, 1971), 91.

35. Howard Thurman, *Creative Encounter: An Interpretation of Religion and the Social Witness* (New York: Harper & Bros., 1954), 32.

36. Ibid., 67–68.

37. Ibid., 70–72. Surrender in the Thurmanian sense is not necessarily oppressive and may be very liberating. From a Womanist perspective, however, commitment seems to be a better term.

38. Ibid., 74.

39. Ibid., 82.

40. W. R. D. Fairbairn, "On the Nature and Aims of Psychoanalytical Treatment," *International Journal of Psychoanalysis* 39 (1958), 376.

41. W. R. D. Fairbairn, "Freud, the Psycho-Analytical Method and Mental Health," *BJMP* 30 (1957), 61.

42. Jay R. Greenberg and Stephen Mitchell, *Object Relations in Psychoanalytic Theory* (Cambridge: Harvard University Press), 1983.

Notes to Chapter 13

1. See "The History of the Bethlehem United Methodist Church" in the 111th Church Anniversary booklet of the Bethlehem United Methodist Church, Sunday, October 11, 1987. Much of the history of the congregation has not been recorded. It remains in the form of oral history, and may never be significantly reconstructed.

2. Ibid.

3. Ibid., 2.

4. Ibid.

5. *Minutes of the Eighth Session of the Georgia Annual Conference, Methodist Protestant Church (Colored)* (Atlanta, Georgia, November 4, 1885), 12.

6. *Minutes of the Ninth Session of the Georgia Annual Conference, Methodist Protestant Church (Colored)* (Campbellton, Georgia, November 17, 1886), 11.

7. *Minutes of the Thirty-eighth Annual Session of the Georgia Annual Conference of the Methodist Protestant Church, Colored, of Georgia* (Adamsville, Georgia, November 16–17, 1916), 19.

8. The membership of 31 people during the year 1913 is as reported in the *Minutes of the 35th Annual Session of the Georgia Colored Methodist Protestant Conference* (College Park, Georgia, November 5–9, 1913), 32.

9. James S. Thomas, *Methodism's Racial Dilemma: The Story of the Central Jurisdiction* (Nashville: Abingdon Press, 1992), 44–46.

10. *Minutes of the Sixth Annual Conference of the Methodist Protestant Church (Colored) for the Georgia District* (1883), 13.

11. *Minutes of the Eighth Session of the Georgia Annual Conference, Methodist Protestant Church (Colored)* (1885), 12.

12. *Minutes of the Tenth Session of the Georgia Annual Conference of the Methodist Protestant Church (Colored)* (Rocky Head, Georgia, [1887]), 4.

13. *Minutes of the Fifty-first Session of the Annual Conference of the Methodist Protestant Church (Colored) of Georgia* (Ben Hill, Georgia, November 20–24, 1929), 12.

14. Ibid., 10.

15. See *Minutes of the Thirty-eighth Session of the Georgia Annual Conference of the Methodist Protestant Church Colored, of Georgia* (1916), 10. Similar statements were made in subsequent years.

16. *Minutes of the Forty-seventh Session of the Methodist Protestant Annual Conference (Colored) of Georgia* (Rocky Head Methodist Protestant Church, November 18–24, 1925), 11.

17. For the complete text see the *Minutes of the Ninth Session of the Georgia Annual Conference, Methodist Protestant Church (Colored)* (Campbellton, Georgia, Nov. 17th, 1886), 13–14. The term "stationing committee" was used more or less interchangeably with "itineracy and orders committee" down through the years. Appointment of ministers was recommended by this committee to the President of the Conference in session. Presidents

were restrained from changing or otherwise manipulating appointments between the annual conference sessions.

18. *Minutes of the Sixth Annual Conference*, 11.

19. This reference rests on an interpretation of Gayraud Wilmore's idea of the deradicalization of the Black Church in his book *Black Religion and Black Radicalism* (Maryknoll, NY: Orbis Books, 1983). Despite the deep immersion of Black people into Methodist belief and practice, the White Methodist churches never fully received and appreciated the presence, participation and gifts of African American people. Slavery occasioned the first compromise in the eighteenth century. The second compromise came with segregation in the nineteenth century, in order to maintain some sort of unity in a supposedly universal church and union of states that summarily marginalized and dehumanized Black people in particular. The decision of many Black people to stay and morally persuade White people to change—in relative silence—epitomized a deradicalized Black Methodist Protestant Church.

20. It seems most likely that there was contact between the historically Black congregations of the Methodist Protestant (Colored) Conference and the Black Mission/Annual Conference of the Methodist Episcopal Church in Georgia. The latter was formed in the year 1867 and the former in 1877. Existing Methodist Protestant records, located to date, do not report much about the fact or the nature of the contact that almost certainly took place. Both were absorbed and pressed into the Central Jurisdiction of The Methodist Church in 1939.

21. For a well-documented description of the economic situation in Atlanta see Jonathan W. McLeod's *Workers and Workplace Dynamics in Reconstruction-Era Atlanta: A Case Study* (Los Angeles: Center for Afro-American Studies, UCLA, 1989), 33–34.

22. Ibid.

23. John Hope Franklin and Alfred A. Moss, Jr., *From Slavery to Freedom, A History of Negro Americans*, sixth edition (New York: Alfred A. Knopf, 1988), 224–38.

24. "Datelines of Atlanta History," Part II, 1866–1950 (Atlanta: The Atlanta Historical Society, 1980).

25. For a full description see James P. Brawley, *Two Centuries of Methodist Concern: Bondage, Freedom and Education of Black People* (New York: Vantage Press, 1974), 81–121.

26. *The Social and Economic Status of the Black Population in the United States: An Historical View, 1790–1978* (Current Population Reports, Special Studies Series P-23, No. 80, U.S. Department of Commerce, Bureau of the Census), 96.

27. W. E. B. DuBois, ed., "The Negro Church: Report of a Social Study made under the direction of Atlanta University; together with the Proceedings of the Eighth Conference for the Study of the Negro Problems, held at Atlanta University, May 26th, 1903" (Atlanta: The Atlanta University Press, 1903); compiled in *The Atlanta University Publications, Nos. 1, 2, 4,*

8, 9, 11, 13, 14, 15, 16, 17, 18 (New York: Arno Press and the *New York Times*, 1968), 38–48.

28. Thomas, *Methodism's Racial Dilemma*, 45.

29. Ibid., 46.

30. The conference *Minutes* of the Georgia and other southern conferences of the Methodist Protestant Church, and the General Conference Journals—up to the Civil War and Reconstruction period—are revealing sources of the temper of the times as concerns slavery and the Methodist Protestant Church. Much sentiment against slavery was memorialized through resolutions. There is little evidence that it made any difference in the practice of the church, especially in the American South, regarding the toleration of slaveholders. In the *Minutes* of the Black mission/annual conferences of the Methodist Protestant Church, there is no mention of the social evil of legally enforced racial segregation and the related patterns of injustice which were part of the taken-for-granted practice of the "reconstructed" South and United States of America and its social institutions. The spirit of protest against racial oppression and injustice in church and society was subdued. One is inclined to believe that this apparent situation was more a tactic for survival and development rather than capitulation to social, cultural, and economic oppression at the hands of White people.

31. Conventional wisdom held that, in addition to the legal ramifications of mixing the races, such a move would have fractured the White Methodist Protestant organization and rendered it utterly impotent in the competition with the Methodist Episcopal Church, South.

32. In the *Proceedings of the General Conference of the Methodist Protestant Church* (Lynchburg, Virginia, May 4, 1858), the tension between the Northern and Western Conferences and the Southern Conferences is palpable. On pp. 14–15 a memorial was brought to the MP General Conference from an 1857 Convention of Representatives of Northern and Western Conference held in Cincinnati. It stated in part:

> We devoutly respect the injunction contained in one of the elementary principles of our Constitution, that it is the duty of all Ministers and members of the Church to maintain godliness, and oppose all moral evil. Now, it is our clear conviction, long since and repeatedly expressed by all our Annual Conferences, that the traffic in slaves, and the voluntary holding of slaves, does conflict with the rights of humanity, and with the morality of the Holy Scriptures. Hence, we regard it the bounded duty, as well as constitutional right of all ministers and members of the Meth. Prot. church, to oppose the practices alluded to. But it has ever been a source of grief and mortification to us, that in the entire Southern section of the Meth. Prot. Church, slave-holding and slave-trading are continually practiced without rebuke. We have, for a series of years, again and again, in our respective Annual Conferences, expressed to our Southern brethren our kind remonstrance against the continuance of these practices, entreating them to put away for ever this sin, and relieve us of a humiliating reproach. But our

expostulations have ever been deemed not only unacceptable, but highly offensive to our slave-holding brethren. All prospect and hope of their regarding our appeals have well nigh fled—they seem more and more fixed in their purpose to sustain and perpetuate in the Church what we are constrained to deem a more wrong. Hence, we are in difficulty. . . .

On p. 15 the call was made for "modifications of the Constitution and Discipline":

First—The word "white" should be stricken from the Constitution, Art. XII, Sections 1 and 2, as establishing an invidious distinction, not in accordance with the principles of the Gospel of Him who made of one blood all the nations of men, to dwell on all the face of the earth."

Second—The third item and annexed proviso, embraced in the section of Art. VII, should be stricken from the Constitution, because it is understood and used to protect ministers and members of the Church in the practice of slave-holding and slave-trading.

Third—A clause should be inserted, specifically setting forth that the practices of voluntary slave-holding and slave-trading, will be henceforth a barrier to Membership in the Meth. Prot. Church.

On pp. 16–17, a report on the impending failure of Madison College in Uniontown, Pennsylvania, is presented with the lament that the withdrawal of the Southern professors and students and the refusal to continue funding activities had removed any hope for the survival of the college.

Notes to Chapter 14

1. J. Daniel and G. Smitherman, "How I Got Over: Communication Dynamics in the Black Community," *QJS*, 62 (1976), 26–39.

2. C. Eric Lincoln, ed., *The Black Experience in Religion* (New York: Anchor Press/Doubleday, 1974), 311.

3. L. Barrett, "African Religions in the Americas," in Lincoln, 311–54.

4. Ibid., 313.

5. Ibid.

6. Ibid., 314.

7. Ibid.

8. Ibid.

9. Lawrence Levine, *Black Culture and Black Consciousness* (New York: Oxford University Press, 1977).

10. Ibid., 60.

11. B. Malinowski, *Magic, Science and Religion and Other Essays* (Garden City, NY: Doubleday, 1954).

12. Levine, 63.

13. V. P. Franklin, *Black Self-Determination: A Cultural History of the Faith of the Fathers* (Westport, CT: Lawrence Hill & Co., 1984).

14. Ibid., 4.

15. Cf. James H. Cone, *The Spirituals and the Blues* (New York: Seabury, 1972); see also the works of Lincoln, Levine, and Franklin cited above.

16. Lincoln, 44.

17. John Wesley Work, *Folk Songs of the American Negro* (Nashville: Fisk University Press, 1915), 110.

18. Franklin, 67.

19. Levine, 35.

20. Ibid.

21. Ibid., 37.

22. Ibid., 50.

23. Ibid., 51.

24. Ibid., 26.

25. James H. Cone, Black Theology and Black Power (New York: Seabury, 1969), 35.

26. Cone, *The Spirituals and The Blues*, 58.

27. Ibid., 63.

28. Ibid.

29. Ibid., 64.

30. S. Brown, "Negro Folk Expression: Spirituals, Seculars, Ballads, and Work Songs," in A. Meier and E. Rudwich, eds., *The Making of Black America* (New York: Athenaeum, 1969), 215, 216.

31. Cone, *The Spirituals and the Blues*, 73.

32. Ibid., 74.

33. Ibid.

34. Ella P. Mitchell, "Oral Tradition: Legacy of Faith for the Black Church," *RelEd* 81 (Winter 1986), 93–112.

35. Levine, 44.

36. A. Haley, *Roots* (Garden City, NY: Doubleday, 1976), 95.

37. Ibid., 96.

38. Mitchell, 99.

39. Ibid.

40. Ibid., 101.

41. Ibid.

42. J. W. Blassingame, *The Slave Community* (New York: Oxford University Press, 1972), 79.

43. Mitchell, 102.

44. Ibid., 103.

45. Franklin, 147.

46. W. E. B. DuBois, *The Autobiography of W. E. B. DuBois: A Soliloquy on Viewing My Life from the Last Decade of Its First Century* (New York: International Publishers, 1968), 236.

47. Mitchell, 105.

48. J. Daniel, *The Wisdom of Sixth Mount Zion from the Members of*

Sixth Mount Zion and Those Who Begot Them (Pittsburgh: Limited Edition Publication, 1977).

49. Ibid.

50. Jack Daniel and Geneva Smitherman-Donaldson, "How I Got Over: Communication Dynamics in the Black Community," *Quarterly Journal of Speech* 62 (February, 1976), 35.

51. Daniel, *Wisdom*, 35.

52. L. Hughes, "Mother to Son," in *Selected Poems of Langston Hughes* (New York: Alfred A. Knopf, 1926), 52.

CONTRIBUTORS

Randall C. Bailey, Ph.D., is Associate Professor of Old Testament and Hebrew at the Interdenominational Theological Center. He is the author of *David in Love and War: The Pursuit of Power in 2 Samuel 10–12* (Sheffield Academic Press, 1990).

G. Murray Branch is Professor Emeritus of Old Testament at the Interdenominational Theological Center, Atlanta. He last served as Pastor of Dexter Avenue–King Memorial Baptist Church, Montgomery, Alabama.

Katie Geneva Cannon, Ph.D., is Associate Professor of Religion at Temple University, Philadelphia, Pennsylvania. She is the author of *Black Womanist Ethics* (Scholars Press, 1988) and is an alumna of Johnson C. Smith Seminary at the Interdenominational Theological Center, Atlanta, Georgia (Class of 1974).

Octavius A. Gaba, Ph.D., is Minister of Covenant Presbyterian Church, Norfolk, Virginia. He is an alumnus of Gammon Theological Seminary at the Interdenominational Theological Center, Atlanta, Georgia (Class of 1981).

Jacquelyn Grant, Ph.D., is Professor of Systematic Theology at the Interdenominational Theological Center, Atlanta, Georgia. She is the author of *White Women's Christ, Black Women's Jesus* (Scholars Press, 1989). She is an alumna of Turner Theological Seminary at the Interdenominational Theological Center, Atlanta, Georgia (Class of 1973).

Janice E. Hale, Ph.D., is Professor of Early Childhood Education at Wayne State University, Detroit, Michigan. She is the author of *Black Children: Their Roots, Culture and Learning Styles*. She is an alumna of Morehouse School of Religion at the Interdenominational Theological Center, Atlanta, Georgia (Class of 1972).

Carolyn L. McCrary, Th.D., is Associate Professor of Pastoral Care and Counseling at the Interdenominational Theological Center, Atlanta, Georgia. She is an alumna of Turner Theological Seminary at the

Interdenominational Theological Center, Atlanta, Georgia (Class of 1977).

H. Wayne Merritt, Ph.D., is Associate Professor of New Testament at the Interdenominational Theological Center, Atlanta, Georgia. He is the author of *In Word and Deed: Moral Integrity in Paul* (Peter Lang, 1993).

Stephen Breck Reid, Ph.D., is Associate Professor of Old Testament at Austin Theological Seminary, Austin, Texas. He is the author of *Experience and Tradition: A Primer on African American Biblical Hermeneutics* (Abingdon Press, 1992), and a former faculty member of Area I: Bible at the Interdenominational Theological Center, Atlanta, Georgia.

David Rensberger, Ph.D., is Associate Professor of New Testament at the Interdenominational Theological Center, Atlanta, Georgia. He is the author of *Johannine Faith and Liberating Community* (Westminster Press, 1988).

Boykin Sanders, Ph.D., is Associate Professor of New Testament and Greek at the School of Theology of Virginia Union University, Richmond, Virginia. He is an alumnus of Morehouse School of Religion at the Interdenominational Theological Center, Atlanta, Georgia (Class of 1969).

James M. Shopshire, Ph.D., is Professor of Sociology of Religion at Wesley Theological Seminary, Washington, D.C. He is an alumnus of Gammon Theological Seminary at the Interdenominational Theological Center, Atlanta, Georgia (Class of 1966).

Abraham Smith, Ph.D., is Assistant Professor of New Testament and Early Christian Writings at the School of Theology at Boston University. He is the author of *The Book of Consolation: A Rhetorical Analysis of 1 Thessalonians* (Westminster/John Knox Press, 1994), and is an alumnus of Morehouse School of Religion at the Interdenominational Theological Center, Atlanta, Georgia (Class of 1982).

James W Waters, Ph.D., is Pastor of the Greater Solid Rock Baptist Church, Riverdale, Georgia. He is a former faculty member of Area I: Bible at the Interdenominational Theological Center, Atlanta, Georgia.